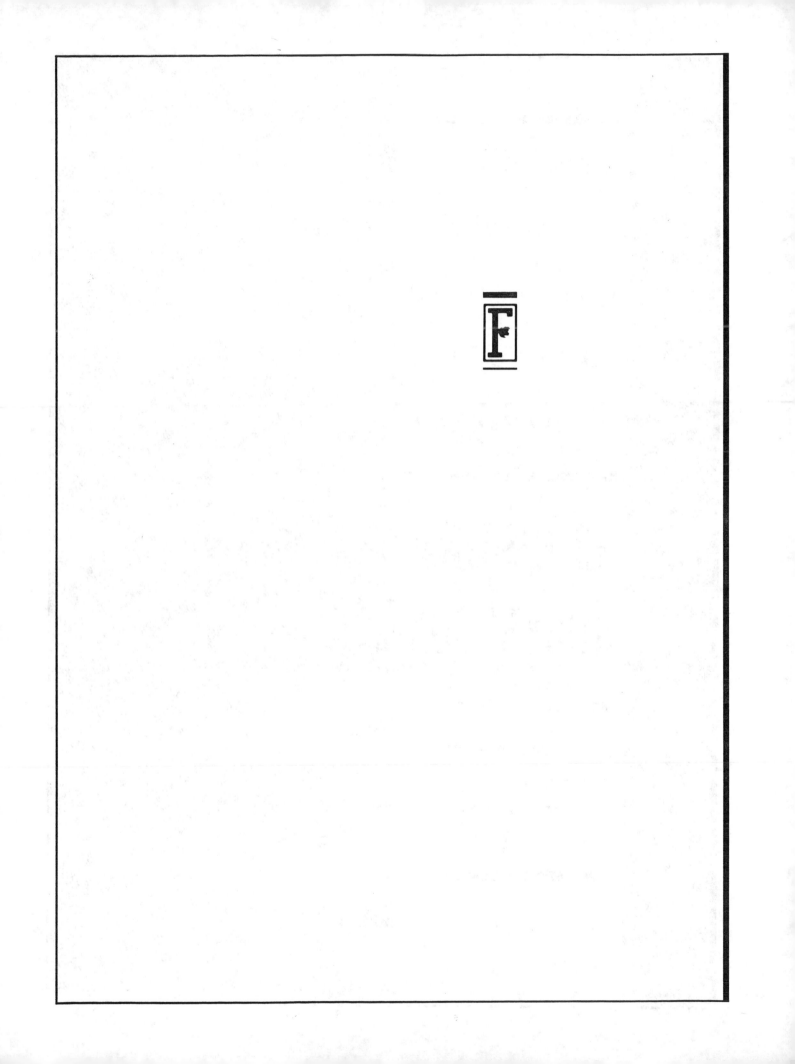

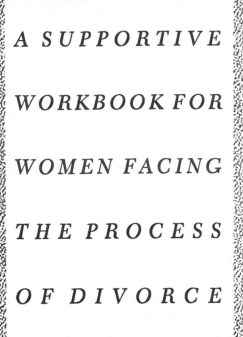

A SUPPORTIVE

WORKBOOK FOR

WOMEN FACING

THE PROCESS

OF DIVORCE

CHRISTINA ROBERTSON

A FIRESIDE BOOK

Published by Simon & Schuster Inc.

NEW YORK LONDON TORONTO

SYDNEY TOKYO SINGAPORE

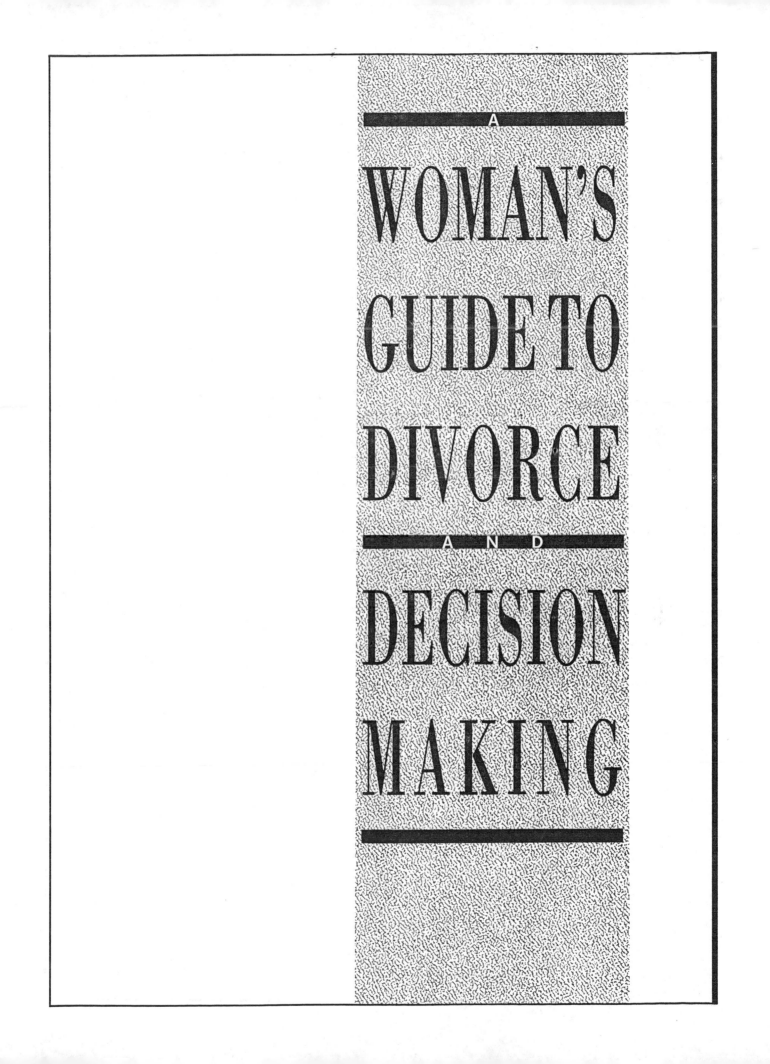

A WOMAN'S GUIDE TO DIVORCE AND DECISION MAKING

FIRESIDE
Simon & Schuster Building
Rockefeller Center
1230 Avenue of the Americas
New York, New York   10020

FIRESIDE and colophon are registered trademarks
of Simon & Schuster Inc.

Designed by Kathy Kikkert
Manufactured in the United States of America

10   9   8   7   6   5   4   3   Pbk.

Library of Congress Cataloging in Publication Data
Robertson, Christina, 1944–
    A woman's guide to divorce and decision making:
a supportive workbook for women facing the process of divorce / Christina Robertson. —1st Fireside ed.
        p.   cm.
    Previous ed. published as: Divorce & decision
making. ©1980.
    "A Fireside book."
    Bibliography: p.
    1. Divorced   women—Life   skills   guides.
2. Divorced women—United States—Life skills
guides.   3. Divorce—Decision making.   I. Robertson, Christina, 1944– Divorce & decision
making.   II. Title.
HQ814.R62   1989
306.8′9′088042—dc19   88-29083
                                        CIP
ISBN 0-671-67009-3 Pbk.

*TO MY CHILDREN,
AMANDA AND NATHANIEL,
WHO HAVE STRUGGLED
WITH THEIR PARENTS'
DIVORCE AND HAVE
DEVELOPED INTO STRONG,
INDEPENDENT, AND
WONDERFUL
INDIVIDUALS.*

ACKNOWLEDGMENTS

Special thanks go to:

Amanda and Nathaniel Edmunds, my children, who have given challenge, meaning, and joy to my life.

The members of my family who have always been supportive and have encouraged me to go after what I've wanted.

My women friends who are always there, ready to share the good times as well as the bad and who provide a special kind of "shared understanding."

Jane and Fred Catalano, who served as "second grandparents" to my children.

Shamus Misek, my son's "big brother," who exemplified for Nathaniel very special qualities for a man to have.

John Francis Marion, who has been a lifelong friend and who always gives so much of himself.

Wil Roberts, who offered moral support and expert advice.

Laura Yorke and Sydny Miner, my editors, who provided valuable editing assistance.

CONTENTS

PREFACE

This book is intended for women who have decided to obtain a divorce and who are in the process of making major decisions concerning their futures. Although divorce is becoming more and more common, the adjustment from a married to a single status is difficult for most people. If you have felt loneliness, anger, fear, anxiety, and insecurity, you have felt emotions that are commonly experienced by people in your situation. While these feelings are normal and a necessary part of your emotional adjustment, they make planning and decision making difficult.

While men and women go through similar processes in adjusting to divorce, women are faced with unique problems during their period of adjustment to a single life. You will probably, if you have not already been, be faced with problems such as discrimination, child care, finding suitable employment, and retaining a lawyer.

However, these problems are not insurmountable. Solving the problems you currently face may be easier if you follow a logical process of planning and decision making. If yours has been a traditional marriage, you may have had little or no experience in making plans and decisions for yourself. The purpose of this book is to provide you with planning and decision-making models that you can then use as tools to help you with the decisions you now face.

This book consists of two major sections. Part 1 deals with your emotional supports, your values, your plans for the future, and your decision-making ability. Part 2 deals with specific decisions you may have to make.

There are many ways to use this book. You can complete:

1. Part 1 as a basis for the decisions you will be asked to make and proceed to Part 2 to make those decisions
2. Chapters that deal with decision areas of current concern to you
3. Activities that deal with specific decisions of current concern to you
4. Activities that deal with the practical aspects of divorce when you find the emotional aspects too painful
5. Activities that deal with the emotional aspects of divorce when you feel the practical aspects are too numerous and overwhelming
6. Sections of the book that are assigned to you by a professional such as a counselor, lawyer, or group leader
7. Activities dealing with decisions you have already made to check your decision-making process and to reaffirm these decisions
8. Activities several times during your adjustment process to see if your values and decisions have changed or if they have remained the same.

As you work through this book, you may find it helpful to write out your answers to certain activities. Keeping a notebook may be of help to you. You may be tempted not to write down your answers to the various activities. However, writing out your answers will provide you with a record of your thinking that might be useful should you use the book again at different points during your adjustment process. Writing out your responses may also force you to clarify your thoughts and feelings concerning given decisions. If a particular activity has been significant for you, take the time to briefly summarize what you learned from it. After you complete a chapter, review what you learned.

If you are more comfortable not writing out the answers to the various activities, do not feel compelled to do so. The book should be of help to you in making decisions for your future. The decisions you will make as you use this book are yours—there are no *right* or *wrong* decisions.

The book cannot provide you with answers; it can only provide you with a process to use in making your own decisions. You will be asked to do some thinking, research, evaluating, planning, and decision making. The payoff for the time and work you invest is the likelihood that the decisions you make will be well thought out and right for you. While decision making involves risk and uncertainty, it also involves growth and taking responsibility for yourself. That is what this book is all about.

INTRODUCTION

WHERE ARE YOU IN THE ADJUSTMENT PROCESS?

When I was first separated, I was at a complete loss. I felt unprepared and incapable of tackling decisions which had to be made. I thought I'd never be able to make it. Three years later, I feel I know myself better and have a feeling of accomplishment and self-confidence. If someone had told me then that I'd feel this way, I never would have believed them.

Emotional and legal divorce rarely occur simultaneously. Some women are emotionally divorced before they have their divorce decree whereas others may take months or even years to become emotionally divorced. Estimates vary concerning the length of time it takes women to adjust to divorce and become fully functioning, single individuals; most estimates fall in the range of from two to four years. The length of the adjustment period depends on many things: the individual woman, her resources, how long she was married, the state of her marriage prior to her divorce, and so on. The important thing to remember is that adjustment takes time. It does not happen overnight. Give yourself time to recover from divorce and to learn the new ways of being and doing things that a single life requires.

Rather than talking about adjustment to divorce in terms of months or years, it may be more helpful to consider the stages that most individuals—men and women—experience. The divorce process may be seen as one of both grief and growth. The time an individual spends on each stage varies. Although the stages may overlap, one stage is more or less completed before the individual moves on to the next one. There are no good or bad stages and most people go through each stage in the divorce process. If one stage is skipped, overall adjustment may take longer and be more difficult. At times during the adjustment period, an individual may return to a previous stage. This does not necessarily mean that the individual has regressed; it may mean that new situations trigger emotional aspects of a given stage or that certain issues of a stage need to be reworked. It is important to remember that it is impossible to force yourself to be at a given stage if you are not emotionally ready to be there. It is paradoxical that a prerequisite of change is accepting where you are, even though you are anxious to move on.

Reva S. Wiseman, a family medicine specialist, developed a list of stages people typically go through during their adjustment to divorce and their readjustment to a single status. A brief description of these stages follows. As you read the descriptions, ask yourself which stage(s) best describes you at this point. If you feel you have completed or are in a given stage, try to give examples of your feelings and behavior in that stage.

1. DENIAL

In order to keep the marriage going, the individual insists that he or she has adjusted to the relationship with all its liabilities. External rationale such as finances or children keep the individual from considering divorce. In some cases, a spouse may refuse to face the reality that the partner has left and acts as if the marriage were still intact. Denial can serve as a buffer that allows a woman to accept the idea of divorce gradually and to mobilize her resources.

2. LOSS AND DEPRESSION

The occurrence of stress, either internal or external, makes it impossible to continue denying that something is wrong with the marital relationship. The situation has come into conscious awareness and must be dealt with for the first time as a reality. The reaction encompasses loss, outright grief, feelings of depression and isolation, and an inability to communicate. Loss and depression are natural reactions to the end of a marriage, a life-style, and the expectations that went with it. Even though a woman may have wanted and initiated the divorce, it is still a normal reaction to experience these feelings. By experiencing initial loss and depression, a woman may become prepared for impending losses she may experience once her divorce is final.

3. ANGER AND AMBIVALENCE

As the ending of the marriage becomes a reality, there is a movement away from depression toward the feeling that underlies it—anger. Feelings of overt anger toward the spouse often alternate with intense ambivalence about the idea of ending the marriage. Spouses often ask themselves if they have done enough to save the marriage and they may even try a last attempt at marriage counseling. Anger, which may be uncomfortable and frightening, facilitates the break. At this stage, there are usually legal negotiations, which often serve as sources of dispute, to contend with. A resurgence of adolescent conflicts may coincide with the anger phase—one spouse behaving like a rebellious teenager and the other acting out the role of the indignant parent.

Anger indicates a healthy sense of self. It is not fair that something we thought would last did not. It is understandable that a woman may be angry with her husband, her lawyer, or other people. At times a woman may be angry and blame herself for having stayed in the marriage as long as she did, for allowing herself to be treated poorly, to have made the decision to marry her spouse in the first place, and so on.

4. REORIENTATION OF LIFE-STYLE AND IDENTITY

As the divorcing individuals work through their anger and ambivalence, each spends less time looking back in anger and more in focusing on present and future planning and functioning. The primary task of this stage is the reworking of identity in all areas touched upon by the marriage: personal, vocational, sexual, and social. There may be a need to experiment in these areas. Sexual experimentation, for example, is common. There is the need to rebuild a damaged self-concept by seeing oneself as sexually desirable again. New friendships are often formed with others who are coping with the process of divorce.

5. ACCEPTANCE AND NEW LEVEL OF FUNCTIONING

Acceptance comes about gradually as the divorced person begins to feel adequate as a person socially, sexually, and vocationally. There is a move from casual and transitory relationships to those that involve one other person for a longer period of time and with a deeper degree of emotional commitment. Feelings of anger toward the former spouse begin to abate and the divorced person begins to accept the former partner and terminated marriage as they really are. In some cases, there will be a new marriage; in many more, an adjustment to divorced life will be more or less permanent and comfortable. Difficulties arise when a new marriage is entered into before the ending of the old one is completely worked through. Remarriage involves a new and different set of adjustments that should not be subordinated to those involved in the working through of the divorce.

While the first three stages may be the most difficult for individuals to experience in adjusting to divorce, they are part of the process that people must go through. The objective is to arrive at stage five (acceptance) but this is not possible if other stages are short-circuited. If an individual feels trapped in a particular stage and is unable to move on, she may want to consider help through counseling.

Which stage(s) best describes where you are in the adjustment process? Give examples of your behavior and/or feelings in the stage(s) you feel best describes you at the present time. If you feel you have completed a stage(s), give examples of your behavior and/or feelings in that stage(s).

Because each stage is different, your needs during each stage vary. Consider the stage(s) you are in and think about your answers to the following questions. If you think it would be helpful to write out your answers, do so on a separate sheet of paper or in a notebook.

1. In what ways can you be understanding and accepting of yourself during this stage?
2. Which of your friends can be most helpful to you during this stage? Why?

If you feel stuck in a particular stage, answer these questions.

1. Approximately how long, in terms of months or years, have you been in this stage?
2. Are you really "stuck" in this stage or are you being impatient with yourself and not allowing the time you need to complete this stage?
3. What concrete actions can you take to help you move on to the next stage?
4. What people might help you move on to the next stage? Why?

Sometimes individuals at stage 1 or 2 emotionally find that reality is forcing them to make plans and decisions that are more characteristic of stage 4. It is difficult to accomplish tasks for which you are emotionally unprepared. The activities in the chapters that follow will encourage you to accept and respect where you are at the present time. At the same time, they will help to prepare you to move on to the next stage when you are ready to do so.*

*The stages of the adjustment process are discussed in Reva S. Wiseman's "Crisis Theory and the Process of Divorce," *Social Casework* 56 (April 1975): 205–12. The stages Wiseman gives are similar to Elisabeth Kubler-Ross's stages of adjustment that terminal patients and their families experience when dealing with their impending loss. Kubler-Ross lists the stages of denial and isolation, anger, bargaining, depression, and acceptance in her book, *On Death and Dying* (New York: Macmillan, 1969).

17

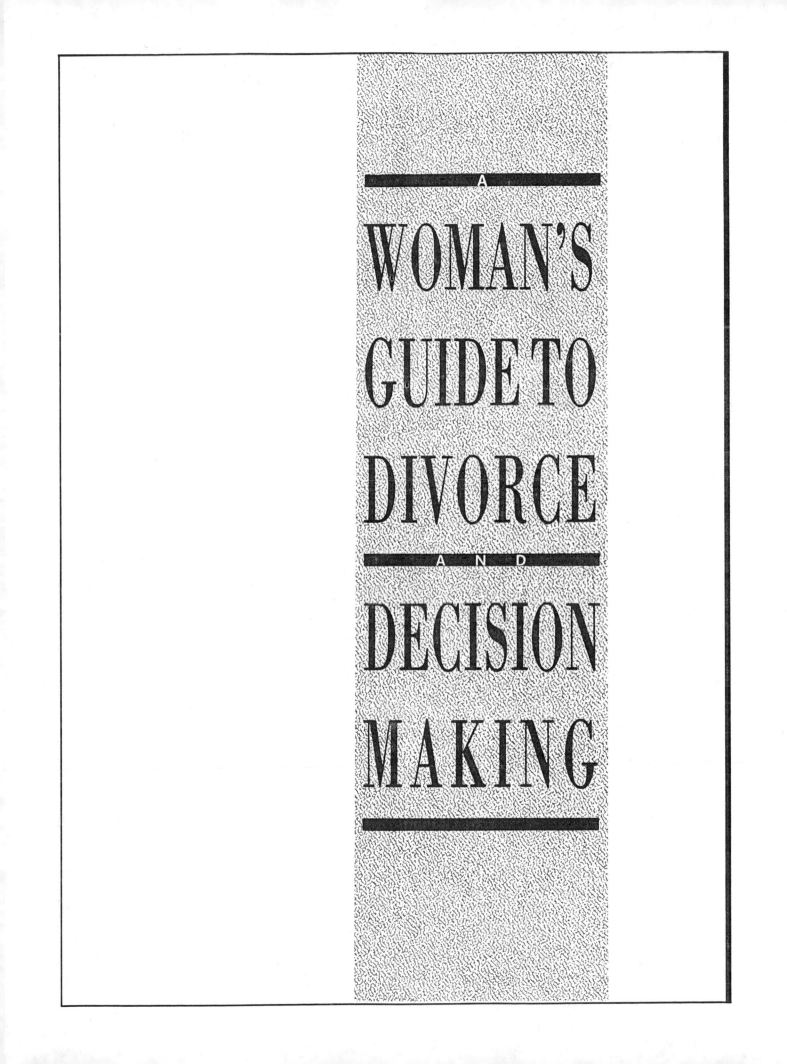

A
WOMAN'S
GUIDE TO
DIVORCE
AND
DECISION
MAKING

PART

ONE

WHERE DO YOU GET EMOTIONAL SUPPORT?

Since I've been divorced I've made closer friends—friends I can really confide in. Not only do I have female friends but male friends as well. When I was married I never had any male friends.

After I became separated, I became very close to my parents even though our relationship had been strained for years. Something about my situation made it easier for us to communicate with each other and made it possible to develop a relationship where we were supportive of each other.

I don't know what I would have done without my counselor who was my major source of support when I divorced. Many women feel they can't afford counseling at this time, but I can't see how they can afford not to have it.

Everyone needs a personal support system—a group of people to turn to for friendship, understanding, help, and reassurance. Being newly separated or divorced may create in you a new sense of vulnerability that can be expressed in apprehensiveness, anxiety, fear, or even panic.

When you married, you may have assumed that your husband would always be there to offer security and emotional support. Your needs for emotional support are still there. A first step in the readjustment process is to find people who will be able to provide you with the support you need. Some women have been emotionally divorced for a long time and are fortunate enough to have friends and relatives who give them encouragement and support. Others, when they separate or divorce, find that they have few people to whom they can comfortably turn for friendship. Regardless of your marital status, it is helpful to have close relationships with several people who can be of help to you in different ways.

WHO GIVES YOU EMOTIONAL SUPPORT?

To help you examine where you get emotional support and to help you evaluate why you might hesitate to talk honestly about your marital problems and/or divorce to others, ask yourself the following questions. It will probably be helpful to write out the answers.

1. Who were the first people you told about your marital problems and/or divorce?
2. Are there people you would like to turn to for friendship and support but you avoid because you are uncomfortable discussing your marital situation? Who are they?
3. There are many reasons people may hesitate to mention marital problems or divorce to others. Which of these apply to you?

   a. Fear that people won't understand
   b. Fear that people will offer unwanted advice
   c. Fear that people won't keep what you say in confidence

d. Fear that people will think less of you when they learn you have marital problems

e. Fear that discussing marital problems would make things difficult should you decide to reconcile

f. Fear that people would be judgmental

g. Fear that people who knew you were divorced would consider you "different" or an "outsider"

h. Fear that your divorce would not be accepted by people opposed to divorce on religious grounds

i. Fear of facing things threatening to you

j. Fear that you would lose composure, break down, and cry

k. Fear that your image will be damaged or that your status will suffer

l. Fear of "washing your dirty linen in public"

m. Fear that you will burden others with your problems

n. Other

While these fears are common to people who are experiencing divorce, there is much you can do to make them manageable. If statements *a.* through *h.* apply to you, you are concerned about the way others will react. Being honest and open with others involves risk. By carefully choosing those you confide in and deciding upon qualities you need to have in people you approach for emotional support, you minimize those risks. Statements *i.* through *m.* deal with how you feel about yourself. This too is under your control. You will be asked to examine your feelings about yourself in greater depth later.

You may not be talking to anyone concerning your divorce because you are not ready to do so. This is perfectly acceptable. The purpose of this chapter is to have you identify people you feel would be supportive if you felt the need for emotional support. When there is a divorce or a separation, some people feel they have a right to know all the details. Just as you have a right to discuss the details of your marital problems and/or divorce with the people you choose, you have a right *not* to discuss your divorce or separation. It is your divorce—don't let people pressure you into discussing things you might not be willing or ready to discuss.

List three people with whom you would *not* want to discuss your divorce or separation. List three people whom you would consider calling upon should you decide you would like some emotional support.

WHO DO YOU FIND SUPPORTIVE?

To help you identify the qualities you like and do not like in people you turn to for support, answer these questions.

1. Which three people would you turn to first if you felt depressed, frightened, scared, or lonely?
2. What is it about these people that made you choose them?
3. Which three people would be the last people you would turn to if you felt depressed, frightened, scared, or lonely?
4. What is it about these people that made you choose them last?

From your answers to questions 1 through 4, you should have the beginning of a list of the qualities you would and would not want in close friends you could turn to for support. Other qualities that you might want to list may come to mind. It might be helpful to draw up a chart of these qualities. Simply separate a sheet of paper into two columns and list qualities that you would want in friends in one column and qualities you would not want in the other.

Now go back and look at the people you listed in answer to question 1. Do these people have the qualities you have identified as desirable in people you could turn to for support? If these people do not have the qualities that you need in supportive persons, why are you turning to them for support?

Do the people you list as being the *last* people you would call on for support have any of the qualities you listed as undesirable?

Before you proceed with your assessment of what you do and do not need in terms of support, it may help to examine what you receive and what you contribute to your present friendships. To help you do this, make a list of the people you consider to be good friends—people you can confide in and turn to for help and support. For each person, examine what you "get" from your relationship with that person and what you "give" to the relationship. For example,

	GET	GIVE
MARY	*Willing to listen without offering advice*	*Willing to listen; am supportive*

If you feel a chart format might be helpful, draw up a chart.

Did you find it difficult to think of people you consider to be your good friends rather than just acquaintances? Is what you receive from each friend approximately equal to what you give each friend? Are you getting the kind of friendship you need from each person?

Which of the people on your friendship list are easy to give to? Which people on your list, if any, would you like to avoid because they drain you and "use your energy"? Why do you keep up friendships with people who drain you? Is there anything you can do to make these relationships less draining?

Being good to yourself means developing friendships that are nourishing for you. Many people have no close friends, only acquaintances. It helps to have several friends you can turn to for help and support. If you found it difficult to answer the preceding questions, or if you found no equity in the getting-and-giving exchange, you may want to consider the possibility of developing friendships that are good for you.

NEW FRIENDSHIP POSSIBILITIES

To help you examine your present friendships and to consider possibilities for new friendships that could provide emotional support, list the good friends you presently have. You may wish to refer to the list you made in the previous exercise.

1. How many people on your list are members of your family? Did you list your father or mother? Siblings? Children?
2. How many on your list are male? Are they family members? Friends?
3. How many people on your list are female? Are they family members? Friends?
4. How many people on your list are friends

you and your husband had as a married couple?
5. How many people on your list are single?
6. How many people on your list are divorced?
7. How many people on your list are primarily your friends (rather than your ex-husband's)?
8. How many people on your list are members of the "helping professions"? Did you list a counselor, psychologist, or psychiatrist? Minister, priest, or rabbi? Doctor or lawyer?
9. How many people on your list are members of groups which offer you support? Are there members of a women's group? Of a group for divorced or single people? Of a therapy group? Of a church group? Of a group at work?

The questions you just answered may provide you with information concerning who you choose to be your friends and serve as sources of support. Look over the list that follows and decide which categories might be potential sources of new friends for you.

—*family members*   —*doctors*
—*men*   —*lawyers*
—*women*   —*women's groups*
—*divorced people*   —*singles' groups*
—*single people*   —*therapy groups*
—*counselors*   —*church groups*
—*social workers*   —*occupational groups*
—*psychologists*   —*other*
—*psychiatrists*
—*members of the clergy*

If all your friends and support come from a particular group, for example your family, you may want to consider possible disadvantages of getting your support from that one group.

HOW NOURISHING ARE YOUR FRIENDSHIPS?

At this point, it would probably be helpful to examine how nourishing your friendships are for you considering your present stage of growth and development. Before you begin, state briefly how you presently feel about your divorce. Then list the people who are most important to you and examine briefly their reactions to your divorce. You may find it helpful to write out this list.

Now rate the people on your list as follows:

- Excellent for me considering my present stage of adjustment to divorce
- Average for me considering my present stage of adjustment to divorce.
- Poor for me considering my present stage of adjustment to divorce.

In what ways is your present reaction to your divorce similar to or different from the reactions of the people you listed?

On page 17 you were asked to identify your present stage of adjustment to divorce. How do your friends help or hinder you in this stage of adjustment? Considering your present stage of adjustment, are the people you turn to for support good for you?

Some friends continue to be nourishing for us as we grow and move through different stages of development. It is a rare and delightful experience when we can pick up a friendship and be on another's "wavelength" after months or even years have gone by and a multitude of life experiences have occurred. More often we find that as we change or our friends change, the friendship no longer offers us what it once did. When this happens, the friendship usually is phased out and new friendships develop that give us what we need at that particular time.

Do you have any friends whom you feel you have outgrown or with whom you no longer have much in common because of your marital status? If your answer is yes, what is it about this person(s) and yourself that makes your relationship less rewarding than it once was?

Do you continue to invest time and energy in relationships even though they are less rewarding than they once were? If your answer is yes, why do you continue to do this?

You will probably find that your time and energy as a divorced woman are more valuable to you than they ever have been before. Try to consider relationships as investments. If they consistently do not return what you invest in them in terms of your time and energy, examine your reasons for continuing them. Most people divorce because they feel their marital relationship no longer yields what it once did and because the emotional investment needed to continue the marriage is too great. Because time

and emotional energy are at a premium, avoid spending these limited resources on friends who no longer "fit" or who are "dead weight."

Evaluate the time and emotional energy you feel you presently *have* available to give to others by finding the appropriate point on this scale.

NO TIME OR EMOTIONAL ENERGY		LIMITED TIME AND EMOTIONAL ENERGY			UNLIMITED TIME AND EMOTIONAL ENERGY

```
+--+--+--+--+--+--+--+--+--+--+
0  1  2  3  4  5  6  7  8  9  10
```

Evaluate the time and emotional energy you presently *want* to give to others by finding the appropriate point on this scale.

NO TIME OR EMOTIONAL ENERGY		LIMITED TIME AND EMOTIONAL ENERGY			UNLIMITED TIME AND EMOTIONAL ENERGY

```
+--+--+--+--+--+--+--+--+--+--+
0  1  2  3  4  5  6  7  8  9  10
```

The time and energy you will have available or will want to share may vary greatly. At times, you may find that you need every bit of your time and energy for yourself. At other times, you will find yourself wanting to share your time and energy with others. Some women find themselves giving so much to others that they have nothing left for themselves. It is wise to keep a favorable balance of time and energy for yourself by periodically evaluating how much you have and want to give to others. Make offers and respond to others' needs with yourself, as well as the other person, in mind. Most successful relationships involve two people who give to and receive from each other.

MARRIED AND DIVORCED FRIENDS

To examine the married and divorced friends you may have in terms of the support they can offer you considering your present stage of growth and development, answer the following questions:

1. Which of your friends are married?
2. In general what has been their reaction to your divorce?

The following phases are used by Robert S. Weiss in his book *Marital Separation* (New York:

Basic Books, 1975) to describe typical reactions of married friends to a person who divorces.

PHASE 1

Married friends are very supportive. They may be *too* understanding and solicitous; this may cause the separated person to feel she is helpless.

PHASE 2

Married friends begin to recognize that the separated individual is moving toward a new way of life in which she will be confronted by the freedom and anxieties of being alone. The reactions of friends may vary from being supportive to being envious or threatened.

PHASE 3

Mutual withdrawal takes place. The divorced person and her friends realize that her life is now different and that the friendship is less rewarding than it once was.

Are you experiencing any of these phases with your married friends? If yes, which friends?

Some women find that their married friends continue to be a source of support. If you find, however, that you are drifting away from some of your married friends and vice versa, remember that this is a common occurrence when one divorces. It does not mean that they are deserting you or that you are deserting them. It simply means that because your situations and lives are different, you may not have as much in common as you once had. You may choose to turn to other people, such as divorced persons, with whom you would have more in common. Answer the following questions:

1. Do you have any divorced friends to whom you turn regularly for support?
2. Who are they?
3. Which stage of the adjustment process do you think best describes them?
4. Which friends are in the same adjustment stage as you?
5. Which friends are in a different adjustment stage than you?

Many divorced people find that the new friends they make are divorced—simply because it is easier to share experiences and problems with individuals in a similar situation. If you find yourself becoming friends with people who are divorced, consider the advisability of having friends who are in different stages of the adjustment process. The following chart lists some of the advantages and disadvantages of having friends in the same and in different stages of the adjustment process than the one in which you presently find yourself.

	ADVANTAGES FOR YOU	DISADVANTAGES FOR YOU
FRIENDS IN SAME ADJUSTMENT STAGE	*Can empathize and be supportive of each other*	*Can play games that keep them stuck in a given stage. Example: In the anger and ambivalence stage, friends may support each other indefinitely in the games "Isn't he a rat!" and "Ain't it awful!"*
FRIENDS IN STAGES AHEAD OF YOU	*Can empathize and be supportive because they have "been there"*	*You may compare yourself unfavorably with individuals who are at a later stage—they always seem "one step ahead"*
	Can serve as a model of someone who is growing and moving through the adjustment stages	*Friends who are a stage or two ahead of you may become impatient with you if they feel you are in a given stage too long*
	May be helpful in "showing you the ropes" of a stage you are just entering	
FRIENDS IN STAGES BEHIND YOU	*May help you realize how far you've come and how much you have grown by comparison*	*May drain you of your time and energy—people in stage 1 or 2 may be more "needy"*
	May contribute to your feeling competent and capable when you are able to help them or "show them the ropes"	*May trigger issues that are unresolved with you; this may cause discomfort and anxiety*

If you are at stage 4 or 5 of the adjustment process, you are busy pursuing goals and defining your identity. The time you may have to give to an individual in the beginning stages of the divorce process may be limited. You may want to limit the number of friends who require a great deal of your time and emotional energy. The advantage of giving emotional support to another woman who is in the beginning stages of the divorce process is that she is a potential source of future support. Hopefully, she will progress through the divorce process and will ultimately be able to give to you. Women are just learning to support and help each other; men have been trained to use the "Old Boy" network to help others. Women can benefit from developing a "New Woman" network of their own and utilizing it to help each other with emotional and practical needs.

EXAMPLE 1

When Sandy's husband left her for a young secretary in his office, leaving her with a four-year-old daughter and a three-month-old son, their married friends who lived in their neighborhood were most supportive. They helped Sandy through the first few months when she was trying to cope with the reality of her situation and with deciding what she wanted to do. Her married friends and neighbors were shocked. Sandy had appeared to have the "perfect marriage." Not only were they shocked that the "perfect couple" had problems, but they couldn't understand how Sandy's husband "could do such a thing."

After her divorce, Sandy felt it difficult to be with her married friends. The women either looked at her with pity or they tried to avoid her. They were afraid to be faced with the question of what *they* would do if their husbands left them. They talked about recipes at their get-togethers; Sandy talked about graduate schools. They no longer had much in common. The men were either protective of Sandy or made passes at her. When couples asked her to parties attended by other couples, she began to feel they were doing so out of pity—rather than giving to the United Fund that year they'd ask her over for dinner. On the occasions when Sandy would bring a date, she would sense the jealousy of her married friends. What adolescent pleasures was she now experiencing that they were not? Sandy was just beginning to realize some of the positive aspects of divorce—a chance to examine her goal for a career, an opportunity to develop her relationships with men, and time to determine what her values and identity really were. When she was by herself, she was beginning to feel alive and positive about her future. When she was with her married friends, she felt victimized and depressed about her past. Gradually, Sandy formed a new circle of friends who were divorced. They seemed to understand her. They neither pitied her nor were threatened by her activities as a single person.

Three years after her divorce, Sandy evaluated her friendships again. She had a circle of friends, both men and women, who were divorced. Since she was the first one in her circle of friends to get a divorce, women called her when they were having problems with their marriages or were going through the divorce process. Sandy realized that more and more of her time was being consumed by friends who were getting divorced and who needed a great deal of support. She was at a period in her life when she wanted more time for herself, her family, and her career. Gradually, she decided to maintain one or two limited friendships with friends who were going through a divorce and selected friends who were less energy- and time-consuming. She was able to be understanding, yet assertive about her present need for time for herself.

EXAMPLE 2

Judy was married to a college professor. Their married friends were all professors or employees of the college. Judy believed that their friends were her friends as well as her husband's. When she and John got divorced, she was disappointed to find that her friends from the college didn't continue to call her. She tried asking them over to the house but the invitations were rarely accepted. When they were, they weren't returned. Gradually Judy made new friends. It took a long time for her sense of hurt to diminish and for her to realize that her former friends were not rejecting her, they were just rejecting an awkward situation—one that made them uncomfortable.

BEING FRIENDS WITH YOUR FAMILY

One obvious source of friendship people may overlook is their family. Some adults are never quite able to resolve issues they had with their parents when they were growing up. Somehow, many adults still feel like children around their parents. Because it is difficult for many reasons to end our relationships with our parents if they are less than satisfactory, many of us continue shallow or polite relationships with them.

Some women find it possible to form new relationships with members of their immediate family during a divorce. In some instances, where relations with parents were strained prior to the divorce, new supportive relationships are developed. The point of the following exercise is not to tell you that you *have* to get support and friendship from your parents—for many reasons this may not be possible—but to point out that your parents may be a potential source of support to you. You may find this a good time to develop your relationship with them.

To help you examine potential sources of support within your family, briefly answer the following questions. If you find that writing out the answers is helpful, do so.

1. Carl A. Witaker, a well-known marriage counselor, feels that all first marriages are on the rebound from our separation from our family of origin. We marry so that we will not be alone.

   What were the circumstances surrounding your separation from your family of origin? Did you leave home to marry?

2. Often when we start a family of our own when we marry, certain issues we have with our family of origin remain unresolved. Were there any issues, arguments, or hurt feelings with your family that were left unsettled when you married?

   Can you share with your parents some of the issues or problems that may have gotten in the way of your relating to them? If not, why not?

3. Attending to those issues that were not resolved can serve as a first step to getting in touch with the person you were beginning to become before you may have stopped the process to become someone's wife. Did you know who you were and have a clear sense of your identity when you married?

   Did your parents approve of your marriage? Why or why not? What is your parents' reaction to your divorce?

   How supportive are your parents of you at this

point? Very supportive? Somewhat supportive? Not supportive?

4. Sometimes people complain that their parents treat them like children without considering that they may unconsciously be asking and encouraging their parents to treat them in this way. What do you feel the chances are of having an adult-adult relationship with your parents? If you feel the chances are "not good," what reasons can you give for feeling this way?

5. At the beginning stages of any crisis, it is very natural to feel overwhelmed and to want to be taken care of. Even when you are not in a crisis, it is sometimes nice to have someone "take over." Do you feel free to tell your parents when it is all right for them to do things for you? Do you also feel free to tell them when you want to do things on your own?

   Do you have a sense of when it is good for you to do things on your own and when it is good for you to allow others to help you? Give examples if possible.

6. You may want to "educate" your parents as to how they can best help you at this point. The qualities you decided you want in friends to whom you turn for support can also apply to your parents. Frequently we make the mistake of thinking that someone who loves us or really knows us should know what we want and need. People may often want to be supportive but for many reasons may not know how to go about it. It may be a relief for them to be told just how they can be helpful and supportive.

   How can your parents be most helpful to you at this time? What directions could you give to your parents to tell them how they can help you most? For example, you might want to say, "Mother, I really need you to listen to me and serve as a 'sounding board.' I'm not asking for advice at this point."

EXAMPLE

Janet had a guarded relationship with her parents during her nine-year marriage to Frank. She married at twenty when she was in her junior year of college after dating Frank exclusively for three years. Her parents were not pleased by the marriage—it wasn't that they disliked Frank, they just didn't think he was right for Janet or that Janet was right for him. They wanted her to date a number of men and have fun before she settled down to washing socks and diapering babies. Janet and Frank sensed their disapproval but walked down the aisle anyway. In order for Janet to feel loyal to her husband, she began to reject her parents and the life-style they presented as models. Her parents had stimulating careers and were open to the adventures that life offers.

The nine years of Janet's marriage were spent in having three children and moving them every two years when her husband was transferred. The only adventures she and her husband were open to were new split-levels and memberships in Newcomers' clubs. It was easy for Janet to ignore her parents' fun-loving life-style when she lived several states away.

When Janet and Frank divorced, she was able to reestablish a relationship with her parents. Janet felt that her parents rejected Frank. She did not understand that they felt he was too somber and conventional for her. Her parents felt that she had rejected them. They did not understand that it created a conflict to be close to a husband and parents who were so different in their outlooks on life. Janet gradually became the woman she had stopped becoming when she married Frank—fun-loving, adventurous, and capable. She was able to admit that while there were things she didn't like about her parents, she was essentially more similar to them in nature and what she wanted for her life than she was to her ex-husband. Janet's parents were pleased to see Janet change from the suburban matron who appeared to be ten years older than she really was into a thirty-year-old single woman who was enthusiastically examining who she was as she became her own person. Janet was able to develop a friendship with her parents where they were supportive and respected her new independence.

EDUCATING PEOPLE TO BE
THE FRIENDS YOU NEED

Often we expect people to know automatically what we need. Have you tried telling people what you need from them? It is possible that people may want to be supportive but may not know what you need at this time. We may give up on relationships when we do not get what we need. Sometimes ending relationships that we do not find nourishing is a good idea. At other times, with an investment of some time and energy, we can educate people to be the kind of friends we need.

To help you examine how you can educate people to be supportive and the kind of friends you need, work through the following activity.

List present relationships that you feel are unsatisfactory to you or could be improved. Then list the ways in which you would like each relationship to be improved. For example, what does the person(s) do who "turns you off," or what do you want that you are not getting from the relationship? Ask yourself these questions about each relationship.

Have you shared with this person(s) how you feel about the relationship? If yes, what was the result? If no, why do you hesitate to talk about your feelings concerning the relationship?

What would be the possible risks of such a discussion? What would be the possible gains from such a discussion? What do you think would happen?

Select one of the relationships you thought of as "unsatisfactory" or "could be improved" and decide what you could say to that person to instruct her or him in the kind of friendship you need at the present time. For example, you might want to say: "If you have expectations of me, I appreciate your telling me. That way I can decide what I want to do and we can talk about it. If I don't know what your expectations are, there is no way I can meet them even if I would like to. I end up feeling angry and frustrated."

Remember that people may receive your suggestions more readily if you speak in terms of your needs rather than in terms of people's failure to meet your needs. For example, "I really need you to listen," will be better received than, "You never listen to me."

It may be that people will choose *not* to act in ways you feel would be most helpful to you. There may be several reasons for this.

- You are asking them to act in new ways which may take time for them to learn.
- You are asking them to change, which might be threatening and uncomfortable for them.

• They may have their own need to continue relating to you in the ways they have been (they feel their need is stronger than your need).

If after repeated attempts you fail to get the support you need, you may decide that it would be best to turn to others for support. The time and energy you spend in trying to educate people in how they can be supportive of you will depend upon who the person is, how important that person is to you, how much time and energy you have to invest, and how much time and energy you have already invested in the relationship.

WOULD COUNSELING HELP YOU?

Almost all individuals could use counseling at some point in their lives. Psychiatrists, psychologists, social workers, clergy, and counselors all offer counseling that may be of help to you at some point during your adjustment to divorce. To determine if counseling might be helpful to you, decide which of the following statements apply to you.

—*feel stuck*
—*feel no one understands*
—*feel tired, lifeless, and run-down*
—*feel unable to relate to others*
—*don't know what is best for me*
—*don't know what I want*
—*feel confused by major decisions*
—*feel my life is over*
—*feel I have no identity*
—*feel I am worthless*
—*feel overwhelmed*
—*have no one to turn to*
—*am unable to function*
—*am always depressed*
—*can't handle my children*
—*don't know how to handle my anger*

Many of us feel these things from time to time when we are coping with divorce. If you feel that a number of these statements apply to you, you may have a special need for support and friendship. It may be that emotional support is not available to you at the present time and that you feel incapable of developing the friendships you

need. Or, you may need more from your friends at this point than they can or are capable of giving. A solution to this problem may be to get professional counseling for yourself. A counselor won't make your problems go away but she or he may be able to help you get to the point where you are more capable of dealing with your problems. Counselors are trained to be "expert friends." They may be able to provide you with the friendship you need at this point.

Some people have negative images of counselors and the counseling process, which causes them to dismiss the possibility of counseling. What preconceived impressions, if any, do you have of counseling?

You may want to check out these impressions with people who have experienced counseling or with counselors themselves. The book *Women in Transition: A Feminist Handbook on Separation and Divorce* (New York: Scribner's 1975) has excellent suggestions for selecting a counselor; see especially pages 401–12 and 464–65. It also has an excellent chapter on "Emotional Supports."

If you think you might be interested in counseling, you may want to contact some of the following:

• Community mental health agencies
• Family service agencies
• College counseling centers
• Members of the helping professions—recommendations from clergy, doctors, lawyers, social workers
• Friends who have had counseling
• Pastoral counseling centers
• Women's organizations

If you look hard enough, you can find the right counselor for you to suit your budget. Usually, when you make an appointment with a counselor in private practice, you can discuss fees and decide during the first few visits if you would feel comfortable with that person. If you visit an agency, fees are usually discussed during an initial session and a counselor will be selected with your particular needs in mind. Not all counselors are right for all people. If you find that you don't like a particular counselor, you can change and find one you do like. If you think counseling might be helpful, it is worth a try.

This chapter has encouraged you to examine your need for support and what you can do to get the support you need. The support will not come to you; you may have to be active and assertive in getting what you need. Here are some additional suggestions concerning places to go in search of support:

- Parents Without Partners—national organization with local chapters
- Young Single Parents—branches in the Chicago area
- Local singles' groups—consult magazines and guides of your area
- Church groups for single and divorced people
- Therapy groups for single and divorced people—contact your local community health or family service agency
- College courses in single living—check offerings in local adult education programs, community colleges, and colleges

- Women's centers
- YWCAs
- School social workers
- College counseling centers
- Consciousness-raising groups

If you can't locate a group that is right for you, start your own group. Team up with a friend or two who have similar needs. Try calling organizations such as the ones listed and tell them what you need in terms of a group. If they are unable to help you, put notices on bulletin boards or ads in appropriate papers. The point is that if you want and need support, it is up to you to decide what you need and to see that you get it. This might require some work on your part, but you will probably find it worth the effort. After all, what will you have if you do nothing?

HOW MUCH EMOTIONAL SUPPORT DO YOU GIVE YOURSELF?

I have really learned to watch the way I talk to myself. I used to talk myself down, and never be supportive of myself. My relationship with myself wasn't so great! I depended upon my husband to say encouraging and nice things to me. When I didn't hear them, I decided I must be no good. Then I started in on me. It is a new idea for me that I can be kind to myself. I'm working on it. It really feels good!

In the first chapter you examined the emotional support you get from others. This chapter will encourage you to examine the emotional support you give to yourself. In marriage, people often depend upon a partner for support. When the marriage ends, it may seem as if all emotional support is gone. Most people do not consider that they can provide support for themselves. This does not mean that we can do without other people. It does mean, however, that most people are capable of being kinder and better to themselves than they are. This chapter will help you examine three ways you can be supportive of yourself. First, it will ask you to consider what kind of friend you are to yourself. Second, it will ask you to examine how you talk to yourself. Third, it will ask you to acknowledge the resources that you have.

DO YOU NOURISH YOURSELF?

In the last chapter you were asked to examine the kinds of relationships that are nourishing for you. In *Creative Intimacy* (New York: Simon and Schuster, 1975), Dr. Jerry Greenwald talks about relationships that are nourishing and toxic. Just as it is important to have nourishing relationships with others, it is important to have a nourishing relationship with yourself. Greenwald states, "When we are on intimate terms and enjoy a loving relationship with ourselves, then whatever the course of our relationships with others, we can always in times of adversity or rejection turn inward to our own resources and find the comfort and security that come from loving ourselves and knowing who we are."

To help you determine whether you have a "nourishing" or a "toxic" relationship with yourself, decide which statement in each of the following pairs best describes you.

1.a. I love and accept myself even though I am aware that I want to change some of my attitudes or behavior.

b. I feel unloving and rejecting toward

myself when I am in touch with parts of me that I don't like.

2.a. I feel elation and excitement when I discover things about myself of which I was previously unaware.

  b. New experiences make me feel anxious and afraid that I will discover things about myself that will also be unacceptable to me.

3.a. I choose and develop friendships that are good for me.

  b. I find myself in relationships that offer little and use up time and energy I could spend on myself.

4.a. I have the ability to be assertive, to stand up for what I want for myself, and to say no to those things I don't want.

  b. I am rarely assertive and seldom stand up for what I want for myself; I always let the needs and wants of others come first.

5.a. I know what my goals and values are and am moving in a direction that is consistent with them.

  b. I set no goals and am unaware of my values; my activities often seem purposeless and I have no sense of direction.

6.a. I take care of myself physically and avoid activities that are detrimental to my health and vitality.

  b. I pay little attention to what is good for me physically and often find that I lack energy and vitality.

7.a. I can distinguish between being lonely and alone and can enjoy my own company.

  b. Being alone for me means being lonely; I'll go to great lengths to avoid being alone.

8.a. I am interested in expanding my own awareness of myself in my quest for greater intimacy.

  b. Even if I feel full of discontentment and frustration, I would rather leave well enough alone for fear that knowing myself will only make things worse.

9.a. I feel that there is no thought, feeling, or impulse within me, however upsetting, that could shake my self-love and belief that I am in control of myself.

  b. I am afraid that deep within me there are dreadful thoughts or impulses that might emerge and destroy me or isolate me from other people.

10.a. I feel that I can take better care of myself and my needs than anyone else, however loving, possibly could.

  b. I use my time and energy looking for someone who can take over the responsibility of taking care of me and my needs.

11.a. I allow my thoughts and feelings to emerge into full awareness.

  b. I squeeze myself when I become aware of some unfamiliar thought or feeling emerging that might make me uncomfortable.

12.a. I am comfortable with the thoughts and feelings I decide to share with others as well as those I will not share with anyone.

  b. I feel guilty when I am unwilling to share parts of myself even with my most intimate friends.

13.a. I am in touch with my inner resources and strengths and turn to these to resolve my anxieties, conflicts, and frustrations.

  b. I attempt to manipulate others into solving my problems and relieving my frustrations and anxieties.

14.a. My quest for greater inner intimacy is centered on my own growing acceptance of myself as lovable.

  b. I keep hoping that if I can get others to love and approve of me that this, in turn, will lead to an increased acceptance and love within myself.

15.a. I feel eager to initiate activities and thereby take responsibility for generating new experiences that may be growth-enhancing.

  b. I frequently wait passively for external stimulation or other people to relieve my boredom and make my life more exciting.

16.a. I give myself rewards when I achieve the realistic goals I set for myself and am kind to myself when I fall short of my goals.

  b. I set impossible goals for myself and constantly berate myself for getting nowhere.

17.a. I offer myself the same care, kindness, and consideration that I offer to other people.
   b. I always give others more care, kindness, and consideration than I give to myself because they are more important.
18.a. I accept my mistakes as an inevitable part of learning.
   b. I attack myself with ridicule, disgust, or self-punishment when I make mistakes.
19.a. I function as best I can in the present.
   b. I cling to the misfortunes of my past—real or imagined—and use these as excuses to avoid taking responsibility for myself in the present.
20.a. I see myself as continuing to grow to the last day of my life.
   b. I create artificial cutoffs (e.g., "after thirty it's all downhill") and live as if my opportunities for new discoveries and joys were over.*

The first statement in each pair is obviously representative of a nourishing relationship with oneself; the second statement is representative of a toxic relationship with oneself. If you chose the second statement consistently, you need to develop your relationship with yourself. Try to be aware of and avoid things you do that are toxic to yourself.

ARE YOU A GOOD FRIEND TO YOURSELF?

Many of us feel it is important to be good friends to other people but do not work on being good friends to ourselves.

Look again at page 23 in chapter 1 where you were asked to list qualities that are important to you in close friends. After reviewing the qualities you stated were important to you, answer the following questions. This will help you assess the kind of friend you are to yourself.

1. Which of the qualities that you feel are important in people you turn to for support do you find you use in your relationship with yourself? For example, if you seek understanding friends, are you understanding of yourself?
2. Which qualities that you feel were important in friends could you use in your relationship with yourself to a greater extent?
3. Review the qualities of people that "turn you off." Do you find any of those qualities in your relationship with yourself? Which ones?
4. Give the name of a person to whom you are a good friend. In what ways do you show yourself the same respect, kindness, and consideration as you do to that friend?
5. In what ways do you *not* show yourself the same respect, kindness, and consideration as you do to that friend?
6. If you were asked to make a contract to improve your relationship with yourself, what would the contract include? Be as specific as possible.

EXAMPLE

I am going to be kinder and less critical of myself when I make mistakes at work.

Signed_____

Write out your contract with yourself and try to keep it.

Most of us find it easy to praise other people or to give them pep talks when they are discouraged. We are told it is good to praise others but immodest to praise ourselves. Therefore, when we need some praise and there is no one around to supply it, we may feel lonely and unappreciated. To help assess this feeling, practice praising and being supportive of yourself.

Spend approximately five minutes writing down accomplishments, skills, abilities, attributes, and characteristics for which you praise yourself.

Anticipate the next time you will feel "down." Write a brief pep talk for yourself.

---

* This questionnaire adapted from Jerry Greenwald's *Creative Intimacy: How to Break the Patterns That Poison Your Relationships* (New York: Simon and Schuster, 1975), Jerry Greenwald's *Be the Person You Were Meant to Be* (New York: Simon and Schuster, 1973), and Marie Edwards's *The Challenge of Being Single* (Los Angeles: Tarcher, 1974).

HOW DO YOU MANAGE STRESS?

One reality about adults is that they don't like change. Rarely do people decide to make major changes. Change occurs when people are forced to change or when maintaining the status quo becomes too painful.

The degree of change, and the number of changes that occur at one time, determine the degree of stress you will experience. Stress occurs when an individual is required to react to a change in the environment, in others, in oneself, or in one's life situation.

There are few events in life that are as stressful as divorce, perhaps because divorce may create change in almost every area of a woman's life. The woman experiencing divorce may be changing her financial condition, her relationship with friends and family, her relationship with her children, her sex life, her place of residence, and so on. Any one of these changes can be monumental in themselves. When numerous changes occur at once it can be overwhelming and thus overly stressful.

Too little stress can lead to a lack of functioning. Too much stress, or overwhelming stimuli to react to, can also render a person dysfunctional. Shock is a common reaction when a person has to cope with overwhelming change and consequently too much stress. Stress is not always bad, however. So the objective is not to eliminate it but to learn how to manage it. The adjustment stage of denial, for example, allows a person to acknowledge only the change they are capable of dealing with at a given time. Therefore, denial serves as a protection against too much stress. Ultimately, a person should develop more productive stress-coping methods.

There are a number of coping mechanisms people commonly use in dealing with the stress that accompanies change. Some of the coping mechanisms can be harmful if done to excess. Some of them can be helpful. Check the coping mechanisms you have used to deal with the stress you have experienced.

COPING MECHANISMS

—*Drinking*   —*Exercise*
—*Drugs*   —*Counseling*
—*Overeating*   —*Avoidance*
—*Shopping sprees*   —*Using humor*
—*Crying*   —*Religion*
—*Support groups*   —*Always talking in posi-*
—*Talking with*   *tive, encouraging*
  friends   *terms to oneself*

Some of the ways people cope with stress such as drinking or drug abuse can make things worse. Now is the time to take good care of yourself. Be sure to watch your diet, get plenty of exercise, and get any medical help that is needed.

How you look at change greatly affects your ability to manage it effectively. Change has two aspects: crisis and opportunity. Hopefully the exercises in this book will help you to manage the crisis aspect of change and to optimize the opportunities that divorce provides to determine who you are and what you want your future to be.

Ask yourself, "Do I manage stress?" or, "Does stress manage me?"

Only you can decide the answer!

HOW DO YOU VIEW DIVORCE?

You are the person who can offer yourself the most support and encouragement. Pay attention to how you talk to yourself. Do you pay yourself compliments and give yourself pep talks when you are down? Or, do you scare yourself to death and tell yourself that you'll never be able to handle your new responsibilities as a single person? You may find that your thoughts and attitudes toward your divorce make a difference in how you grow as a single person. You have the ability to choose what you think about divorce. Some people choose to look at divorce as a tragedy and manage to be miserable for the rest of their lives. Others recognize the difficulties that come with divorce but are also willing to look at its positive aspects.

Examine your views on divorce and how they affect your adjustment to divorce. How do you view the positive aspects of divorce? To help assess your views, work through the following exercise:

1. Honestly describe how you presently feel about divorce and your divorce in particular.
2. How have your views affected your adjustment to divorce?

3. The following list of positive aspects of divorce was adpted from Marie Edwards's *The Challenge of Being Single* (Los Angeles: J. P. Tarcher, 1974). Answer yes or no to indicate if you have experienced any of these positive aspects.

   a. An opportunity to develop skills, cultivate talents, develop goals and pursue them more single-mindedly

   b. An opportunity to better evaluate what you want and need out of life

   c. More freedom to make your own decisions without having to compromise, to set your own schedules, to pursue your own interests

   d. An opportunity to try new things, new places, new ideas

   e. An opportunity to develop new relationships with people of both sexes

   f. Privacy to think and create with less interruption and interference

Make a contract with yourself to experience one of the positive aspects of divorce that was listed. State specifically what you plan to do and when you plan to do it. Write out your contract.

EXAMPLE

To experience divorce as an opportunity to try new things, new places, and new ideas, I am going to go on an architectural tour this Saturday.

Signed _____

WHAT RESOURCES DO YOU HAVE?

When women first separate or divorce, they often find that a sense of security is missing. A husband may represent financial security, provide emotional support, and help with major decisions. When a husband is no longer present, one may feel abandoned and without certain strengths and abilities to depend upon. Because there is often a tendency to dwell on what is missing in one's life after divorce, women may find that they are not examining the resources and strengths that they have.

To help you evaluate your present resources and additional resources you will need during the adjustment process, compile a list of your assets and resources. In other words, list the things, both tangible and intangible, that you can draw upon and that are in your favor.

A partial list of general categories of assets and resources follows. Note those that you feel you may have.

—*money*　　　　　—*skills*
—*time*　　　　　—*job experience*
—*material posses-*　—*special abilities*
　sions　　　　—*personal experience*
—*family*　　　　—*personal qualities*
—*friends*　　　　—*other*
—*education*

You may not be identifying some of the assets and resources you have because you are considering them in too narrow a sense. The following explanations and questions may help.

MONEY—Most people feel that they suffer from a lack of this particular resource. Do you have enough money to provide you and your children with the basics of food and shelter? For how long? You may not have the money for a Mercedes or a Pucci outfit but, if you have enough money for immediate survival, you can focus on other things. Are you able to borrow money from a bank, parents, or friends? You may want to examine how you spend your money. The way to have more money is to earn more or spend less. Are there ways you could earn more money? What things for which you presently spend money could you do without? The resource of money will be examined at length in chapter 10.

TIME—If you are not forced to go to work immediately, or are not forced to make immediate decisions concerning your future, you may consider time as a resource. If you do feel you must make immediate decisions, ask yourself who or what is forcing you to do so. Time can enable you to feel better about yourself, make better decisions, and put your life in order.

MATERIAL POSSESSIONS—Do you own the things that you consider to be necessities? Material possessions can be converted into cash in some cases to provide a sense of security.

FAMILY—Do you have family members who are willing to support you emotionally and/or financially? Don't automatically assume that if you have had trouble with your family in the past you cannot count on them now. A crisis can often provide an avenue for renewed communication in the most strained relationships. You may have to tell your family members what you would find helpful at this point.

FRIENDS—Do you have any special friends in whom you can confide or who will give you emotional support? You may find that if you risk asking for help, your friends will be willing to help. Again, you may have to define what they can do to help you.

EDUCATION—Do you have a college education or an education that will prepare you for a job or career? If you do, count this as a resource.

SKILLS—Do you have a special skill that has been developed? Have you been trained to perform a special job? If you can answer yes, count this as a resource.

JOB EXPERIENCE—If you have held jobs in the past, the experience will serve as a resource. Don't forget to include volunteer or community jobs that required you to develop certain abilities and talents.

SPECIAL ABILITIES—Do you have any special talents? Do you do something particularly well? Count these as resources if your answer is yes.

PERSONAL EXPERIENCE—If you have experience that might help you in the future—be it experience on the job or general living experience that has helped you learn more about yourself and life—consider this a resource.

PERSONAL QUALITIES—Most people have special personal qualities that make life easier. If you have a sense of humor, determination, courage, or any qualities you consider special, count them as assets or resources.

In order to evaluate your assets and resources, study the following chart and check the appropriate column to indicate if you feel the resources you have in a given area are adequate or inadequate. If you are not certain of the status of a given asset or resource, check "uncertain." For example, if you are in the beginning stages of divorce, you may be unsure of what your material or monetary assets will be.

Next, consider how important these assets and resources are to you in your present situation. Put a "1" in the "Importance" column if you feel the resource is very important. Write a "2" if you feel the resource is somewhat important, a "3" if you feel it is of little importance.

RESOURCES	ADEQUATE	INADEQUATE	UNCERTAIN	IMPORTANCE
MONEY				
TIME				
MATERIAL POSSESSIONS				
FAMILY				
FRIENDS				
EDUCATION				
SKILLS				
JOB EXPERIENCE				
SPECIAL ABILITIES				
PERSONAL EXPERIENCE				
PERSONAL QUALITIES				
OTHER				

IN WHAT WAYS ARE YOU SPECIAL?

Sometimes women need help in thinking positively about themselves and in identifying the personal resources they have. To encourage you to examine ways in which you are special, examine the following list* of words. Write out the words that you feel apply to you. It does not matter if others would agree—if *you* think you have a particular quality, be sure to list it.

* This list is from James I. Briggs, Career Development Seminar, Director of Career Planning and Placement, Georgetown University, Washington, D.C., July 14, 1976.

academic	conscientious	goal-directed	open-minded	reflective	supportive
accurate	conservative	healthy	opportunistic	reliable	sympathetic
active	considerate	helpful	optimistic	resourceful	tactful
adaptable	cooperative	honest	organized	responsible	tenacious
adventurous	courageous	idealistic	outgoing	retiring	thoughtful
affectionate	daring	imaginative	painstaking	robust	tolerant
aggressive	deliberate	independent	patient	self-confident	tough
alert	determined	informal	peaceful	self-controlled	trusting
ambitious	dignified	intellectual	persevering	sensitive	unaffected
analytical	discreet	intelligent	poised	serious	unassuming
artistic	dominant	introspective	polite	sincere	understanding
assertive	eager	kind	practical	sociable	uninhibited
attractive	easygoing	leisurely	progressive	spontaneous	verbal
broad-minded	emotional	lighthearted	punctual	spunky	versatile
businesslike	farsighted	likable	quick	stable	warm
calm	firm	loving	quiet	strong	witty
capable	flexible	loyal	rational	strong-minded	zany
cautious	forgiving	mature	realistic		
charming	formal	meticulous			
cheerful	frank	moderate			
clever	friendly	modest			
competitive	generous	natural			
compulsive	gentle	obliging			

Now, return to the list and indicate the qualities you would like to have. What could you do to develop these qualities?

WHAT DO YOU VALUE?

One positive thing about divorce for me was that for the first time in my life I was forced to examine my values. I learned that the way I had been living in marriage really didn't represent my values at all!

Planning for your future involves knowing what your values are. Everything you do, every decision you make, and every course of action you take is based on your consciously or unconsciously held beliefs, attitudes, and values. When you set goals or make decisions, you are making a statement about who you are and what you believe to be important. Many women faced with divorce realize that they are unsure of their values. They may never have been forced to consider their values. They may have lived according to their husband's values or may have patterned their lives upon the way things *should be*. Still other women are overwhelmed by the multitude of values from which to choose. In their "new freedom" they are totally confused. Deciding what you value is a first step in deciding the person you want to be and the direction you want your life to take. You may find people who tell you what you should value—perhaps your ex-husband, parents, friends, or children. While it may initially seem easier to accept the values of another, in the end it is self-defeating. Finding out what you value provides you with a greater sense of identity.

There are three major ways we make statements about the values that are important to us. First, we prize our beliefs and the behaviors that are determined by the values we hold. We may publicly affirm our values when appropriate. Second, we choose our beliefs and behaviors from alternatives after considering the consequences. The choices we make reveal our values. Third, we act on our beliefs with some consistency and repetition in our daily lives. The activities in this chapter will help you consider what you affirm, the decisions you make, and how you act in order to examine your values.

In order for the exercises to help you determine what you value, it is necessary for you to complete them honestly. In other words, give *your* answers, not the answers you feel others want you to give. Keep in mind that *values are neither right nor wrong in themselves*. You may disagree with the values others hold and others may disagree with the values you hold, but the important thing is to face yourself honestly concerning your values. This is often hard for women to do. Stereotypes of women suggest that they should hold certain values. You may find after completing these activities that the values you *thought* you held are not really yours. If, for example, you find that the value of achievement is more important to you than the value of nurturing others, don't apologize. If you try to center your life around a value that you feel you should have, you, and those around you, will be miserable. Consider the woman who forces herself to stay home with her children when she really wants a career. Not only does she become increasingly frustrated but her children sense that she would really rather be elsewhere. So be honest! If the values you decide are important to you surprise you, it is enough just to recognize them as your values. Later you will be asked to implement them and will receive help in assertively standing up for what you value.

HOW DO YOU AFFIRM YOUR VALUES?

Many people value the items listed below:

—honesty	—success
—intelligence	—money
—achievement	—popularity
—pleasure	—health
—power	—independence
—security	—service
—family happiness	—personal relationships
—religion	—recognition
—adventure	—personal development

What things are important to you? Make a list of these things. Now look at the list of things you value. Write a *P* next to those values you affirm or have affirmed publicly. Put a *D* next to those that played a part in an important decision you may have made. Put a *C* in front of those you wish to continue in life with some consistency.

Now think about your decision to get a divorce. What values were involved with that decision? If you feel the decision was your ex-husband's, what values are involved in the particulars of your situation, for example, your agreement to get a divorce, your reluctance to get a divorce, and so on.

What do you consider to be the three most important values to your ex-husband? Do you share these values? If not, what part, if any, did a conflict of values play in your marital problems and ultimate divorce?

EXAMPLE

June always felt that her values and her husband's were identical. They had started dating at age fifteen and had grown up together. When they started to have marital problems and June began to examine who she was through counseling, she was surprised to find that her values differed from her husband's. She valued achievement—her achievement. Any ambition she had ever possessed had been transferred to her husband and her children. When she got a divorce, she also realized that her personal growth was most important to her. She was unwilling to put it on a back burner to save the marriage. She learned that she was a risk taker who wanted to experience all the pleasures life had to offer.

George, on the other hand, valued security. His main ambition was to climb the corporate ladder, which he did quite successfully. He was a dependable person. He saw no necessity for looking inward; this might only stir things up and he was satisfied with the way things were. He wanted his wife to be a "traditional wife"—to put him and the family first and to derive satisfaction through meeting their needs. He was an excellent provider. He just couldn't understand why his wife wasn't satisfied.

Which values are most important to June? Which values are most important to George? How do you think a difference of values contributed to marital problems that ended in their divorce?

RELATING ACTIVITIES TO VALUES

We often show what we value by the activities we enjoy. Use the chart* on page 41 as a guide to help you analyze the activities you enjoy. Make up a similar chart for yourself. List twenty things you enjoy doing on the chart. Put a check in the following columns if they describe each activity. Rank the twenty activities you enjoy (#1 being the most important) to indicate their importance to you.

* This exercise is adapted from Sidney B. Simon, Leland W. Howe, and Howard Kirschenbaum's *Values Clarification: A Handbook of Practical Strategies for Teachers and Students* (New York: Hart Publishing Co., 1972). Used by permission of A & W Publishers, Inc.

RANK	20 THINGS I ENJOY DOING	COSTS MORE THAN $10 $	ENJOY ALONE ENJOY WITH PEOPLE ENJOY ALONE/PEOPLE A P A/P	REQUIRES PLANNING PL	WANT TO DEVOTE MORE TIME MT	INVOLVES RISK R	INVOLVES INTIMACY I	ACTIVE ACTIVITY PASSIVE ACTIVITY AT PS

SYMBOLS

Col. 1: **$** if it costs more than $10 each time it is done

Col. 2: **A** if you enjoy doing it alone
P if you enjoy doing it with other people
A/P if you can enjoy the activity alone or with other people

Col. 3: **PL** if the activity requires planning

Col. 4: **MT** if you want to devote more time to this activity in the future

Col. 5: **R** if the activity involves some risk—physical, emotional, or intellectual risk

Col. 6: **I** if the activity involves intimacy with another person—man or woman

Col. 7: **AT** if you regard this as an active activity
PS if you regard this as a passive activity

What does your chart tell you about yourself? Your values?

NOTE: If you found it difficult to list twenty things you enjoy doing, it may indicate that you have not had the time, opportunity, or encouragement to determine what is important to you. Some of the positive aspects of divorce listed on page 36 may provide you with a new opportunity to pursue those things you enjoy and value.

TIME AND VALUES

How we spend our time can be an indication of what we value. The circle below represents a typical day. Each slice represents several hours. To help you examine how you spend your time and to consider how your use of time reflects your values, estimate the number of hours or parts of an hour you spend on each of the following activities:

- Sleep
- With family, including mealtimes
- With friends
- Work
- Chores
- Alone—reading, watching TV, doing things for yourself
- Other activities

Your estimates will not be exact, but they should add up to twenty-four hours. Draw slices in a circle to represent proportionately the part of the day you spend on each category.

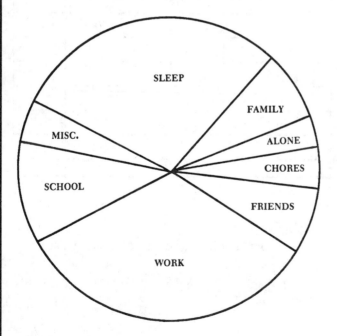

Write brief answers to the questions that follow.

1. Are you satisfied with the relative sizes of your slices? Why or why not?
2. Do you spend your time on what you want to do or what you think you *should* do?

3. What does the way you spend your time say about your values?
4. Refer to the exercise on page 40 that asked you to list your values. On which values do you spend time?
5. Is your circle consistent with your values? For example, if a close family life is an important value for you, do you spend part of your day with your family?
6. If you do not devote time to the things you value, why not?
7. Ideally, how big would you want each slice of your pie to be? Draw your *ideal* pie.
8. Realistically, is there anything you can do to change the size of your slices?
9. Do you see major future changes in your pie because of your divorce?
10. In what ways can you use your time more efficiently?
11. What are the chief interruptions you have when you are doing something that is important to you?
12. What can you do to minimize those interruptions?

NOTE: A distinction may be made between "time" and "quality time." It is not just the hours you have available but how you use them that counts. For example, you may have less time to spend with your children than another person but, while you are with them, you may make that time very meaningful.

HOW ACTIONS REVEAL YOUR VALUES

The following activity* will help you consider your values in relation to what you do. Make a chart for yourself like the one on page 43. On the chart, write ten things you have done during the last year *in order of their importance to you*. Put the thing that was most important to you first. You may include both activities for which you were paid and for which you were not paid,

* Adapted with permission from *How to Decide: A Guide for Women* by Nelle Tumlin Scholz, Judith Sosbee Prince, and Gordon Porter Miller, copyright © 1975 by College Entrance Examination Board, New York.

TEN THINGS YOU HAVE DONE IN THE LAST YEAR	PRIORITY OF VALUES									
	1	2	3	4	5	6	7	8	9	10
1.										
2.										
3.										
4.										
5.										
6.										
7.										
8.										
9.										
10.										
TOTAL										

things you do for pleasure, and things that relate to work and/or leisure. Following the chart, you will find a list of ten common values. Rank order these values according to their importance to you and put the most important value in column 1 at the top of the chart, the second-most important value in the second column, and so on. Then follow the directions given for each value.

VALUES

INTEREST—In the column you have labeled "Interest," put a check next to any activity on your list that you did because you really liked doing it.

INDEPENDENCE—In the column you labeled "Independence," put a check next to any activity you did because you like to do things on your own without having to follow a lot of orders and directions.

SELF-EXPRESSION—In the column you labeled "Self-expression," put a check next to any activity you did because you feel that using your natural talent or ability helps you express who you really are and what you do well.

SERVICE—In the column you labeled "Service," put a check next to any activity you did because it had meaning for others or because it was for another person's benefit.

LEADERSHIP—In the column you labeled "Leadership," put a check next to any activity you did because you like to use your leadership abilities.

REWARD—In the column you labeled "Reward," put a check next to any activity you did because you expected to receive money or some other kind of reward.

ACHIEVEMENT—In the column you labeled "Achievement," put a check beside any activity you did because advancement and growth are important to you.

RECOGNITION—In the column you labeled "Recognition," put a check beside any activity you did because recognition of your work by others is important to you.

VARIETY—In the column you labeled "Variety," put a check beside any activity you did because you like to do new and different things.

SECURITY—In the column you labeled "Security," put a check beside any activity you did because you feel comfortable doing it, it was familiar to you, and you found it easy to do.

After you have checked the ten activities for the ten value columns, total the responses in each column. Now check for consistency between the values you said were most important to you and the activities you said you enjoyed most.

1. Are your totals in the first several columns the highest?
2. Do you have the greatest number of check marks in the boxes at the upper-left section and the lower-right section of the chart?
3. If your answer to either of these questions is no, there is an inconsistency in what you say you enjoy doing and the values you have rank ordered. What might account for your inconsistencies? You may find, for example, that "Things I have done have not really reflected my values" or "The priority I originally assigned to the values does not really reflect me."

YOUR VALUES IN RELATION TO THOSE OF OTHERS

We often find that we have been influenced by the values of important people in our lives. Sometimes we adopt the values of others as our own without really asking whether they are our values too. Sometimes we decide that we really do share values of people who have been important to us; sometimes we discover our values are in conflict with the values of those around us.

You will probably find it helpful to examine your values in relation to values of others who have played an important role in your life. To do so, list five people who have played, or who presently play, an important role in your life. Next to each person's name, list the three values that you believe are most important to that person.

Now write brief answers to the following questions:

1. Do any of these people have values that you share? Who?
2. Do any of these people have values that you may think you *should* share but that you really do not share? Who?
3. Have any of these people pressured you, either directly or indirectly, to share their values? Who?
4. If your answer to the last question was yes, how did you react to this pressure? Did you conform, rebel, or ignore the pressure?
5. Do you feel conflict with any of the people on your list? If yes, name them.
6. Do your values conflict with those of any of the people you listed? If yes, list the name(s) or the person(s) and the value(s) that conflict with yours.
7. If you listed an individual in the last question, will you be dealing with that person in the future? Do you think your conflict of values will be an issue with that person? How do you plan to deal with your conflict of values?

VALUE EXPECTATIONS

To help you examine your values and the values others may expect you to have, make a list of those values below that are important to you.

VALUES

—security	—emotional	—achievement
—cooperation	awareness	—education
—family life	—risk taking	—activity
—service to others	—independence	—objectivity
—sensitivity	—competence	—competition
—compassion	—logical thinking	—power
—tenderness		
—passivity		

How many of the values in the left-hand column did you list? How many in the right-hand column?

The values listed in the left-hand column are those which people who hold a traditional view of a woman's role would ascribe to women; those in the right-hand column are values that people traditionally ascribe to men. ***There are no right or wrong answers to this exercise.*** Many people, men and women, would list values from each column. Women are often pressured into feeling they *should* hold the values in the left-hand column. If you listed values in the second column, you may encounter some resistance from people who have fixed ideas about what men and women *should* be. Stereotypes of what is masculine and what is feminine affect the opportunities you have available to you as a woman as well as your aspirations and your beliefs about yourself. Some women have been prevented from becoming what they could have become because of myths concerning what men and women should be.

Have you restricted yourself in any way because you felt you had to hold values that were traditionally viewed as feminine? In what way? Have you ever been judgmental of men because they held values that were traditionally viewed as feminine?

Remember that both men and women have suffered from outworn myths of what men and women should value. You may want to think about things you can do in your relationship with yourself, with men and with women in order not to perpetuate these myths.

ORDERING YOUR VALUES

Think about the values you said were important to you in the activities you just completed. Make a list of these values. Check those that you indi-cated were important to you in more than one activity.

Now select the ten values that you believe are most important to you at this time. Rank order them according to their order of importance *to you*. Put the most important value first, the second-most-important value second, and so on. Write out your list.

HOW DO YOU IMPLEMENT YOUR VALUES?

In order to examine the role the values you stated were important to you play in your life, try to analyze these values. You may want to draw up a work sheet for each of the ten values. At the top of each work sheet write the value. Then answer the following questions:

1. How do I define this value?
2. What do I do to implement this value in my life?
3. What do I refrain from doing in my life due to this value?
4. Am I consistent or inconsistent in my implementation of this value?

A FINAL NOTE
ABOUT VALUES
As you continue to grow as a single individual, you may find that your values, or the priority of your values, change. Therefore, it is a good idea to periodically assess your values in order to see if the values that are most important to you at the time are being implemented in your life.

HOW DO YOU PLAN FOR YOUR FUTURE?

Planning for the future was at once thrilling and terrifying for me. For years I had just gone along, moving when my husband was transferred and just fitting in with other people's plans. It was hard to get used to the idea when divorced that I was planning for my future—that I had to decide what I wanted for myself and then act on it!

Now that you have identified and examined the values that will play an important part in the plans and decisions you will make concerning your life as a single individual, you will be introduced to a planning model that will ask you to set goals for your future. The model will also help you formulate objectives to meet those goals that are consistent with your values.

You have probably known people who seem to have a knack for getting what they want from life. Often what differentiates people who accomplish things from those who do not is that the doers know where they want to go and have a plan for getting there. For many women faced with divorce, planning for the future is a new, and often a frightening, experience.

In the past, planning for the future may have revolved around your husband. It may be that in reality you were planning for his future rather than your own. Or, you may have been "just going along" without doing much planning on a conscious level. Because you are a woman, society has encouraged you "not to make waves," to "go along with things," and "be the woman behind the man." When you are suddenly forced to plan for your future it may seem like a foreign process—one for which you are totally unprepared. Because men have been culturally conditioned to be the leaders and women the followers, you may need special help when thrust into a position that requires you to plan for your future.

Although planning for your future may seem frightening initially, the realization that you are responsible for your life and future also has its rewards. Hopefully, you will begin to feel that you have more control over your life. A positive aspect of divorce is that it is possible for you to make *your* plans without having to compromise with or follow the plans of another person that might conflict with yours. The activities in this chapter will help you plan for the future in the following ways:

1. They will ask you to examine what you want.
2. They will ask you to assess your present situation and what your future will be like if you do nothing to change your present direction.
3. They will ask you to set goals for your future.

4. They will ask you to formulate objectives to help you reach the goals you have set.

YOUR DREAMS FOR THE FUTURE

Many of us find it difficult to plan creatively for the future because practical restraints of the present, such as money, put a ceiling on our dreams. To free you from practical considerations so that you can dream of a future you would like to have, imagine that you will be given, tax-free, one million dollars per year for the next twenty years. Write a description of what you would do during the first year after receiving the money. Then describe what your life would be like—where you would live, how you would spend your time, what you would do for pleasure, the people with whom you would spend time, the work you would do, and so on.

Which of the activities you mentioned would be a possibility without the million dollars? Which activities would be possible but would take you longer to achieve?

Are your dreams for your "million-dollar future" consistent with the values you stated were important to you in the last chapter?

How did the million-dollar gift influence the way you look at your future? Is there any way you could get money to accomplish your dream on a more limited scale?

YOUR LIFE FIVE YEARS FROM NOW

When women divorce, they may be so caught up in the problems of the present that they spend little time thinking of what they want their future to be like. Take time to think about what you would like your life to become. Imagine a typical day in your life five years from now. Write a description of your day from the time you get up to the time you go to bed. In your description you may want to include where you imagine yourself to be living, the important people in your life, the way you feel about yourself, the career or job you may have, what you do for fun, in short, what your general life-style will be.

What parts of your description do you feel you will be unable to attain? What obstacles will prevent you from attaining them? Is there anything you can do to eliminate those obstacles?

Compare your description of this future with that of your million-dollar future. Were there major differences between your two descriptions? If so, what were these differences? Were there any similarities in the descriptions you wrote for the two futures? If yes, what were the similarities you noted?

Which parts of the description of your five-year future do you think you will realistically be able to attain? What will you have to do to attain them?

YOUR PERSONAL IDEAL

Most of us have ideal images of what we would like to be. The areas listed below are important in most people's lives. To help you define your personal ideal, be as definite as possible in describing what you would like to achieve in these nine areas over the next five years. Think in terms of optimum achievement, but be realistic. For example, in the physical/personal health area, you might like to be ten pounds lighter. This would be possible to achieve.

1. PHYSICAL/PERSONAL HEALTH—What do you want in terms of weight, physical condition, absence of harmful activities such as smoking and drinking, and so on?
2. FINANCIAL STATUS—What do you want in terms of money to live on, material possessions, investments, insurance, and so on?
3. EDUCATION/INTELLECTUAL—What level of education and intellectual development do you want to achieve? Consider both degree and nondegree education.
4. PROFESSIONAL/CAREER STATUS—What do you want to achieve in terms of a job or career?
5. SPIRITUAL LIFE—What kind of relationship do you want with yourself? What role, if any, do you want traditional religion to play in your life?
6. FAMILY RELATIONSHIPS—What kinds of relationships do you want to have with family members?
7. FRIENDS—What kinds of relationships do you want with friends? How many friends, of what sex, and what kinds of friendships do you want?
8. RELATIONSHIP(S) WITH A MAN AND/OR MEN

—What would be your ideal status with regard to men? Do you want to be married, single, single with male friends, married with male friends, without male friends, etc.?

9. LEISURE-TIME ACTIVITIES—What do you want to do with your leisure time?

WHAT DO YOU WANT TO BE AND ACCOMPLISH?

Although we know that we won't live forever, many of us do not use that knowledge to help us decide how we want to live and what we want to accomplish with our lives. Take time to examine the quality of your present life and to decide what you want to do with your future.

In their book *Values Clarification* (New York: Hart Publishing Co., 1972), Simon, Howe, and Kirschenbaum suggested the following activity as a way of determining future goals. On the left-hand side of a sheet of paper, write your obituary as it would appear in the paper if you were to die today. On the right-hand side of the paper, write your obituary if you were to live to age eighty. You may want to incorporate the following suggestions or you may wish to use your own ideas.

SUGGESTED LEADS

- Mary Jones died yesterday from . . .
- She was a member of . . .
- She is survived by . . .
- At the time of her death she was working on . . .
- She will be remembered for . . .
- She will be mourned by . . . because . . .
- The world will suffer the loss of her contributions in the areas of . . .
- She always wanted, but never . . .

Some people may experience discomfort in completing this exercise. Did you feel uncomfortable? If yes, what do you think caused your discomfort?

Did your present and future obituaries differ? What did you add to your future obituary? Did your future obituary contain some of the things you previously mentioned as being of value to you?

YOUR GOALS

Review your answers to the activities in this chapter up to this point. Select key phrases from these activities to help you determine your goals for the future. Write your goals in no more than three sentences. State your goals for a time *three to five years in the future*.

Your goal statement should

- Be written so that they can be understood by you and by others
- Specify a deadline
- Be statements of outcomes you can achieve
- Be stated in specific terms so you can ultimately determine if they have been achieved

It helps if goals are:

- *Your* goals—not those of others
- Thought through—consider the results and consequences, the costs and benefits of your goals
- Within your control—something you believe you can do
- Based on your personal values—what need are you trying to fulfill? What personal value are you meeting?

Challenge yourself and be creative in setting goals for your future. Women often aim too low in their goal setting. Goals are important because they can motivate you to work toward a future that is a more desirable and creative alternative to the present.

After you have written out your goals, rank order them in order of their importance to you.

Consider any roadblocks that might prevent you from reaching your goal or that might make it difficult to do so. Roadblocks may be tangible, such as small children who need care, or they may be emotional, such as a long-term lack of self-confidence. See if you can arrive at possible solutions to the roadblocks that exist.

Next consider the resources you will need to reach your goals. Remember, resources include money, time, energy, special talents, friends, and so on. Decide if you have the resources necessary and how you could obtain them if you do not.

List the rewards that make the goals worth

working toward. Seeing the rewards that come with meeting your goals can help motivate you.

What personal values are involved in your goal? In other words, what value are you meeting or what need are you trying to fulfill?

Be sure to indicate how long it will take you to achieve each goal. Set a realistic time limit for yourself.

The following chart summarizes points to consider when you set a goal. Complete the chart for each of your major goals.

GOAL (STATE SPECIFICALLY):

ROADBLOCKS	
WAYS AROUND ROADBLOCKS	
RESOURCES NEEDED	
HOW RESOURCES WILL BE OBTAINED	
REWARDS	
PERSONAL VALUES INVOLVED IN GOAL	
DATE GOAL IS TO BE ACHIEVED	

SETTING OBJECTIVES TO ACHIEVE YOUR GOALS

Look at the goals you have set for yourself. Ask yourself how you are going to reach each goal. What actions does the goal require?

Objectives should be

- Clearly stated so that you and others can understand them
- Stated in such a way that achievement can be measured
- Stated in terms of who is going to take what action and indicate by what time it will be completed
- Realistic
- Stated in terms of the resources available

Rank order your objectives; be aware of the rationale of your order of priority. An objective may be of primary importance because it is important for many reasons. Perhaps it is important to who you are as a person. Maybe it is a response to a crisis. Perhaps it is particularly appropriate for a specific time and place. Or, maybe it must be achieved so that other objectives are possible.

It is suggested that each goal be broken down into four to eight objectives. If more objectives are needed it may be that the goal statement is too broad; perhaps the statement encompasses several goals.

Sometimes a divorce thrusts so many decisions and plans upon a woman that she is overwhelmed and doesn't know what to do first. In this situation, it may help to write out the goal which you gave first priority and determine the objectives needed to reach that goal. At this point, it will help to rank order the objectives. Deciding which goal is most important and which objective must be completed first to achieve that goal can provide a sense of direction and help mobilize your energies.

EXAMPLE

GOAL:
To be a registered nurse and employed in the nursing profession within the next four years.

OBJECTIVES	ORDER OF PRIORITY
Personally collect materials by Friday of coming week from the two colleges in the area that grant R.N. degrees.	3
Read and evaluate materials and decide which program suits me best.	4
Register by required date for two courses for the coming term leading to my degree.	5
Arrange with neighbors to care for children while I am in school.	2
Ask boss tomorrow if work schedule can be arranged so that I can take courses.	1

You may find it helpful to deal with your objectives in chart form. The sample chart on page 50 could be used.

BREAKING HABITS THAT NO LONGER FIT

Often when taking a new direction in life it is necessary to plan to discontinue past habits and activities that are no longer appropriate.

When women divorce, they often find that they have established practices and ways of doing things when married that are impossible to continue or that are not appropriate for a single life-style. Think about times that are difficult for you emotionally or practically because they remind you of times when you were married. For example, some women experience loneliness during what used to be a cocktail hour with their husbands or on Sundays, which were devoted to family activities. Develop a plan that will discourage habits or traditions you followed when you were married that are either no longer possible or that you wish to discontinue. Make a list of the practices you wish to discontinue. Remember to include an alternative or substitute action.

EXAMPLE

OLD PRACTICE TO BE DISCONTINUED	PLAN
Holiday dinners are difficult—gathering seems small without husband and in-laws	*Get together with single friends—each person brings a dish. Guests will help me focus on my new life and friends; dinner will be cheaper and less work for me!*

The planning process you have just been introduced to is most effective if it is a continual process in your life. Check yourself at frequent intervals.

First, see if you have met the objectives you have set for yourself. Since objectives are to be stated in measurable terms, this should be easy for you to do. Objectives are meant to be achieved.

Second, you will want to check if you have achieved your goals. If you have not, ask yourself the following:

1. What has interfered with achieving the goals I have set for myself?

2. Did I order my goals according to those which are most important to me?
3. Do I still have the same goals?
4. Are my goals realistic?
5. Are my values the same as when I set my goals?

Periodically, you will want to repeat the planning process to see if your goals are the same or if you have new ones. Goals are blueprints for the future and are meant to be changed. You may find, for example, that based on new information, other goals are more appropriate than the ones you originally selected. If you find that you are not achieving your objectives, it may be that the original goal toward which you are working is no longer relevant. Evaluating the progress you make toward achieving your objectives and reaching your goals and repeating the planning process will keep your planning current. It will also help you to assess if you are on target.

GOAL:

OBJECTIVE	ACTION REQUIRED BY WHOM	DATE TARGET ACTUAL
RESOURCES REQUIRED		BY WHEN

FIVE

HOW DO YOU FEEL ABOUT DECISION MAKING?

In the last chapter you were introduced to a planning process. Decisions must be made throughout the planning process. As a divorced woman, you are required to make major decisions concerning your future. Perhaps this is the first time in your life that you have been required to make major decisions. You may find the responsibility for making your own decisions frightening; it is not unusual to feel anxious in new situations with new responsibilities. In this chapter you will be asked to examine your attitude toward decision making and to accept responsibility for making your own decisions.

When I was married I left all the major decisions to my husband—where to live, how to spend money, the friends we would have, and so on. I made all the minor decisions such as what to have for dinner, what color drapes to buy, and how to arrange the furniture. Now that I am divorced I make all the decisions. While it was scary at first, the first time I made a major decision I realized how much more powerful I felt. I may make mistakes once in a while, but at least I make the mistakes when it comes to major decisions affecting my life—not someone else. I like it better this way.

WHAT'S YOUR ATTITUDE TOWARD MAKING DECISIONS?

Take three minutes to think about a major decision you are making now or will soon have to make. Write down as many words as you can describing how you feel about making that decision. Pay attention to any physical sensations you may have. Do not try to be consistent, just describe how you feel about making this particular decision.

Now look at the words you have chosen to describe your feelings about making the decision you chose.

1. How many words indicate that you feel that decision making is an anxiety-producing, *negative* experience?
2. How many words indicate that you feel that decision making is a challenging, *positive* experience?
3. How many words indicate that you feel capable of making major decisions on your own?
4. How many words indicate that you do not feel capable of making major decisions on your own?
5. What percentage of you feels that decision making is an anxiety-producing, negative experience?
6. What percentage of you feels that decision making is a challenging, positive experience?

EXAMINE YOUR DECISION-MAKING ANXIETY

Decision making can be tension filled and frustrating for a variety of reasons. If you indicated in the last activity that it is an anxiety-producing, negative experience for you, it may help to examine your reasons for feeling anxious about making major decisions. List as many of these reasons as you can think of.

Now reconsider the reasons you gave for your decision-making anxiety. Can you think of any steps you could take to reduce your anxiety?

If you consider decision making to be primarily an anxiety-producing, negative experience, the following suggestions may be of help to you.

SUGGESTION 1

All decision making involves anxiety. Anxiety can be good or bad. It can be good if it helps alert you to some of the risks and consequences of major decisions. It can also serve as an impetus, urging you to do what is necessary to make a decision and see that the decision is carried through. Anxiety can be bad if it is totally consuming. In this case, you may not be emotionally capable of following a logical decision-making process. If you are faced with a major decision, check where you are on the anxiety scale.

RELAXED AND CONFIDENT   **NERVOUS, YET ABLE TO COPE**   **OVERWHELMED WITH ANXIETY**

If you feel unable to cope with anxiety that seems overwhelming, seek help from a friend or a professional person you trust. It may be that concerns underlying the decision and not the decision itself are the source of your anxiety. Ask yourself if it is possible to postpone your decision; if it is, set a future time when you think you will be better able to cope with that decision. Do not allow yourself to be bullied, forced, or embarrassed into making decisions you are not ready to make. If postponing a decision means increasing the likelihood that you will make a more rational one when you are calmer, by all means consider this alternative.

WARNING:—If you feel unable to cope with a decision due to overwhelming anxiety, *do* get help

and *do* set a time target by which you hope to be able to make a decision. Some people postpone major decisions for years because they "just aren't up to it."

SUGGESTION 2

If you feel some anxiety that is uncomfortable when making a major decision, try to look at the anxiety in a positive fashion. Your anxiety is a signal that there are risks and consequences involved with the decision. Positive anxiety tells you that you are alive, facing a challenge, and growing. It can give you the impetus to do what you have to do for yourself.

SUGGESTION 3

Decision making may be considered a nerve-wracking, necessary evil to be avoided at all costs, or it may be considered a challenging opportunity to further define oneself. You have a choice concerning your attitude toward decision making. Try looking at the positive aspects of decision making. After all, what do you have to lose by assuming this attitude?

SUGGESTION 4

Some people fool themselves into believing that they are avoiding the anxiety of decision making by not making a decision. Refusing to make a decision is a decision in itself—it is a decision not to make a decision! This decision is not necessarily good or bad. It is important for you to be aware, however, of your decision not to make a decision and the consequences of that decision. Sometimes not making a decision will give you more time to gather needed information or be to your advantage in other ways. Sometimes, if someone else makes a decision for you or if you decide by default, the outcome is not to your advantage.

WARNING:—If you decide *not* to decide, make sure that decision is to your advantage!

SUGGESTION 5

Very few decisions are irrevocable. If the outcome of a decision is unfavorable, you can usually make another decision. Certainly, it is to your benefit to try to avoid the necessity of a new decision that can be costly and time consuming, but sometimes this is necessary.

WARNING:—Don't paralyze yourself with fear by treating a decision as if it were a life-or-death decision when it is not. Even if you are deciding whether or not to have open-heart surgery, for example, excess fear will stand in the way of following a rational decision-making process. Be realistically aware of the possible risks a decision involves, but don't scare yourself to death!

SUGGESTION 6

In chapter 2, you examined how supportive you are of yourself and how you talk to yourself. You may be scaring yourself needlessly concerning your ability to make decisions. Some people are terrified of making decisions because they fear they will make the wrong decision. People who make decisions often know that, inevitably, there are times when the outcome of a decision will not be favorable. In the next chapter, you will be introduced to a decision-making process that will help maximize the possibility that the outcomes of the decisions you make will be in your favor. If you fear making decisions because you fear you will make the wrong decision, perhaps you have unrealistic expectations for yourself. No one is perfect and you are bound to make some mistakes in the decision-making process. Would you rather run the risk of making a decision and having an undesirable outcome, or of doing *nothing* and having an undesirable outcome?

WARNING:—Decision making involves risk. Good decision makers have had lots of practice in making decisions—they have allowed themselves to make mistakes and to learn from them. You have the right to make mistakes!

WHAT AVOIDANCE STRATEGIES DO YOU USE?

In the book *Without Guilt and Justice: From Decidophobia to Autonomy* (New York: Wyden, 1973), Walter Kaufmann lists ten strategies people use to avoid making their own decisions. Read the strategies he listed and decide which apply to you.

KAUFMANN'S AVOIDANCE STRATEGIES

1. Taking up religion (I'll let God solve my problems—He knows best.)
2. Following the status quo (I'll just continue to go in the direction I've been going—it isn't so bad.)
3. Forming an allegiance to a movement (If I follow the leader and/or the cause, I won't have to make decisions.)
4. Forming an allegiance to a school of thought (I'll let certain philosophies established by others be my guide.)
5. Reading your own meaning into what an authority says (I'll listen to the experts, interpret them, and *then* decide on that basis.)
6. Choosing between black and white alternatives (It's either this or that—I don't want to be confused by alternatives in between.)
7. Assuming logic will dictate values (The logical alternative is best for me.)
8. Becoming absorbed in minute distinctions (If I busy myself with trivia, I can forget that a decision has to be made.)
9. Having faith in the future (All things are solved in time.)
10. Taking up marriage (I'll let him decide.)

List any additional strategies you may use.

Now think about specific times when you have been afraid to make a decision. Why were you afraid to make that decision? What strategy did you use to avoid that decision? What were the consequences of avoiding that decision?

HOW DO OTHERS INFLUENCE YOUR DECISIONS?

Each of us is influenced by other people. The degree of influence varies from situation to situation according to our intellectual and emotional makeup. Letting others influence your decisions is not necessarily good or bad. Life would be less rewarding without concern and consideration for others. On the other hand, constant deference to the wishes and priorities of other people can lead to a life of frustration and unhappiness. The important thing is to maximize control over your life by understanding who influences your decisions and by deciding the extent to which that influence is acceptable to you.

To examine who influences your decisions, in what areas others have influence, and to what extent you want to be influenced, work through the following activity. This exercise was adapted from Loughary and Ripley, *Career & Life Planning Guide* (Chicago: Follett, 1976), pp. 79–81. The chart below lists 8 decision-making areas. Draw a similar chart for yourself and in column 1 list people who influence(d) you in each decision-making area. In the next column, opposite the name of each person listed, use the following point scale to rate the degree of influence of each person:

(1) very high   (4) low
(2) high   (5) negligible
(3) average

	INFLUENTIAL OTHERS, SOCIAL INSTITUTIONS, NORMS	DEGREE OF INFLUENCE
EDUCATION		
SOCIAL LIFE		
SEX LIFE		
CAREER		
FINANCIAL—SPENDING HABITS		
CHILD REARING		
TERMS OF DIVORCE DECREE		
WHERE TO LIVE		
OTHER		
OTHER		

In some cases, we may be influenced by social institutions or norms. For example, many of our decisions in the areas listed may have been influenced by the church we were raised in or social norms concerning how women "should be." List social institutions or norms that may have influenced your decisions.

After you have completed the chart, rank the people you listed from most influential to least influential. Then answer these questions:

1. Do you see yourself as more or less independent than you thought?

2. In what areas would you like to have more influence from other people?
3. In what areas would you like to have less influence from other people?
4. Which of the people you mentioned do you influence? How?
5. To what degree did social institutions or norms influence your decisions?

You may want to make a contract with yourself if you wish to change the degree of influence a given individual has on the decisions you make. Write out the contract.

YOUR MAJOR DECISIONS

To examine major decisions in your life, draw a lifeline.* Although your lifeline will be unique in shape, it should begin at a point you consider to be the beginning of your life and should terminate at a point you consider to be the end of your life. Write in the events that shape the lifeline you draw. After you have plotted your lifeline to the present, continue shaping it by projecting the shape you would like it to take in the future. A scale on the left-hand side of your lifeline will help indicate the experiences you consider to be peak periods and low periods in your life. Use the example on page 55 as a model.

Now locate the following symbols on your lifeline:

! the greatest risk of your life
X an obstacle encountered
O a critical decision that was made for you by someone else
+ the best decision you ever made
— the worst decision you ever made
? a critical or important decision coming up in the future
Δ a decision you made by default, by just letting it "happen," or that happened by "accident"

WARNINGS
The last two exercises helped you examine the influence others may have on your decision making. Some women have never made a major de-

* Adapted with permission from *How to Decide: A Guide for Women* by Nelle Tumlin Scholz, Judith Sosbee Prince, and Gordon Porter Miller, copyright © 1975 by College Entrance Examination Board, New York.

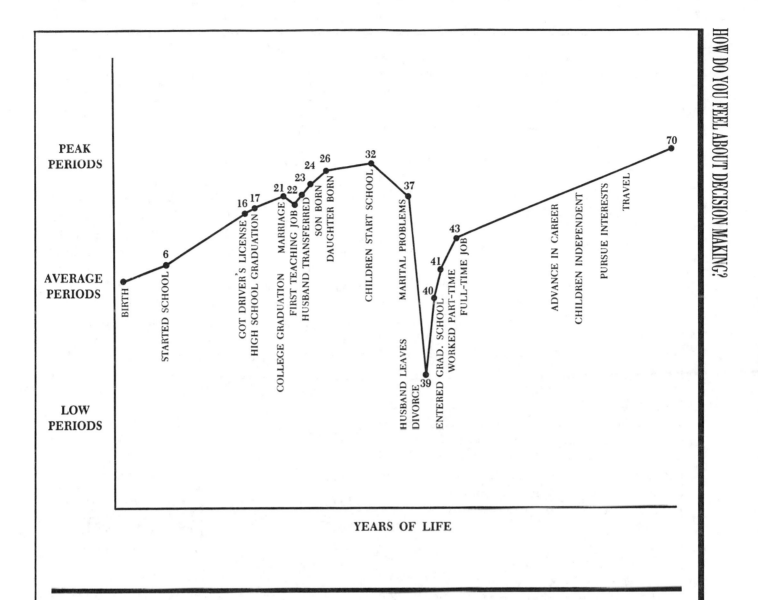

PEAK
PERIODS

AVERAGE
PERIODS

LOW
PERIODS

BIRTH

6 STARTED SCHOOL

16 GOT DRIVER'S LICENSE

17 HIGH SCHOOL GRADUATION

COLLEGE GRADUATION

21 MARRIAGE

22 FIRST TEACHING JOB

23 HUSBAND TRANSFERRED

24 SON BORN

26 DAUGHTER BORN

32 CHILDREN START SCHOOL

37 MARITAL PROBLEMS

HUSBAND LEAVES

DIVORCE

39

40 ENTERED GRAD. SCHOOL

41 WORKED PART-TIME

43 FULL-TIME JOB

ADVANCE IN CAREER

CHILDREN INDEPENDENT

PURSUE INTERESTS

TRAVEL

70

YEARS OF LIFE

cision for themselves. They have left the major decisions to their parents, husbands, the "experts," or other people. If you let other people greatly influence or make your decisions for you, read the following warnings.

WARNING 1: If you find yourself saying, "I have no choice," look at what you are saying. Rarely is *no* choice available to you. Be careful that you are not automatically allowing others to make decisions for you by kidding yourself that you have no say in a decision that involves you. You may not like the choices available to you, but you still have an opportunity to choose between alternatives.

WARNING 2: If you allow others to make decisions **for you,** be aware that you are making *this* decision. The decision to allow another person to decide for you is not in itself good or bad. Do not

automatically assume, however, that other people know what is best for you. This does not mean that you should not get advice from others or profit from their expertise. Since you will have to live with the decisions that are made, be aware of who is making them.

WARNING 3: Be aware of your reason for allowing another person to make a decision for you. While other people may be experts on subjects about which you know little or nothing, you are the expert on yourself. Don't expect others to know more about you than you do. You are the one who can best decide how a decision will affect you.

WARNING 4: Be wary of people who want you to leave the decision making to them. What do they gain by making your decisions? How well do they know you? Are they meeting your needs by making your decisions or are they meeting their personal needs for control? Upon rare occasions you may be emotionally upset and unable to cope with decisions that must be made; on these occasions, it may be wise to allow someone you trust to make a decision for you. Remember, such occasions are rare! If other people insist on making decisions for you, they may be saying they do not feel you are competent enough to make your own decisions.

WARNING 5: Ultimately, it is impossible to avoid making decisions. You may try to avoid account-ability for decisions by allowing others to make them for you. You may say, "But I didn't make the decision—so-and-so did." However, you made the decision of allowing another to make your decision for you. We are all responsible for our decisions, or lack of them.

WARNING 6: While it is important to consider the ways in which major decisions will affect important people in your life, do not be afraid to make a decision that might be good for you even if another person won't like it. When you are afraid, you may be saying that another person is more important to you than you are to yourself. Although this may occasionally be true in special relationships, the person who consistently does this may be expecting some types of repayment from others that they are not prepared to give. If you base a decision on pleasing another person and expect something from that person in re-turn, discuss your expectations with that person. This will help you avoid the "After all I've done for you!" syndrome.

VALUES AND DECISIONS

Every decision we make is based on the con-scious or unconscious beliefs, attitudes, and val-ues we hold. Therefore, we define ourselves and tell other people what is of value to us by the decisions we make. Use the following activity to help you examine values underlying past deci-sions. List three important decisions you have made. Remember, even decisions you let others make are decisions and could be used for this activity. Think about these decisions and the val-ues involved. What values would have been in-volved if you had made a different decision? Are the values that were involved with the decision important to you today?

EXAMPLE

DECISION	VALUES INVOLVED
To move from Atlanta to Chicago when husband transferred	*Professional achievement (husband's); increased earnings (husband's)*

The analysis procedure you have just com-pleted can also be used to analyze future deci-sions you will have to make. Examining alternatives often puts the decision you eventu-ally make into sharper perspective.

HOW DO YOU MAKE DECISIONS?

Many people are afraid to make a decision because they fear their decision will not be a *good* one, or that the decision they make will be *wrong*. Women, in particular, may need help with decision making—especially if, in the past, they have had all their decisions made for them or if they have only had practice in making minor decisions. With the decision to divorce come many major decisions that will affect your future. Therefore, it is necessary to assess your decision-making skills and to examine the manner in which you make decisions.

A decision is possible when there are two or more alternatives or courses of action to follow. Some people feel that decision making consists of sheer luck—either you select the correct alternative or you do not. Such people are afraid that they are not magically endowed with a sixth sense to "pick the right answer" to a problem. This chapter will introduce you to a logical process that you can use in making decisions important to you.

WHAT ARE *GOOD* AND *BAD* DECISIONS?

To begin your decision-making evaluation, think of a bad decision you have made. Why do you think this was a bad decision? What is your definition of a *bad decision*?

Now think of a good decision you have made. Why do you consider it a good decision? What is your definition of a *good decision*?

Most people believe that a decision is a good one if the result is what they wanted it to be or if it is in their favor. Actually, although a person has control over the decision, she does not have direct control over the outcome. A *decision* is the act of choosing or selecting one of several possibilities based on personal judgments. An *outcome* is the result or consequence of a person's act or decision. A good decision does not guarantee a favorable outcome because outcomes cannot be directly controlled. A good decision will, however, increase the probability of the outcome's being a good one—one that is favorable to you.

Major decisions threw me at first when I got a divorce—I was so afraid that I'd make a wrong decision. Now I'm more confident about making my own decisions. I've learned to actively seek the information I need to make intelligent decisions for myself.

A good decision is one in which the skills of decision making are used and a logical decision-making process is followed to choose the alternative that is best according to the decision maker's values and preferences.

Does your definition of a good decision differ from the one given here? If yes, in what way?

Reread the definition of a good decision. How would you evaluate your examples of "good" and "bad" decisions according to this definition of a good decision? Remember to examine the manner in which the decision was *made*, not the result. Give an example of a good decision you have made according to the definition provided.

WHAT IS YOUR DECISION-MAKING PROCEDURE?

People make decisions in different ways, which can affect the decisions' outcomes. This activity will help you examine how you make decisions.

Identify a major decision you have had to make. On a sheet of paper, list the steps you took to reach that decision. In other words, how did you go about *making* the decision? Why did you choose one alternative over another?

The following steps are involved in a logical decision-making process:

Step 1—Define the decision to be made as specifically as possible. Decide when the decision must be made and what will happen if it is not made.

Step 2—Clarify what you want to accomplish and what you value.

Step 3—Study what you already know and determine what additional information you will need to make a decision. Determine how you will obtain this additional information.

Step 4—Identify alternatives and predict the outcomes of each alternative.

Step 5—Compare the possibilities and the risks of the available alternatives.

Step 6—Make the decision.

Step 7—Develop a plan of action that specifically describes how the decision will be implemented and carried out.

Is the process you outlined for making your decision similar to this process? Is your process different? In what way(s) is it similar or different?

Can you think of a major decision you have made that would have been different if you had followed the decision-making process presented here?

Following a logical decision-making process increases the probability that the outcome of the decision will be favorable to you. Unfortunately only merchants give guarantees. Even if you do follow a logical decision-making process, there is no guarantee that the outcome of your decision will be favorable to you.

You can only hold yourself responsible for the decision you make and the process you follow to make that decision. You cannot hold yourself responsible for the outcome.

Following a logical process in decision making can help you relieve decision-making anxiety. It can also protect you from falling into the trap of "second-guessing" decisions you have already made. You probably know people who, years after making a decision, say, "If only I hadn't made that decision," or, "If only I had made another decision, my life would have been different." These people are wasting energy they could use to live in the present by regretting a past that cannot be changed.

An example may help to make this point clearer.

EXAMPLE

DECISION—Brenda and Tom were getting a divorce. Brenda had a decision to make. She could choose to have a suburban house turned over to her in the divorce settlement in lieu of alimony, or she could elect to receive half the profits from the sale of the house in addition to alimony for a five-year-period with child support at the end of that period. With the help of her lawyer, who was an expert on matters involving divorce, real estate, and taxes, she approached the decision in a logical fashion. She knew the decision had to be made in order to obtain a divorce and that Tom was willing to accept either alternative. Other alternatives had been considered and these two seemed the most sensible.

Brenda had two children, aged two and four. Although she had a college degree in elementary education, she decided that to prepare herself for the career she really wanted, she would need a graduate degree in counseling. The suburban home, with the time and money to keep it up, was no longer important to her. If she kept it, she would have to go to work to make the mortgage payments and she would not be able to go to graduate school.

She decided to accept half the profits from the house and alimony for a five-year-period. Brenda moved into an apartment. The alimony payments were adequate for her current living expenses. Tom could afford to pay her more alimony since he could deduct it from his taxable income. Brenda and Tom worked out an agreement whereby he would pay half her taxes since alimony was taxable for her. Brenda had no intention of marrying within the next five years. She wanted the assurance of a five-year period to complete her graduate degree, get her career started, and place both her children in school. Once she began working, she would be able to live comfortably on her salary and the child support that would begin when the alimony stopped. Receiving alimony payments for five years seemed an ideal arrangement. Tom, who had an excellent job with a corporation he had been with for eight years, agreed to the alimony alternative.

Did Brenda follow the steps given in the logical decision-making process mentioned earlier? Did Brenda make a good decision?

OUTCOME—Six months after Brenda's divorce was final, Tom lost his job. There was a radical reorganization in his corporation due to a merger with another company. Tom had not expected this and the shock was devastating to him. He was determined to find a job with another firm at approximately the same salary, but jobs in his field were scarce and the competition was keen. It took him a year of job hunting and interviewing to realize that he would have to accept a much lower salary than the one to which he had been accustomed. Unfortunately, Tom's career crisis affected Brenda's alimony payments. During the time he was unemployed, he could not afford to send her the alimony payments they had originally agreed upon. When he did get a job, the payments were based on his lower salary and were thus reduced. Brenda was forced to get a part-time job, reduce the number of graduate courses she was taking, and dip into the savings she had received from her half of the house.

Does the outcome of the decision Brenda made make it a poor decision? Was there any way she could have anticipated what happened to her ex-husband?

Brenda did achieve her goals—she just had to work harder and use her savings. Occasionally her mother would say, "If only you had taken the house and sold it, you would have been better off." Brenda paid no attention to her mother. She had followed a logical decision-making process. There was no way for her to know what would happen to Tom's company and thus to his job—this was beyond her control. She had made the best decision she could, given the information available.

WARNING:—Be sure you know what you value when you make a decision. Often values are not made explicit when decisions are made although they comprise a decision rule. A *decision rule* is a directive that indicates a clear choice among the alternatives that exist. An example of a decision rule would be an economy rule where an individual selects the least expensive feasible alternative. Decision rules can be helpful if they are explicit and acknowledged. It is important to decide if such rules are acceptable to you and if they can act as useful guides when you make decisions. Sometimes women use decision rules without being aware of them. Decision rules women may use include:

- Authority Rules—To select the alternative that an authority would suggest
- Deference Rules—To select the alternative that would most please others who might be affected by a decision.
- Conflict Avoidance Rules—To select the alternative that would produce the least amount of conflict or produce the fewest waves
- Logic Rules—To select the alternative that is most logical and makes the most sense

Can you think of any decision rules that might be operating when you make a decision?

EVALUATING ALTERNATIVES

Sometimes women may find it difficult to decide which alternative they have developed is best for them. Analyzing the forces that work for or against a decision and assigning a point value to

OBTAINING HOUSE AND KEEPING IT

FORCES FOR (BENEFITS)	POINT VALUES*	FORCES AGAINST (COSTS)	POINT VALUES*
		House expenses & utilities (costly & sometimes unpredictable)	5
Good investment	4	*Could invest money elsewhere*	3
		Need money to be liquid to pay for graduate school	5
Provide sense of security & continuity for children	3	*Better to move children now than when they start school*	5
Neighbors nearby for help	2	*Need to surround myself with new friends—neighbors can only relate to the married person I was*	4
Like the house	3	*Do not want the responsibility and time required to maintain the home— particularly as a single parent who will be involved in graduate studies*	5
POINTS FOR OBTAINING HOUSE AND KEEPING IT:	12	POINTS AGAINST OBTAINING HOUSE AND KEEPING IT:	27

* POINT VALUES: Brenda assigned point values to indicate how important each factor was in her decision, ranging from 5 (very important) to 1 (of least importance).

the facts, feelings, and values involved with the decision may help to objectively assess the costs and benefits of that alternative.

EXAMPLE
Let's return to the decision Brenda had to make. Although there may have been more than two alternatives, she narrowed the alternatives to two: to have the house owned jointly with her husband turned over to her, or to sell the house and receive half the profits and alimony for a five-year period. Brenda could do a cost-benefit analysis for each alternative, as seen on the chart below. Brenda could have completed a similar analysis for obtaining the house and selling it versus obtaining half the house and alimony instead. She may in this case have compared actual dollar figures, the chances of her husband not being able to pay the alimony, tax ramifications, and so on.

NOTE:—In the example given, the points Brenda assigned strongly suggest that the alternative of

not obtaining and keeping the house was preferable for her. In cases where the points indicate no clear preference, a woman must ask what decision, in her heart of hearts, she truly prefers. Then she can examine ways to realistically reduce the costs or maximize the benefits to support the decision she prefers.

RATE YOUR CURRENT DECISION-MAKING SKILLS

The process suggested for good decision making requires certain decision-making skills. To evaluate your present skills and abilities in decision making, use the scale that follows to rate your skill in making decisions.*

A = I think I am very similar in ability to an excellent decision maker.
B = I think I am close to the best but not quite as skilled as the best.

* This exercise was adapted from H. B. Gelatt, Barbara Varenhorst, Richard Carey, and Gordon P. Miller, *Decisions and Outcomes* (New York: College Examination Board, 1973).

C = I still have to learn more about how to do this in order to become really good.

D = I need a great deal more experience before I will be able to do this satisfactorily.

Decide which letter applies to your ability to use the following skills:

1. To go about getting the information I need
2. To differentiate between important and nonimportant information
3. To use the information and to apply it to a decision
4. To become aware of and to clarify my values
5. To be able to rank my values and apply them to a critical decision
6. To know what an objective is and how to set one for myself
7. To be able to use my goals, values, and beliefs to establish clear objectives for myself
8. To be able to develop new alternatives or possible actions when the available ones are not satisfactory
9. To be able to narrow down the number of alternatives when a confusing array or too many are available
10. To estimate the chances that certain outcomes will occur
11. To rank various possible outcomes of a decision on the basis of their desirability to me
12. To be able to analyze the special nature of a critical decision including its long-range consequences and the closing off of opportunities
13. To use a strategy for making critical decisions

You probably rated yourself high in some skills, low in some, and average in others. You are very unusual if you rate high in most skills. The remaining chapters of this book will deal with important decisions that divorce forces a woman to make. You will want to pay special attention to those skill areas in which you rated yourself low when it comes to making decisions.

The skills needed to make decisions usually fall within one of the four areas listed.

- Values—Knowing what you value and how your values influence the decision
- Information—Knowing what information is presently available, what additional information is needed, how to obtain additional information, and how to evaluate information
- Alternatives—Identifying alternatives, assessing the probabilities and risks of each alternative, and choosing among alternatives
- Planning—Developing a plan of action to implement the decision you have made

In which areas do you feel you need help with your skills?

PART

TWO

DECISIONS CONCERNING LEGAL HELP: HOW TO GET IT AND HOW TO USE IT

Choosing a lawyer is an important decision. The lawyer you select is your representative in the legal system and is a resource person concerning legal matters pertaining to divorce. I realized after I got a divorce that I did not utilize my lawyer as effectively as I could have—I was too passive in the process and expected him to make the right decisions for me. I didn't question him when I had doubts about parts of the divorce decree—I simply let him take over because he was the authority.

If you have definitely decided to get a divorce, one of the first things you will ask yourself is, "How do I go about getting a good lawyer?" Sometimes people say, "I want a divorce but I don't know a good lawyer," or "I want a divorce but I can't afford the legal fees." If you are one of these people, consider what you are saying. If you really have decided to divorce (remember making a decision implies taking the necessary steps to implement that decision), the decision of how to proceed legally will not stop you indefinitely in your decision to get a divorce. You may be at the point where you are *really* examining the question. In that case, you will find this chapter helpful. If you are using the excuse of "I can't afford or find a good lawyer" to postpone getting a divorce, you may not find this chapter helpful. You may be dealing with the questions of "Do I want a divorce?" "Can I make it on my own?" and "How will I support myself?" which keep you from actually making the decision to get a divorce and acting on it.

If these are the issues with which you are struggling, and most women do struggle with them, you may find the remaining chapters helpful. You can return to this chapter if you decide that divorce is the right decision for you and that you are prepared to act on it.

Selecting the legal help that best suits your needs is an important decision in beginning and completing the formal process that ends a marriage. Unfortunately, there is no sure way of finding the right lawyer for you. Many women discover that they do not know where to turn for legal help. If you have never dealt with legal issues or consulted a lawyer on your own, the whole process may seem intimidating and overwhelming. This chapter will help you examine the kind of legal help that is best for you, how to choose and use a lawyer, and how to avoid common pitfalls that may interfere with your getting what you want.

WHEN TO CONSULT A LAWYER

Which of the following statements apply to your situation?

1. You have decided that you want a divorce.
2. Your husband has told you that he wants a divorce.
3. Your husband has been violent with you and/or the children.
4. Your husband does not provide support for your children.
5. Your husband has consulted a lawyer concerning a possible divorce.
6. Your husband has left you.
7. You do not know your legal rights.
8. You do not know how the divorce laws affect your particular situation.
9. Your husband has threatened to take or has taken the children.

If any of these statements apply to you, it would be wise to seek the advice of an attorney if you have not already done so. Seeing an attorney does not mean that you must proceed immediately with a divorce or that you have decided to use the attorney you see if you decide to get a divorce. You may need to consult an attorney simply to obtain information.

Sometimes people do not initially consult a lawyer when there are marital problems because they hope that their marriage still has a chance. They are afraid that once lawyers enter the picture conflict will increase and a reconciliation will become impossible. If your husband continues to support you while you are separated and you are both considering reconciliation, you may decide it is in your best interest not to take legal action. If you consult a lawyer, you may want to stress that you are there for information only and that you do not want anything done on your behalf until you instruct the lawyer to do so. If your husband is not responsible and tends to be unstable, it may be wise to see a lawyer concerning your rights and to ask for separate maintenance. *Separate maintenance* is an order from a court requiring a husband to support his wife and family while they are living apart. The marriage remains intact, the spouses can reunite at any time, and there is no division of property.

The advantages of seeing an attorney when marital problems first suggest that you may eventually need one are as follows:

1. You can learn your legal rights and gain information that pertains to your particular situation.
2. You can feel prepared with a lawyer you trust should you need a lawyer in a crisis situation.
3. You can go on record that certain problems exist; this might be helpful if and when you decide on divorce.
4. You can be advised on certain procedures to follow that might legally be in your best interests.

Know why you are seeing a lawyer. If you want advice and information, keep that in mind. You cannot be forced to file for a divorce if you are not ready to do so or if you do not feel that it is in your best interests at the present time. It is wise, however, to have legal advice available should you need it.

If you have a tendency toward passivity, of not acting until absolutely necessary, guard against this tendency if you feel you need legal advice. Ignoring your problems will not make them go away. Waiting until you are forced to obtain legal help may not be in your best interests. It is best to be prepared.

LEGAL DIVORCE: ADVANTAGES AND DISADVANTAGES

Some people who have been separated or emotionally divorced for years fail to take any legal action to end the marriage. Answering the following questions will help you examine reasons for not divorcing legally as well as the advantages and disadvantages of legal divorce.

1. What are the advantages for you of being separated but not legally divorced?
2. What are the disadvantages for you of being separated but not legally divorced?
3. Are you legally divorced? If your answer is no, what is the reason you are not divorced?
4. The charts on page 66 list some of the advantages and disadvantages of legal divorce and of "informal" divorce through separation, desertion, or emotional divorce. Which advantages and disadvantages apply to you?

LEGAL DIVORCE

ADVANTAGES	DISADVANTAGES
Agreements are spelled out legally so woman has recourse if they are not kept	Bitterness may develop during legal process where one person must be labeled "at fault"
Each party knows what is required of him or her	Legal procedure may be expensive
Legal divorce can prompt woman to establish own life, own means of financial support	May have to give up property, income
Legal status may make it easier to date and establish new social life	
Remarriage possible	

"INFORMAL" DIVORCE*

ADVANTAGES	DISADVANTAGES
Avoid bitterness and emotional trauma of divorce process	Keeps the individual in a dependent state where she may avoid taking responsibility for her own life
Do not have to pay costs of legal proceedings	Woman may have little recourse if agreements are not legalized
May have financial advantages for wife such as Social Security benefits, keeping family home, being covered by husband's insurance, etc.	May not be free to date and develop social relationships
Don't have to deal with negative reactions from children, church, parents	

*Informal divorce through separation, desertion, or emotional divorce.

There is a difference between deciding not to take legal action to end a marriage for a definite reason and postponing the decision indefinitely because of fear of the unknown. For some people there may be real advantages to waiting to legalize divorce.

EXAMPLE
Mary is twenty-eight and has been married for eight years. She has three children. Although she has resigned herself to a divorce, she really doesn't want one. She learned that, during the last year, her husband has had a series of affairs—all with women in their late teens. He isn't pressing her for a divorce, hasn't filed for one, and has no plans to file for one in the near future. Mary went to counseling alone because her husband said he didn't need or want it. Through counseling, Mary realized that there is nothing she can do to change her husband—he wants to continue his present affairs, doesn't want to change, and doesn't want to work at a marriage with her. Mary realizes that, as things are at the present time, there is no hope for the kind of marriage she wants with her husband. Her husband has his own apartment and continues to support her and the children. Mary has decided to wait for two years to get a divorce for the following reasons:

1. If she remains married for ten years, she will be eligible for Social Security. Since she has never worked, she has no Social Security of her own. This money represents some security for her future.
2. She has enrolled in a two-year program to become an X-ray technician. She is not presently prepared for work in a career that she feels she would enjoy.
3. She has no interest in remarriage or even in dating at the present time. If she decides she wants to date, she can do so in a prudent fashion while separated.
4. Her husband is continuing to support her and the children and to pay the mortgage; she is financially better off with this arrangement.
5. In two years her children will be in school, which will make it easier for her to arrange for child care.
6. She feels she needs a two-year period to adjust to being independent and responsible for herself.
7. While she has no hope for reconciliation, she still cares about what happens to her husband. Waiting two years to obtain a legal divorce will prevent him from remarrying immediately.

In the example, Mary has specific reasons why it is to her advantage not to legally end her marriage at the present time. Yet, she has taken definite steps, such as deciding upon a career goal and returning to school, toward being responsible for herself. She is using time as a resource. She knows when she will get a divorce and will be better prepared to be independent when she does so.

If you are postponing divorce, what are your reasons?

WHY ARE YOU POSTPONING A DIVORCE?

If you have decided to get a divorce, do not have logical reasons for postponing it, and find yourself putting it off, you may want to examine some of the reasons for your procrastination and the payoffs involved. *Payoffs* are advantages you get from a given decision that may make your life easier at present but may ultimately be to your disadvantage.

Examine your reasons for postponing a divorce and the payoffs you feel you are getting from this decision. Read the following reasons and payoffs for postponing divorce; make a list of those that apply to you.

REASON	PAYOFF FOR POSTPONING DIVORCE
Fear of the unknown	*Staying married, legally at least, means you don't have to face the unknowns and risks of single life. Staying married may feel safer no matter how costly it is to you in terms of growth and fulfillment*
Guilt feelings concerning ending the marriage	*Rather than taking responsibility for what you want to do with your life, you can rely on the values of others or what you feel is your duty to other people*
Being afraid of adverse affects divorce will have on the children	*As long as you center your attention on your children, you have an excuse for not taking responsibility for yourself. You can play martyr and collect "you owe me's" from your children in the future because "Look at what I'm putting up with for you"*
Being afraid of the unpleasant aspects of getting a divorce—dividing property, charging spouse under "fault system" of divorce, personal and legal battles	*Putting off a divorce allows you to escape from those activities which no one finds pleasant*
Wondering if you can raise the children alone	*As long as you worry about it, you can put off dealing with the responsibility or the realization that you may be taking the major responsibility for child rearing already*

continued

REASON	PAYOFF FOR POSTPONING DIVORCE
You can't afford a divorce	*You can continue with your present economic situation, which is safer or more lucrative than your financial situation will be when you divorce. You can avoid taking responsibility for your financial independence*
Divorce isn't accepted by your religion	*Rather than deciding and taking responsibility for what is right for you, you can use religion as an excuse to stay in your present situation*
Fear of loneliness	*You do not have to confront your loneliness. Staying with a marriage—even though it may be dead—at least gives the appearance that there is another person who shares your life*
Fear of being alone	*As long as you stay married, you can avoid confronting the reality that we are all alone and responsible for ourselves, whether we are married or single*

Sometimes women are involved in divorce proceedings and then decide to postpone the divorce or reconsider a reconciliation. If this is happening to you, ask yourself what the reason is. There are times when you are particularly vulnerable and will want to run back to the security of a marriage. The following are times when one may be particularly vulnerable. Which apply to you?

- Holidays
- When you are sick
- When your child is sick or has an accident
- When you break up with a man you have been dating
- When you lose your job or find it difficult to get a job
- When a parent is critically ill
- When you have very young children

Are there any other times when you may be particularly vulnerable?

If you really want a divorce but keep returning to a marriage that you feel is going nowhere, consider your support system.

1. Is there a way you can get the support you may need from others so you can go ahead with what is best for you? How?
2. What can you do for yourself to feel less vulnerable?

THE *PRO SE* DIVORCE ALTERNATIVE

Which of the following statements apply to you?

1. I have no children.
2. My husband and I have agreed to divorce.
3. My husband and I know the terms we want in a divorce and agree on most matters.
4. My husband and I have little property to divide and are in agreement concerning property division.
5. We have been married for a short time and both plan to go separate ways with no obligations.
6. We don't have the money to spend on legal fees.
7. I don't qualify for free legal help yet can't afford legal fees.
8. I can qualify for free legal help but don't want to spend the time on the red tape that is required.
9. I feel competent enough to handle my own divorce.

If any of the statements above apply to you, you may want to consider the alternatives of *pro se* divorce.

WHAT IS *PRO SE* DIVORCE?

Many large metropolitan areas have *pro se* divorce classes and groups where people who want to handle their own divorces can get help in completing and filing the proper divorce forms without a lawyer if the divorce is uncontested. This enables a woman or man to obtain a divorce for much less than it would cost if a lawyer were used. If you decide to get a *pro se* divorce, you may want to consult one or all of the following to determine the financial awards made in your geographic area and to answer questions you may have concerning property settlement, child custody and support, procedure, and so on: a free legal service available in your area, legal services available at minimal cost, and divorce decrees on file.

If you are interested in getting your own divorce, contact the local chapter of NOW, in particular its Marriage and Divorce Committee. Ask

if they can help you or if they can refer you to a group that can help. If there are no legal services in your area and you and your husband agree on the terms of a divorce, you might decide to do the divorce yourself. The following steps are the ones you should be aware of:

1. Look at copies of completed uncontested divorces. Divorces are matters of public record and should be on file at your local courthouse. Ask the county clerk if you can look at uncontested divorce decrees for ideas. Also ask if divorce forms are available.
2. Write a clear, concise statement of how you and your husband intend to settle things. Legal jargon is not mandatory. You should state how you are handling child custody, visitation, support, property, and debt division, and grounds for divorce, if required in your state. You may also want to include something about tax refunds, Social Security benefits, and insurance policies.
3. Type your divorce on legal paper ($8\frac{1}{2}''$ x 13''); number the items on the left-hand side of the page. Be neat.
4. Obtain a copy of your state's divorce law from a law library and read it. It explains the rules but not the procedure.
5. It is your legal right to represent yourself in court.

WARNING:—Don't be surprised if friends or lawyers try to discourage you from deciding upon the *pro se* alternative. Friends may try to convince you that divorce is too complicated for you to handle on your own. Lawyers may try to convince you of the same thing, particularly if they want the fee involved. Base your decision on what is best for you in your particular situation. Don't let others scare you!

The following examples describe women who decided upon the *pro se* divorce alternative. Remember, this alternative works only if the divorce is uncontested (both parties agree to the divorce) and if both parties agree upon the basic terms for a divorce settlement.

EXAMPLE 1

Sue and John had been married for a year. They realized that the marriage had been a mistake and wanted to go their separate ways. They both worked and there were no children involved. Sue wasn't asking for alimony. They each rented an apartment and agreed on how to divide what little property they had. Because they were in agreement concerning the terms of the divorce and since there were no major concerns such as children and property division, they decided that it was senseless to spend money on legal services that they didn't need. Sue went to a *pro se* divorce clinic in their area and took the necessary steps to obtain a divorce.

Do you think this couple made a good decision?

EXAMPLE 2

Brenda had been married for six years and had two children. Her husband was an alcoholic, had never supported her or the children, and had never held a job for longer than two months. Half the time he didn't live with them. Brenda had managed on food stamps, welfare checks, and part-time jobs. Assessing her situation, she finally realized that she had never received any emotional or financial support from her husband and never would. He was agreeable to a divorce, as long as he didn't have to give her anything. Brenda decided to get a *pro se* divorce because it was what she could afford. Even though there were children involved, she knew she could never collect any support payments written into a divorce decree. All she wanted to do was get a legal divorce and go her own way.

Do you think Brenda's decision was a good one?

Which of the following statements apply to you?

1. You expect your husband to contest the divorce.
2. You have children and major decisions concerning their welfare must be made.
3. There is considerable property involved that must be divided.
4. You and your husband disagree about the terms of the divorce decree.
5. You know nothing about your legal rights or about divorce laws.
6. You need help in understanding the ramifications of a divorce decree, for example, how it will affect your taxes.
7. You feel overpowered by your husband—emotionally, physically, or financially.
8. You believe your husband will not be fair and that he will give you as little as possible in the way of property and support.
9. You are in a crisis situation—your husband is harming you and/or the children or he has deserted you and left you without any money.
10. You feel emotionally unable to deal with the decisions of a divorce decree and need legal help.

If any of these statements apply to you, you should seriously consider getting a lawyer to represent you. If you can't afford a lawyer and feel you may be entitled to free legal help, contact your local Legal Aid Society or Legal Services Program. The telephone number should be in your local phone directory. These offices will send you forms to complete to see if you qualify for legal assistance.

IS DIVORCE MEDIATION AN ALTERNATIVE FOR YOU?

Divorce mediation is a process that a couple agrees to participate in with the help of a trained mediator, to establish the terms of a divorce settlement. Mediation is more common in some states, such as California, than in others. Although the concept of using mediation to settle disputes has been accepted in other areas (such as labor-management negotiations), it is a relatively new concept in negotiating a divorce agreement. Lawyers may not react favorably to divorce mediation because they may feel they are losing business, or that the mediators do not have the skill and expertise to guard the best interests of their client. So do not be surprised if your lawyer does not react positively—he or she may be feeling threatened by the competition.

Mediators do not replace lawyers. They are simply trained to help a couple draft their own divorce agreement. Each party then takes the agreement to his or her individual lawyer for an opinion to be sure that it is fair and reasonable. This step of "lawyer review" serves to protect both parties.

HOW DO YOU SELECT A MEDIATOR?

Divorce mediators are often listed in the yellow pages of the phone book or can be recommended through domestic courts, counselors, social service agencies, lawyers, or friends. If you live in a small town, you may have to travel to the urban area nearest you to find a mediator. Mediators may be trained in the following:

1. Counseling/social work/psychology
2. Law
3. Conflict resolution
4. Mediation/arbitration

Sometimes mediators may work as a two-member team. Team members may be male and female, and may have backgrounds in counseling and law. The advantage to selecting a mediator team is that you can have two points of view representing different disciplines, and two mediators may find it easier to monitor the **negotiating** process. If mediators are not trained and competent, they may find themselves caught in the family system of the couple, become overwhelmed, and lose objectivity. If there is great conflict or one party is very powerful, a two-person mediating team may be better able to keep control and facilitate the negotiating process than one mediator. Some people may feel more comfortable with a male mediator, some with a female mediator. A team comprised of a man and woman can address this issue. Remember: a mediator is not a counselor or a lawyer. They should have an awareness of both disciplines to be of help to you. Their major function is to facilitate your agreeing to a fair settlement for both of you.

Do not hesitate to ask a mediator what his or her credentials are to serve in this capacity. Since this is a relatively new field, there are no national regulations or professional requirements for mediators. Training requirements for mediators vary from state to state. Ask yourself the following questions to determine if you are working with a mediator who is right for you:

1. Do they have academic or professional credentials and experience that apply to the legal and emotional aspects of divorce?
2. Have they had any training in mediation or conflict resolution?
3. Do they clearly state the terms of the service such as fees and number of sessions?
4. Do they seem knowledgeable about the divorce laws of your state so they can provide an idea of legal trends and precedents that can be helpful in making realistic settlement decisions?
5. If they do not know certain needed information, do they find the answers or refer you to an appropriate resource or professional who can help?
6. Do they act in a professional way that inspires trust and confidence?

SHOULD YOU USE A DIVORCE MEDIATOR?

The following conditions should be met when deciding to use mediation:

1. Both parties have definitely agreed to divorce.
2. Both parties wish to arrive at reasonable and fair settlement terms and do not wish to use the legal system or the divorce agreement to "punish" the other person or "get even."
3. Both parties feel relatively equal in their power and influence and do not feel they need to hire someone to serve as their "protector" or to "fight" their battles.
4. The property, financial, and child-custody situation of the couple is straightforward and does not require extensive advice from experts such as tax attorneys, accountants, and psychologists.
5. Both parties are mature and intelligent enough to agree to the terms of their divorce with the help of a mediator.
6. The mediator facilitates the negotiating process by remaining neutral or impartial.
7. The mediator is aware of the balance of power and supports and protects involved parties as needed.
8. You feel "safe" in the mediator's presence and feel that you are being helped to negotiate a divorce settlement that is fair to both parties.
9. The mediator has been highly recom-

mended. (Because of confidentiality, they may not supply you with references of other couples they have worked with to negotiate successful divorce contracts, unless they have received permission from those couples.)

10. The mediator keeps accurate records of what is agreed upon from week to week so that time is not wasted and there is no "backsliding."

WHAT AREAS SHOULD BE DISCUSSED AND AGREED UPON IN MEDIATION?

The following areas are commonly considered in negotiating a divorce settlement:

1. Children—Who has custody? What are the best arrangements for visitation? Who pays child support, college and medical costs, insurance, and so on.
2. Assets—How will you divide the following assets?
   a. Investments
   b. Businesses
   c. Pensions
   d. Other property (marital and nonmarital)
3. Spousal support.
4. Tax refunds—Who gets them? How are they divided?
5. Tax considerations—Who declares the children as deductions? Who takes capital gains liability? What is the filing status of individuals?
6. Debts—Who pays them off? How are debts to be divided?
7. Other (as they apply to your special case).

WHAT ARE THE ADVANTAGES OF USING A DIVORCE MEDIATOR?

The following are the advantages of using a divorce mediator:

1. It is a process that allows for maximum participation of both parties to determine the terms of their divorce.
2. It enables the couple to invest energy in arriving at fair divorce terms, as opposed to "combating" one another, which can lead to further disruption.
3. It allows parties to control their divorce.
4. It frequently results in quicker, more expedient divorce settlements.
5. It is often less expensive.
6. It is viewed as a fair and reasonable approach.
7. It is a less formal process.
8. It tends to produce divorce agreements where there are fewer feelings of victimization.
9. It encourages a stance of cooperation and openness.
10. It provides a structure and forum to solve settlement disputes and develop communication involving common areas of concern.
11. It stresses a win/win rather than a win/lose approach.
12. It can be more psychologically healing and less stressful, which helps individuals to create new lives for themselves as single people.

WHAT DOES MEDIATION COST?

Fees for mediation services range from $50 per hour to $150 per hour or more, if you are seeing a two-person mediating team. The number of sessions a couple requires depends upon their cooperation and to what extent they have prepared the necessary financial facts and information. On an average, a couple will spend from three to five sessions lasting from one to two hours each, to come to an agreement on settlement terms.

WHERE CAN YOU GET FURTHER INFORMATION ABOUT MEDIATION?

The professional national organization for mediation is:

Academy of Family Mediators
P.O. Box 4686
Greenwich, CT 06830
(203) 345–1205

This organization has developed standards of practice and has a national referral service of mediators who meet the requirements the organization has established.

A mediator can be used not only to establish terms of a divorce decree but for postdecree decisions as well. If a couple has worked well with a mediator, it can be less expensive and stressful to use mediation rather than lawyers and courts to settle issues that may result after the divorce. Mediation is not a realistic alternative for everyone. If you feel that you and your husband are unable to agree or communicate, if considerable assets are involved, complex tax considerations must be made, or if you feel overpowered by your husband, you will need to obtain a lawyer.

SHOULD YOU AND YOUR HUSBAND USE THE SAME LAWYER?

Some people decide to share an attorney because they can save time and money. This may end up to be false economy. Many lawyers will not represent both husband and wife since they feel it would be difficult to remain neutral and are afraid they will end up acting as a referee. Even if you and your husband agree to the terms of a divorce and if you have a lawyer who is a good friend, it is possible that you may lose that friendship should problems develop. Using the same lawyer may have the following disadvantages:

1. It will be difficult for one lawyer to represent you both should disagreements arise.
2. It is difficult for a lawyer to equally represent both parties in a divorce action.
3. If the lawyer is a man, you may feel intimidated (two men against one woman) should disagreements arise.
4. If your husband and the lawyer are not scrupulous, there is a danger of collusion between them.
5. You do not have a lawyer who is obligated to put your best interests first.

Despite these dangers, some couples do use the same lawyer. However, since the law is based upon an adversary system, it is usually best for a woman to have her own lawyer to represent her.

WHAT DO YOU WANT IN A LAWYER?

Listed below are qualities and qualifications of lawyers that women have said are important to them. Rank these items according to their importance to you. On a piece of paper, write "1" if the quality is of great importance to you, "2" if it is somewhat important, and "3" if it is of little importance. Doing so will help you decide which qualities and qualifications are important in a lawyer who might be representing you. Consider how important the following characteristics are in your choice of a lawyer.

1. Is a specialist in matrimonial law
2. Is empathic and easy to talk to
3. Is thorough
4. Is a good negotiator
5. Is a good fighter
6. Is physically impressive and has a magnetic personality
7. Is an expert on the ins and outs of the judicial system of your area; has firsthand knowledge of the judges and other lawyers
8. Respects women
9. Is an expert in taxes and the tax ramifications of a settlement
10. Is an experienced lawyer
11. Charges reasonable fees
12. Has had extensive experience in litigation (fighting cases in court)
13. Is honest and trustworthy
14. Has an excellent reputation
15. Is a member of a well-known law firm

Keep these criteria in mind when you look for a lawyer. Don't just settle on the first lawyer. Be selective. Your lawyer is going to work for you. You want a good one!

Make a list of the things you want your lawyer to do for you. What are your expectations?

HOW TO FIND A LAWYER

The following referral sources might be able to recommend lawyers and give you some information regarding them. What would be the benefits and risks of referrals from these sources?

—American Academy of Matrimonial
  Lawyers
—coffee shop of your local courthouse
—*Sullivan's Lawyer's Dictionary* for divorce
  law specialists
—Martindale-Hubbell Law Directory (lists
  lawyers throughout the United States)
—the yellow pages of your telephone
  directory
—family or corporate lawyer
—local bar association
—Legal Referral Service and/or other
  lawyers' associations
—Legal Aid
—counselors, doctors, ministers, and other
  members of the helping professions
—members of singles' groups
—women's groups (NOW, YWCAs,
  paralegal groups)
—your husband's lawyer
—law school alumnae chapters
—judges respected in the court where your
  case will be tried
—friends who have used lawyers

When asking for referrals, it helps if you can state what you expect from a lawyer. For example, if you specify that you want a lawyer who is experienced in handling contested divorces, the recommendations you receive may be different from those you receive were you to specify that you and your husband have the details of the divorce worked out and you simply need a lawyer to facilitate the divorce process. You may want to use several of the referral sources listed; keep in mind their advantages and disadvantages. Several you may decide to rule out completely. After consulting a number of referral sources, you will probably discover that several names keep being mentioned. Once you have three to five lawyers' names, there are several ways you can learn more about each.

1. Talk to people who have used the lawyer.
   Ask questions that are important to you
   such as

   a. How did you choose your lawyer?
   b. Do you feel the lawyer is honest?
   c. Are you satisfied with the settlement?
      Or, do you think the settlement is
      fair?
   d. Did the lawyer return phone calls?
   e. Did the lawyer charge for phone calls?
   f. What kind of fees does the lawyer
      charge?
   g. Did the lawyer stick to the fee esti-
      mated in the beginning or did the fee
      amount to more?
   h. What did you like about your lawyer?
   i. What did you dislike about your law-
      yer?
   j. Was the lawyer thorough?
   k. What was the lawyer's attitude toward
      women?
   l. Did the lawyer overlook any major
      points that should have been included
      in the divorce decree?
   m. Would you use the same lawyer
      again?

2. Talk to the lawyer on the phone or in person. Remember to ask what the charge is for an initial visit or a phone conversation.

3. Divorce decrees are a matter of public record. Consult decrees, see what the settlements were like, note the lawyer who handled the case, and call the persons involved to see what they thought of their lawyer. Copies of completed divorces should be on file at your local courthouse. Ask the county clerk if you can look at them.

4. Check local women's groups and YWCAs that may have legal clinics, either free or for a nominal fee. Some women, pleased with the services they receive from these sources, decide to retain one of the lawyers to whom they speak.

5. Local bar associations often have legal referral services that give out names of lawyers who specialize in matrimonial law. Such services should be used with caution. The bar association can only tell you whether the lawyers are "members in good standing;" they do not guarantee that these lawyers are competent. The services give the names of the lawyers who ask to be placed on a referral list. Referral services often arrange for a short interview with lawyers on a referral list for a nominal fee. You are under no obligation to retain a particular lawyer and may talk to several lawyers if you wish to do so. Check with referral services in your particular area for details.

QUESTIONS YOU SHOULD ASK A LAWYER

Read the questions listed below. Which would you want to ask a lawyer before hiring her or him to handle your case? Make a list of these questions.

QUESTIONS PERTAINING TO FEES

1. How much do you charge?
2. Is a retainer required? How much?
3. Do you charge for phone calls?
4. How much do you charge for trial work?
5. On what do you base the fee?
6. How often will I be billed?
7. Will I be charged if I talk to your secretary?

QUESTIONS PERTAINING TO YOUR CASE

1. Do I have grounds for a divorce?
2. How long will it take to get a divorce?
3. Given my situation, how much can I expect to receive in child support and/or alimony?
4. Can I get the family home?
5. How will you handle my case?
6. How strong a case do I have?

QUESTIONS PERTAINING TO THE LAWYER

1. Would you be representing me throughout the case or will other members of your firm take over?
2. Do you practice in the local courts?
3. Do you prepare your own case and do your own research?
4. Do you specialize in matrimonial law?
5. What other type of work do you do?
6. Where do you practice?
7. How much litigation work do you do?
8. How many people do you have in your office?
9. Are they also involved in divorce work?
10. How did you become interested in the law or in your particular area of the law?
11. Do you do your own financial analysis of a divorce situation (a complete analysis of the estate, the tax implications, etc.)?
12. How many cases of my size have you handled in the past year? What have been the results?
13. Is there much difference in how the judges handle cases?
14. Are you an accountant as well as an attorney?
15. What do you think of the attorney my husband has hired?
16. What do you think of attorney X, Y, or Z?
17. What percentage of divorces are appealed? What is the likelihood of success?
18. What college and law school did you attend?
19. For which law firms have you worked?
20. Are you divorced or separated?
21. Do you represent mostly men or women?
22. Are your fees tax deductible?
23. Can you give me the names of clients you have represented?

Pay attention to how the lawyer answers your questions. If he or she tells you that all judges are the same, divorces can be appealed if you don't get what you want the first time around, and that fees are not tax deductible, the lawyer may be uninformed, inexperienced, or trying to handle your case as quickly as possible. Judges may vary greatly, few divorce cases are appealed with much success, and some of the fees may be tax deductible.

COMPARING LAWYERS

Once you have talked to at least two lawyers, you will have to decide which lawyer is best for you. In talking to a lawyer to see if you wish to retain her or him, write down questions that you want answered. It is a good idea to ask several lawyers the same questions so that you can compare their answers. Interview the lawyers within a few days of each other so that the impressions are fresh in your mind. After leaving each lawyer's office, write a review of that lawyer. You may want to draw up a chart similar to the one on page 75. Keep a file of the lawyers on your list, the lawyers you interview, and your comments. If you need to switch lawyers in the middle of your case, you will be better prepared to move rapidly and won't have to start the process of information gathering all over again.

When you talk to a lawyer, honestly state that you are looking for the best lawyer to represent you and mention that you may be talking to another attorney before making a decision. If the lawyer is a reputable and a secure individual, there should be no objection on his or her part to your looking for the best lawyer to represent you. After all, it is best for both of you if you have confidence in your legal counsel.

Be aware of your reasons for choosing one lawyer over another. Are you choosing the lawyer with the lowest fees? The one who is easiest to talk to? The one who is most charming and attractive? Women are sometimes vulnerable to lawyers who are charming and complimentary, particularly if they feel beaten down by their husbands. If you are vulnerable in this way, try to recognize your vulnerability and make sure that it does not affect your choice of a lawyer.

Share your expectations with the lawyers you interview. Some of your expectations may be unrealistic and a lawyer may tell you so. It is better to begin the divorce process with realistic expectations than to have expectations that your lawyer will not be able to meet. If expectations are not discussed, you and your lawyer may be disappointed.

Review the qualities and qualifications you rated as being most important to you in the activity on pages 72. Also review your expectations of a lawyer. Reread the questions on page 74 that you asked the lawyers. Make up a chart to help you compare lawyers. Rate the lawyers on each item you listed as follows:

1 = Poor
2 = Average
3 = Excellent

QUALITY/QUALIFICATION EXPECTATION/QUESTION	LAWYER 1	LAWYER 2	LAWYER 3
1. Is he or she thorough?	2	2	3
2. Has he or she had extensive training in litigation?	1	3	2
3. Is he or she easy to talk to?	3	2	3
4. . . .			
TOTALS			

INFORMATION YOUR LAWYER NEEDS

The following checklist contains items you should have when you first visit your lawyer. You may find it helpful to go over the list and write down each item as you take care of it.

1. A written summary of vital information:
   Your full name and age
   Your husband's full name and age
   Date of marriage (number of years married)
   How long you have lived in your county and state
   Names of children
   Ages of children

2. A written summary of your marital problems: You may find it helpful to write out "what went wrong" before your first visit. This will help you summarize your marital problems and may save the lawyer's time and your money.

3. Copies of important papers and documents: marriage certificates, documentation of former marriages and divorces. Retain the originals for *your* file. If your lawyer needs the original document for a court appearance, turn original documents over to him or her at that time.

4. An inventory of your property and assets

5. A list of your insurance policies

6. An estimate of your husband's annual income and a description of his work history

7. If you work, an estimate of your annual income and a description of your work history

8. Information concerning whether you expect the divorce to be contested (whether you expect your husband to fight the divorce)

9. A carefully prepared budget: explain how much it costs you and any children you may have to live per year. Lawyers may not expect you to have this on the first visit but it would probably facilitate the divorce process for you to have it. Look at the activity on page 144 for help in preparing a budget.

10. A list of questions you may want your lawyer to answer (refer to page 74 for questions you may want to ask)

Since an initial visit to a lawyer is upsetting for some women, you may find it helpful to have in writing information for which your lawyer will ask and questions you may want to ask. You may also find it helpful to take notes.

YOUR LAWYER'S FEES

Because you are a woman, you may have little experience in dealing with financial arrangements with people you employ to work for you. Women are often taught to believe that discussing finances isn't polite. When you fail to discuss finances, you may find that the assumptions you make are not shared by other people, that people are not putting your financial interests first, and that you end up paying more than you wanted or expected to pay. The only way to avoid this is to honestly discuss financial arrangements and agree on a price. If your lawyer is honest and reputable, he or she will appreciate your wanting to spell out financial arrangements before you begin. A lawyer who cares for his or her reputation does not want a client to tell friends, neighbors, and community members that she feels she was mischarged.

To help you consider the financial aspects of using a lawyer, answer these questions:

1. How much money do you have readily available in case your lawyer requests a retainer (a fee, usually paid in advance, that will be considered as part of the total fee)?
2. How much money could you obtain with some effort if you decided to pay a retainer (through borrowing, selling possessions, etc.)?
3. How much money does your husband earn?
4. How much money do you earn?
5. How much property have you and your husband accumulated in the course of the marriage?

There are several systems lawyers use to charge for a divorce. One of these is the *flat fee* system; lawyers who use this system charge a set amount, barring unusual complications. This is usually a favorable arrangement for the woman since she has a clear idea of what the total charges will be. A typical charge for an uncontested divorce amounts to about $750 plus court costs.

Most lawyers are moving toward an hourly charge for divorce work. The charge per hour can range from $90.00 to $160.00 per hour. How much lawyers charge per hour depends upon their experience, if they specialize in matrimonial law, the clients they represent, if they have their own practice, if they are a partner in a major law firm, and if they practice in a rural or a metropolitan area. Since charges vary greatly from area to area and lawyer to lawyer, it is best to conduct a survey to determine the going rate in your location for the kind of legal representation you feel you need. Some women who have the terms of a divorce agreed upon and who do not have much at stake in terms of present or future assets may need a lawyer for minimal advice, simply to take care of the filing and paperwork. Other women with more complex financial situations, who expect the divorce to be contested, may need a lawyer with extensive experience who has the backing of a law firm and other professionals such as accountants.

Most lawyers charge a retainer to begin legal work on a divorce. The amount a lawyer charges depends upon how complicated the divorce will be and how much time the case will require. Retainers can start at $750 for an uncontested divorce, $1,500 for a contested divorce.

WARNING:—There are many lawyers who advertise low-cost divorces. This may be acceptable if you know your divorce will be straightforward with few assets and no children involved. Beware of choosing the least expensive legal advice if you feel your situation is more complex. Choosing a lawyer solely on the basis of cost can be a mistake. Your divorce may be the most important business deal you have made to date. You need to have the legal advice your situation requires. What starts out to be a "good economical decision" can turn out to be more expensive in the long run.

Some lawyers may be interested in taking your case on a *contingent fee* basis, particularly if your husband has a fair amount of property or if you have accumulated property during the marriage. This means that the lawyer will take a percentage of whatever you receive as a result of a property settlement. If you receive very little, so does the lawyer. The advantages of this system are that you don't have to pay the lawyer immediately if you don't have the money and that you won't be charged more than you have. The disadvantage is that your lawyer is encouraged to hold out for the highest possible amount of money for you which may not be realistic. Other considerations, which might be equally or more important to you, such as visitation, child custody, a cost-of-living clause, and the children's education expenses, may not receive as much attention. Because your lawyer is supposed to be realistic during the negotiations between you and your husband, the contingent fee agreement whereby a lawyer is negotiating for his or her fee is not always a good idea.

It is not wise to brag about your assets, your financial situation, or the large salary your husband earns before your lawyer mentions his or her fee. Even if you will not have to pay the fee, it is advisable to keep as many family assets as possible—that way there is more to divide. Although you will have to give your lawyer some idea of your worth and the property you have accumulated, use discretion. If your maiden aunt Mabel is on her deathbed in Duluth and you expect to inherit half a million dollars, don't mention it. Your fee may be more. After all, Aunt Mabel may linger forever or leave her money to her cat.

Before your first visit to a lawyer, decide if you are willing or able to pay a retainer. If your lawyer states it is his or her policy to work on a retainer basis and if you simply cannot afford to pay one, discuss your situation. You may be able to work out an agreement. (A discussion of several advantages and disadvantages of paying a retainer follow.)

ADVANTAGES

1. If your case continues for a long time, your lawyer may be more motivated if he or she feels they have been paid in part for the work they are doing.
2. A lawyer may feel obligated to the party who pays him or her. Should this be the case, the lawyer may feel more obligated and responsible to you if you pay a retainer.

DISADVANTAGES

1. You have used money that you may need for other things.
2. If your husband is going to pay your legal fees, you may not get the retainer fee back on the basis that you have already paid it.
3. If you decide to fire your lawyer in the initial stages, you will have a battle for a refund.

The following questions deal with financial agreements that should be discussed during the first meeting with your lawyer. Can you answer these questions?

1. How much will your divorce cost?
2. For what services will you be charged?
   a. Cost per hour of lawyer's time
   b. Phone calls
   c. Phone calls to secretary
   d. Duplicate copies of documents
   e. Court costs
   f. Research
   g. Court appearances
   h. Postage
3. On what basis will you be charged? By the hour, flat fee, or on a contingent basis?
4. Who will pay the lawyer's fees—you or your husband?
5. Will your lawyer accept payment after the divorce? Will time payments be acceptable?
6. Are the fees tax deductible?

In general, that part of the fees charged for tax advice or taxable alimony is deductible. Ask if your legal adviser keeps time cards on divorce, tax analysis and advice, alimony, asset conservation, and individual assets. The lawyer who glibly states that fees are not deductible may be doing so to save time at your expense.

WARNING:—Some women do not pay attention to legal fees because they feel it is customary for the husband to pay the wife's legal fees. To overlook what your lawyer is charging on the basis of "He can charge whatever he wants—my husband is paying the fees" is a mistake. In the negotiating process, you may end up paying your own legal fees or half of your legal fees, even though you originally did not expect to do so. If you are oblivious to what your lawyer is charging, you are asking for trouble.

If this is the first time you are hiring someone to work for you, you may be somewhat naive. Good business sense dictates that you know what you will be charged for a service in any situation. There are honest and dishonest lawyers, just as there are honest and dishonest members of any profession. Being aware of the financial terms of an agreement before you begin to conduct business with an individual is always wise.

Keeping what you want and what is in your best interest in mind is the best way to guard against people who are unethical and who might take advantage of you. Remember that your emotional state and lack of experience with financial and legal matters may make you particularly vulnerable at this time.

YOUR STATE AND DIVORCE: A TEST

Some women feel that if they have a lawyer, they need not know anything about family law or about the divorce laws of their state. Knowing something about divorce and the laws that affect you will help you ask your lawyer intelligent questions and will make you more aware of what is happening concerning your divorce.

To help you examine what you know about divorce and the laws of your state, see if you can answer these questions:

1. Is your state a "fault" or a "no-fault" divorce state?
2. What are the grounds for divorce in your state?
3. Have new laws recently been passed in your state that might affect your divorce?
4. How long must you be married before you are entitled to Social Security through your husband?
5. How long must you live in your state before filing for divorce?
6. In your state, is fault taken into account when the court determines support and division of property?
7. Does your state have a statute concerning resuming the use of your maiden name?
8. Which is taxable for the woman, alimony or child support?
9. Do you know the meaning of *condonation, collusion,* and *countersuit?*
10. Do you know what separate maintenance is?

If you had ten correct answers, your score is excellent; eight to nine correct, very good; seven to eight, good; five or six, fair; and four or less, poor. If your score was poor, you would be wise to learn more about divorce law, particularly the laws in your state. Be sure to consult a *recent* book that discusses the laws in your state.

MAKING EFFECTIVE USE OF A LAWYER

Answer the following questions with a yes or no. Then compare your answers with those provided at the end of the questionnaire. If your answer differs, read the information accompanying the "ideal" response. Answer the questions honestly!

1. Do you spend a large part of the time you see your lawyer discussing emotional aspects of the divorce such as your feelings toward your husband, your husband's character, and why you don't get along with him?
2. Do you call your lawyer every time your husband says something that makes you angry to tell her or him that you want more in the way of a settlement?
3. Have you given your lawyer all the information and copies of documents needed for him or her to do the necessary work on your case?
4. Do you wait to think about major decisions until you are in the lawyer's office and then expect your attorney to guide you in making these decisions?
5. Do you decide what you want to ask your lawyer, write it down, and wait until you can get your questions answered in one visit rather than making frequent phone calls?
6. Do you find yourself making an extra effort to be attractive when you visit your lawyer (if the lawyer is a man) and find that you are particularly pleased with anything he says that is complimentary to you?
7. Do you expect your lawyer to be on top of every detail of your case and do you refrain from taking the initiative and following through on questions you may have or on things you don't understand?
8. Are you honest with your lawyer; have

you told him or her everything that may have a bearing on your case?

9. Do you treat your relationship with your lawyer as a serious business deal and behave in a businesslike fashion?

10. Do you use discretion in your relationships with your ex-husband and any men you may be dating so that you will be in the best possible legal position?

If you have answered the questions in the following way, you are probably using your lawyer most effectively.

1. **NO.** If you find you are spending considerable time rehashing why your marriage failed, where you and your husband went wrong, your feelings about the divorce, and your fears of being on your own, you may be using your lawyer more as a counselor than as an expert on legal matters. Some lawyers are willing to listen to the minute details of the emotional aspects of your divorce—but they charge you the going rate, which may be $100 an hour or more. Although your lawyer may feel that he or she has special insight into people and the emotional aspects of divorce, he or she is not a trained counselor. Emotional aspects of divorce *should* be dealt with, but it makes more sense to consult a trained counselor than to use your lawyer for this purpose.

2. **NO.** If you spend much of your time with your lawyer discussing your husband's immaturity, the ways he has wronged you, and how you can make him regret what he has done by "socking it to him" in a divorce decree, you may be using your lawyer and the legal system as a vehicle to vent your anger. Again, not only is this an expensive way to deal with your anger but it is also an ineffective method. Anger with one's spouse is normal and should be dealt with. Couples would, however, be wise to seek divorce counseling where they can confront their anger and deal with it, then move on rather than to use the courts as an arena for their battles. If your husband won't agree to divorce counseling, you might consider dealing with your anger in counseling

for yourself. Even playing tennis, where you can whack the ball, or beating a punching bag would be a more effective way of dealing with your anger than regarding your lawyer as the person who is going to help you get even.

3. **YES.** If your lawyer asks for information or legal documents, make sure that he or she has what is needed. Sometimes delays in divorce cases are caused by a client's failure to give a lawyer what is needed. It is a good idea to provide your lawyer with copies of documents rather than the documents themselves. In this way, should you decide to change lawyers, you will have no difficulty should your lawyer refuse to return the documents using them as a "lawyer's lien" in case a dispute concerning fees arises. You can tell your lawyer that you will provide the original documents when you go to court if they are required.

4. **NO.** Beware of the temptation to make your lawyer into a savior who will make the right decisions and spare you the uncertainty and hard work that decision making requires. Your lawyer should be able to discuss alternatives with you and the possible legal and financial ramifications involved, but you are doing yourself and your lawyer a disfavor if you expect him or her to make the final decisions for you. Remember, you will have to live with the decisions that are made—your lawyer won't. If you find that you are tempted to turn over all your decisions to your lawyer, reread chapters 5 and 6 on decision making. Do you really want to pass up an opportunity to define yourself through making your own decisions?

5. **YES.** It is often helpful to jot down questions you want to ask your lawyer so you won't forget what it is you want to ask once you are in his or her office. If you give in to the temptation to call your attorney every time you have a question (provided it isn't an emergency and the question can wait), you may find your bill is higher. Some lawyers charge a minimum time of fifteen minutes per phone call, even if you ask a two-minute

question. So, find out what your lawyer's policy is regarding phone calls. Better yet, try to save your time and his or hers by saving questions that will wait until you see your lawyer. If you guard against calling every five minutes, your chances of getting your attorney's full attention when a crisis arises are increased.

6. **NO.** Some women fantasize about their lawyers. If your lawyer is a man, he may be the only man who is helping you in your life right now. You may want to make him into a knight in shining armor who will ride into battle, defeat your husband, and get revenge for the wrongs your husband has committed. Don't do it! If you find an attraction developing between the two of you, watch out. Try to meet your emotional needs through other people. A word of caution: the last thing you need with a lawyer who is representing you is a sexual relationship. If you find this idea tempting, reconsider. Your lawyer will find it difficult to be objective and you may find that a sexual relationship interferes with your receiving the best legal representation you can get.

7. **NO.** While it is good to have the utmost confidence in your lawyer once you have decided upon one, don't expect your lawyer to be perfect and beyond human error. The best lawyers make mistakes and errors of omission. You are just one of their cases. If you are tempted not to check on something that is bothering you or not to ask about something that doesn't seem right to you, think twice! Many women feel that their lawyers overlooked important items that should have been included in the decree or failed to mention important legal aspects of divorce. The surest way for you to obtain the terms you want is to decide what you want and keep after your lawyer. Remember, too, that laws are constantly changing. You may have heard of a legal aspect pertaining to your case that your lawyer doesn't know about.

8. **YES.** You help neither your lawyer nor your case if you hide information that may be important. If you have done something that is not in your favor, it is best to discuss it with your lawyer so he or she is prepared to deal with it should your husband's lawyer bring it up in court. No lawyer likes to be caught off balance because a client hasn't been honest.

9. **YES.** Your divorce is one of the most serious business deals you will be handling in your lifetime and you should act accordingly. Keep appointments with your lawyer and be prompt. Maintain a personal file of original documents pertaining to your divorce and of correspondence with your lawyer. Your attorney should send you copies of important correspondence he or she has had concerning your case. Also, keep a running log of phone calls and visits to your lawyer, how much time was spent and what business was discussed. Remember, you are paying for your lawyer's time. No matter how sociable you or your lawyer might feel, it is best to confine your discussions to legal matters and find others to socialize with—it is less expensive that way.

10. **YES.** Ask your lawyer how you should act while you are in the process of getting a divorce and then follow the advice. Some women have wiped out the grounds they had for a divorce because they slept with their husband "once for old times' sake" or they jeopardized their cases because their husband saw them entering a motel room with another man. If your conduct jeopardizes your case, you are not helping yourself or a lawyer who is trying his or her best to represent you.

BEING ASSERTIVE WITH YOUR LAWYER

Sometimes women hesitate to tell their lawyers what they want and to be assertive in getting the legal help that is best for them. This may be because they are mystified by the legal process, are looking for someone to make their decisions, feel overwhelmed by the divorce, or see their lawyer as an authority figure, particularly if the lawyer is a man. It is likely that your lawyer is only the first of a number of professional people with whom you will be dealing as a single person. It helps to know what you want and to be informed about the legal system and the divorce laws of your state. Remember that your lawyer is working for you—not the other way around! Your lawyer will not know what is best for you and what you want unless you speak up. You will be doing both yourself and your lawyer a favor if you make your expectations and your feelings known.

To help you examine how assertive you are with your lawyer, answer the following questions with a yes or no:

1. Do you feel free to question your lawyer if you do not agree with the way your case is being handled?
2. Do you feel free to remind your lawyer about certain issues if you feel he or she has forgotten something or is not taking prompt action?
3. Do you feel free to ask your lawyer to explain certain aspects of the law or legal terminology that you may not understand?
4. Do you state what you want in a divorce decree clearly and consistently?
5. Do you allow yourself to feel guilty because your lawyer may disapprove of decisions you make or of certain matters pertaining to your case?
6. Do you feel free to appear intelligent and capable or do you feel it necessary to appear victimized and helpless?
7. Do you insist on making the final decisions after your lawyer has discussed alternatives and the ramifications of those alternatives?
8. Do you allow your lawyer to assume that because you are a woman you will have certain feelings and make certain decisions?
9. Do you discuss financial arrangements openly and question your lawyer when you feel you have been charged incorrectly?
10. When you are displeased about the service you are getting, do you feel free to discuss this openly with your lawyer?
11. Do you feel free to ask your lawyer to explain his or her rationale for the way your case is being handled?
12. Do you object to your lawyer's addressing you as "honey," "dear," or using other terms that are neither appropriate nor professional?

If you answered "no" to any of these questions, you may not be getting what you need and want from your lawyer because you see him or her as an authority figure. While your lawyer is hopefully an expert on the law, you are the expert on yourself. If you take a passive stance, you may not get what you want.

WHEN AND HOW TO FIRE YOUR LAWYER

Some women become dissatisfied with the legal help they are getting but are reluctant to change lawyers because of time and money already invested. If you are dissatisfied with your lawyer, do any of the following situations apply to you?

1. You feel that your lawyer is dishonest.
2. You feel that your lawyer is conspiring with your husband's lawyer for personal economic gain.
3. Your lawyer has failed to keep you informed of developments, such as necessary court appearances, that have been detrimental to your case.
4. You seriously question your lawyer's ability and knowledge of the law.
5. You no longer have any trust or confidence in your lawyer.
6. You feel your lawyer does not act promptly on your behalf.
7. You feel your lawyer is not willing to put enough effort into your case.
8. You feel pressured by your lawyer to make certain decisions that you do not feel are in your best interests.
9. You feel that your lawyer is unwilling to fight on your behalf for the best settlement possible.
10. You feel your lawyer's behavior is unprofessional.

If any of these statements pertain to your situation, you may want to consider changing lawyers. Some objections, such as lack of trust or confidence in your lawyer, are more serious than others and almost necessitate a change.

Ask yourself these questions:

1. Have you told your lawyer what is bothering you about his or her actions and the service you are receiving?

2. Have you tried to discuss your dissatisfactions honestly and rationally with your lawyer?

3. Are you an easy client to work with? If you were a lawyer, would you want to have yourself as a client?

Sometimes clients make it very difficult for their lawyers to act in their behalf. As a client, are you guilty of any of the following?

1. Expecting your lawyer to act upon your demands immediately as if your case were the only case the lawyer had?

2. Calling your lawyer frequently with trivial questions, complaints concerning your spouse, or other matters that could wait?

3. Expecting your lawyer to make all the decisions and then being disappointed by the decisions that are made?

4. Expecting an exorbitant settlement that may be unrealistic considering your husband's financial position?

5. Failing to provide information your lawyer needs to work effectively?

6. Expecting the lawyer to act as a counselor-psychologist who will listen attentively to every emotional aspect of your divorce experience?

7. Neglecting to tell your lawyer what you want or expect and then complaining to everyone else when your lawyer doesn't live up to your expectations?

8. Expecting your lawyer to be your ally in a battle to gain eternal revenge upon your husband?

9. Changing your mind daily and expecting your lawyer to keep abreast of your latest decision?

10. Behaving in a manner that could jeopardize your case, making it more difficult for your lawyer to serve you?

Some women who become dissatisfied never discuss their complaints with their lawyers. If this is true in your case, you would be wise to review the activity on page 81 dealing with how assertive you are with your lawyer. You may also find chapter 13 helpful. You cannot expect your lawyer to represent you adequately if you don't tell him or her what you want.

Unfortunately, divorce is an unpleasant ordeal during which many spouses come to distrust one another and the lawyers involved. It has been said that "A good divorce is one in which both parties feel cheated." You may find it difficult to remain objective and may need another opinion concerning what you are due and how your lawyer is handling your case. Sometimes it is possible to have another lawyer look over a proposed divorce agreement or to ask questions of another attorney if you are wondering whether your lawyer is acting in your best interests. Since lawyers usually tend to be supportive of one another, you will have to be tactful in your approach to getting a second opinion. For example, if you ask a question such as, "Does the proposed amount of child support seem fair and consistent with what courts would award to me given my husband's financial status and our present situation?" you would be more likely to receive an open answer than were you to throw a proposed settlement down on the desk of a second lawyer for comments with the first lawyer's name written on it. Remember, if you decide to keep your lawyer, it may not be in your best interests for him or her to know that you have been questioning the work done on your case by consulting other lawyers.

If you decide to fire your lawyer, it is generally wise to have a new attorney lined up before you do so. Then, if an emergency arises, you will have someone to represent you. Ask your new attorney what papers and records he or she wants. If you have been keeping a file, you should have original documents and copies of all legal correspondence. If you do not have the necessary data, go to your previous attorney's office and obtain copies of the required information. Ask your original lawyer how much time and expense have been incurred to date; try to get this information in writing. It is important that you complete these matters before you fire a lawyer as he or she can retaliate by raising the bill or by refusing to release papers and records pertaining to your case. Once you have your papers and costs tied down, tell your attorney you are making a change for personal reasons. Do not feel obligated to or allow yourself to be pressured into making an explanation, simply state your decision. A Substitution of Attorney Form, which is signed by your former attorney and your new attorney, is usually required. This form is then filed with the court. When you discharge your former attorney, have the form ready and ask him or her to sign it. Then you will be sure the form is signed, that you have concluded all your business, and that you will not have to see your attorney again, a situation that could be awkward and uncomfortable for both of you.

Often, when a client decides to fire a lawyer, the feeling is mutual. It is not in a lawyer's best interests to continue representing a client who will be dissatisfied with the divorce decree and the service she has received and who will let others know this. If, in an extreme case, you feel that your lawyer has been dishonest or has represented you in such a way as to jeopardize your settlement, you can sue him or her. You may have to search for a lawyer who is willing to represent you; lawyers are often reluctant to act against one another. However, if you have proof and a strong enough case, such an action may prove necessary.

As a final reminder, remember that if your lawyer is professional, ethical, and secure in who he or she is, your honesty in stating your initial expectations and your dissatisfactions as soon as they occur will be welcomed and appreciated. Your honesty will make it easier for your lawyer to better serve you.

DECISIONS CONCERNING A DIVORCE SETTLEMENT

When it came time to negotiate the terms of a divorce, I was lost. I had no idea how much it cost to live and what our assets and liabilities were—let alone what I wanted!

Although every case is different, talking to other women who had gone through divorce gave me some idea concerning what I could expect to get in the way of a settlement.

Negotiating a divorce settlement is difficult. No one likes to give up earnings and material possessions. The discussions of "who gets what" can trigger emotional issues and resentments. Couples may find that bitter fights develop at this stage; these may not really be about who gets Aunt Martha's antique clock but may express anger, hurt, and disappointment because the marriage relationship did not work out. Men may try to hold on to as much as they can, women may try to get as much as they can—particularly if there are young children involved and the woman has been out of the work force. The process is often a painful one. Women particularly may feel at a disadvantage at this stage of the divorce process. First, a woman may have little or no property in her name, be unemployed, have no job training, and have small children. This puts her at a decided psychological disadvantage. It becomes her job to get what she needs for herself and her children from her husband. Second, a woman may not understand or be familiar with her total financial picture; she may not know how much her husband earns, how much everyday expenses cost, or what their assets and liabilities are. Third, she may be totally unfamiliar with the world of finances, insurance, bookkeeping, taxes, and so on and feel thoroughly intimidated. Fourth, a woman, forced to make decisions regarding finances for the first time in her life, may feel totally unprepared to do so. Fifth, she may not be a skilled negotiator while her husband may have developed this skill in the business world. Finally, a woman may expect to be taken care of in a divorce settlement and find that recent social trends and laws require that she be more independent when it comes to supporting herself—something she is not prepared to do emotionally or practically.

The reality is that few women receive large settlements that allow them to continue their married standard of living. Divorce means that property is somehow divided and that salaries are shared through alimony and child-support payments. The purpose of this chapter is to help you decide what you want financially in a divorce settlement. Decisions concerning child custody and visitation will be dealt with in the next chapter.

When you separate, you will need to have an accurate account of your expenses should your lawyer find it necessary to go to court to get a temporary settlement for you. Since the temporary settlement often sets the precedent for the final divorce agreement, particularly if the judge is respected, you will want to have an accurate summary of your living expenses at this point. If your husband continues to support you during your separation, making a temporary settlement unnecessary, be sure to collect information concerning your living expenses for use when you begin to negotiate a settlement.

In order to know what you want, you first have to know what there is to divide in terms of assets, liabilities, and income. You will also need an accurate picture of your expenses. This chapter will ask you to gather information, clarify what you value and want, and develop your negotiating skills.

WARNING: Since women are socialized to think of others first and to be understanding, they are often uncomfortable when their husbands seem "unreasonable" and "demanding" when it comes to the terms of a divorce settlement. Many women express the wish to remain "on good terms" with their husbands for the sake of the children. Do not expect to go through a divorce with everyone being fair, and acting agreeably. If you found your husband to be unfair during your marriage, don't expect him to be fair negotiating the terms of a divorce settlement. If you have tended to "keep the peace at any price," be sure you use your lawyer to protect what you are entitled to. You need to put yourself and your needs first. Your husband will be doing the same.

HOW TO PROTECT YOURSELF FROM CREDIT CARDS AND JOINT ACCOUNTS

Make a list of valid credit cards to which you, your husband, or both of you have access. Include all types of credit cards: Visa, Master-Card, American Express, Diners Club, Universal Air Travel Plan (UATP), individual airline cards, individual store charge plates, and oil company credit cards. Then, to examine the dangers of credit cards and joint bank accounts and to learn how to protect yourself, answer these questions:

1. In the last several months, have there been unusual or particularly high credit card bills due to your husband? (You can obtain this information from the credit department of the organization that issued the card.)
2. Do you feel that your husband will use credit cards to incur bills for which you may both be held responsible?
3. Since you have planned to obtain a divorce, how have you used credit cards?

   Some people, realizing divorce is inevitable, use credit to purchase new wardrobes, major appliances for the house, and other items in a last-chance buying spree. If your husband has done this or if you think there is a chance he may do this, it is possible to cancel the card if it was issued to you or to have your name taken off the account so that you will not be held responsible for debts that he might incur. This procedure should be discussed with a lawyer, since card issuers have different procedures for cancellation. If you feel you are being given incorrect information by an issuer, check with your attorney. If cards must be canceled, it is wise to cancel all cards simultaneously to avoid charges on a card that may still be valid.

   Credit companies want your business and are often willing to waive interest charges even if the last few months' worth of card charges are not paid promptly as long as the principal is fully paid and the reason for late payment is explained to the company. If you are removing your name from a joint account, you may want to consider opening a new account under your own name, using the old account as a reference so that you can begin to establish credit as a single person. Discuss any questions or problems you might have with the credit department of the company that issued the card.
4. Have you been using credit established jointly with your husband to make major purchases?

Should you decide to use credit cards to make major purchases before the divorce is final, consult your lawyer. If you have not discussed the purchases with your spouse and arrived at an agreement, be prepared for retaliation on his part. In some cases, major purchases may be valid, necessary, and advisable. However, be sure to check with your attorney. Your husband may not be required to assume your debts and you may find yourself with bills for purchases you would not have made had you known that you would have to pay for them.

5. What joint checking or savings accounts do you have? (Don't overlook children's accounts having both your names.)

If you have a joint checking account that allows either spouse to sign, you may decide to have your spouse's name removed or to withdraw all the money in the account, thus closing the account.

If you think your husband will close joint bank accounts and you have no means of support, consider the risks and benefits of closing the accounts and redepositing the funds in an account under your name only. Another alternative would be to take out the money you think of as your own. If you are considering this, consult your attorney. Before closing an account, consider how well you know your husband presently and how predictable you feel his behavior to be. Stopping charge cards or bank accounts may precipitate full-scale domestic warfare. These actions, which should be considered as defensive maneuvers, are advisable only if you have good reason to believe that your husband will make these moves if you don't. There have been occasions when lawyers have advised these actions unnecessarily and what little goodwill and cooperation existed between husband and wife ceased to exist. A judge awarding temporary support may decide a wife needs less temporary support if she has all the money from the joint savings and checking accounts. If you close bank accounts, safe-deposit boxes, sell stock, and so on for what you feel is a valid reason, make sure the money or assets you remove are inventoried. All withdrawals for living expenses and other costs should be documented. This will prevent your spouse from claiming that you have hidden these assets.

If your husband has stopped your credit cards or closed your bank accounts, ask your lawyer about the advisability of freezing his bank account, safe-deposit box, stock, and so on. If your credit and bank accounts are closed by your husband and you have no available funds, ask your attorney to arrange a court hearing for temporary support. If your husband has cleaned out the joint savings or checking account or if he has sold joint property, your lawyer can get a court order forcing him to reimburse you in a property settlement.

COLLECTING FINANCIAL INFORMATION

In order to make a start in deciding what you want in terms of a property and financial settlement, you will have to collect information. Budget, property, and income information should be gathered as quickly as possible in case your husband may be trying to conceal the information so as to reduce his eventual payments to you. Regardless of the marital situation, women should have this information for their financial independence should they ever have to take over the family finances in an emergency. It may also be necessary to go to court to get a temporary order for support. You will want to document your expenses carefully in order to get a temporary settlement that is favorable to you. Remember that a temporary settlement can set a precedent for the permanent settlement.

If you have paid the bills, been responsible for budgeting, helped your husband with his business, and been familiar with yearly tax preparations, this will not be difficult. If your husband has handled the finances, and has kept his earnings a secret, this data gathering will be more difficult. It is important to have access to financial information. People who separate often take their clothes and cherished personal belongings with them. They may not take financial records and important documents that could provide an important basis for negotiating a settlement. If you feel the negotiations will be difficult or that a court fight will be necessary, accurate business and personal financial data are essential. Estimated assets, income, or expenses can be challenged; estimates are not as good as data that can be documented.

Check to see if you have access to the following records and information you might need to obtain an accurate financial picture. You should have information about these financial books and records for the last two to four years.

—*personal expenses*
—*educational expenses*
—*stock market records*
—*investments*
—*canceled checks*
—*loan statements*
—*tax returns*
—*separate property*
—*debts owed*
—*insurance policies*
—*savings plans (including credit union, "special clubs," 401K plans, etc.)*
—*home expenses*
—*medical expenses*
—*checkbooks*
—*bank statements*
—*paid-bill files*
—*business data (for your business and/or your husband's)*
—*debts receivable*
—*credit cards held*
   other (ask your lawyer or accountant)

You will need this information to reconstruct assets (what you own), liabilities (debts you owe), earnings, and expenses in detail. Without original books and records it is difficult to gain a complete financial picture. Whoever has the books and records, therefore, has an advantage. If you do not have the data, you can ask for information by means of interrogatories and depositions, but only specific answers will be given to questions.

Most individuals are able to provide rough estimates of earnings and expenses. The problem is that rough estimates may be challenged in court and expenses may be overlooked or forgotten unless records are consulted. Begin keeping accurate financial records immediately. Be sure to list all checks, balance your checkbook, and see that your checkbook balance and bank statements agree. If you have trouble, a personal banker at your bank will be glad to help you. Keep a record of all your expenses. Paying by check is a good way to do this. Keep a notebook in which you list all items and bills you pay by cash. Keeping an exact record of cash expenditures is tedious but it is a good way to determine where your cash goes and the cost of incidental and miscellaneous items that mount up. With your records and documents in hand, you are now in a position to obtain the data concerning the financial situation that you need.

DO YOU NEED AN ACCOUNTANT?

This activity will apply to you only if you have many assets, liabilities, and/or businesses that must be considered in order to gain a complete financial picture.

Answer the following questions with yes or no to decide whether or not you need an accountant:

1. Is the estate in question a large one?
2. Do you have many liabilities?
3. Is there a business involved?
4. Do you suspect your husband of hiding earnings and assets?
5. Are numerous tax ramifications involved with your financial situation?
6. Do you believe your financial situation to be very complex?
7. Do you own stocks and bonds?
8. Do you feel entitled to a pension plan or future earnings of your spouse?

If you answered yes to any of the above questions, you may want to consider hiring an accountant to work with you and your lawyer. This will probably be necessary only if your financial situation is a complex one, if you feel your husband is hiding assets or earnings, or if your attorney is weak in tax and financial knowledge. The accountant you select should work for and report to you. Then, should you decide to change lawyers, you will not have to change accountants as well.

The accountant you choose should depend upon your needs and what you want to accomplish. The opinions of large prestigious firms will probably be accepted in negotiation or by a court. Examples of well-known accounting firms are the "Big Eight" listed here in alphabetical order.

- Arthur Andersen & Co.
- Ernst & Whinney
- Haskins & Sells
- Lybrand, Ross Bros. & Montgomery
- Peat Marwick Main
- Price Waterhouse & Co.
- Touche Ross & Co.
- Arthur Young & Co.

Smaller accounting firms generally charge about 30 percent less on an hourly basis. Some people feel they get better, more reasonable service from a smaller firm. A smaller firm may also call less attention to the size of your estate. You will want to know which member of the accounting firm will represent you in negotiations or in court; you will want someone who is skilled in financial presentations and accounting. Ideally, you should deal with an accountant in the tax group of a firm with divorce accounting experience. A person knowledgeable in tax laws can back up your lawyer. He or she can provide a cross-check on the financial and taxation aspects of a settlement. Accounting charges may vary—a junior member of a firm will usually charge less than will a senior member. Ask the accounting firm to send copies of everything they send to your attorney to you as well. This will keep you up-to-date, enable you to be in control of your financial situation, and give you a chance to review the data. Information on accounting firms in your area can be obtained from your bank.

YOUR ASSETS AND LIABILITIES

In order to decide what kind of proposal to make or accept for a settlement, you will need to know the assets and liabilities you have as a couple. *Assets* are your financial resources, or the sum total of what you are worth. *Liabilities* are debts that you owe. A *balance sheet* shows your assets and liabilities.

To determine your assets and liabilities, set up a balance sheet. Unless you have a special situation, set up your balance sheet to be effective on the last day of the month. The reason for this is to produce a cutoff date, simplifying mortgage payment calculations, bank reconciliations, stock pricing, lease payments, loan payments, and pay-

ments that are made on the first, tenth, or fifteenth of the month. Round off your figures to the nearest dollar. In the event that your divorce negotiations or a trial take a considerable amount of time, update the financial statement at the end of each month. Do not consider separate property (property that was owned by you or your husband and was brought into the marriage) in a joint balance sheet.

Look at the categories listed on the following pages and set up your balance sheet to cover these categories.

ASSETS

CASH
What cash do you have in checking, savings, savings and loan, commercial, and thrift plans, 401K, Keogh or IRA plans, brokers' balances, and credit union investments?

    —description
    —value
    —total

REAL ESTATE
If you own real estate, what is your investment worth? You should have a short description of the property, location, lot size, improvements, and a picture. You may want to consider appreciation or depreciation if your divorce proceedings continue for a period of time. Appraisals are based on comparable sales made in your area recently and/or on the cost to duplicate the property. It is wise to get three appraisals from realtors and to use an average of the appraisal figures you receive. Do not feel it necessary to obligate yourself to a realtor who gives you an estimate in the event you plan to sell your home. If necessary, your attorney will suggest a professional appraiser. You will want the following information:

    —date of purchase
    —purchase price
    —down payment
    —equity
    —loans against property
    —present value estimate
    —total value of investment

To figure the total value of investment if the property has appreciated, subtract the purchase price from the present value estimate. Then add the down payment and the equity to that figure.

PERSONAL PROPERTY

It is wise to take an inventory of your personal belongings when you plan to divorce. Taking pictures is an easy method to use. What jewelry, home furnishings, clothing, automobiles, recreation vehicles, art, and so on do you own? Assign a value to major items. Value cars at the wholesale price listed in the Kelly Blue Book (available at banks and auto dealers). If you have a valuable collection, you may want to consider hiring an appraiser acceptable to both you and your husband. In assigning a value to items, consider how much you would get if you sold that item. For jewelry and furnishings in good condition, a reasonable value consisting of retail price minus 50 percent is usually accepted. In dividing property, consider how much it would cost to *replace* an item as well as how much you would get for that item if you sold it.

> —*items listed separately*
> —*value of each*
> —*total*

LIFE INSURANCE

Enter the cash surrender value of life insurance policies. Term insurance has no cash surrender value and should not be listed as an asset. If you have no children, and your insurance is payable to your spouse, talk to your attorney.

> —*policy*
> —*cash surrender value*
> —*total*

STOCKS AND BONDS

If you have many stocks and bonds to consider, you may want to see an accountant. The face or market value of the securities may not be the same as the actual property value because of restrictions or taxes that have to be paid on the sale of securities. You will want the following information:

> —*company and description of securities*
> —*purchase date*
> —*number of shares/bonds*
> —*current market value per share*
> —*total current market value—multiply the number of shares or bonds times the current market price*
> —*total yearly dividend or yield*
> —*total*

RECEIVABLES

What funds of all kinds are to be paid to you; this includes accounts receivable, notes on loans, trust deeds, mortgages, and so on. You will want the following information:

> —*debtor*
> —*original amount of debt*
> —*payment schedule*
> —*amount outstanding*
> —*probability of collection—assign a percent as a possibility of collection*
> —*estimated collection amount—multiply the amount outstanding by the probability factor*
> —*total*

OWNERSHIP OF NONTRADED CORPORATIONS

You will have to assign a value to the company or the stock. Appraisal of a business usually is required.

> —*description*
> —*value*
> —*total*

PROFESSIONAL PRACTICES

Are you and/or your husband a doctor, dentist, lawyer, stockbroker, or real estate broker having sole or partial ownership interest in a business? If so, you may need to have the practice appraised by an appraiser or broker.

> —*description*
> —*value*
> —*total*

CONTINGENT RIGHTS TO RECEIVE

This refers to a right to purchase or receive assets such as options to purchase property, stock options, stock purchase plans, awards from lawsuits, and so on. Regulations concerning contingent rights vary from state to state. Be aware that such assets exist and consult your attorney and/or accountant if you feel they may be part of your assets.

> —*description*
> —*value*
> —*total*

PENSION PLANS

Calculate the present value (if you are retired now) of pension plans belonging to you or your spouse. You may need the services of an actuary to give you an accurate picture of what the plan represents presently or upon retirement. In recent years, spouses have been entitled to a percentage of their spouse's pension based upon the number of years in a marriage. Pension plans vary greatly. They should be considered as part of a couple's assets.

FUTURE EARNINGS

Some women believe that since they have been involved in a partnership, they are entitled to a percentage of future earnings that their spouse will receive. If, for example, a wife worked to put her husband through medical school, she may feel some of his future earnings should be hers. Other rights that have been negotiated are rights to a percentage of royalties received on works (books, movies, etc.) completed during the marriage. If you believe that you may have a legitimate claim to a percentage of your spouse's future income, consult with your lawyer.

At this point you may want to draw up a summary of your assets. You might use the summary presented here as a model.

SUMMARY OF ASSETS

ASSET	VALUE
CASH	
REAL ESTATE	
PERSONAL PROPERTY	
LIFE INSURANCE	
STOCKS AND BONDS	
RECEIVABLES	
OWNERSHIP OF NONTRADED CORPORATIONS	
PROFESSIONAL PRACTICES	
CONTINGENT RIGHTS TO RECEIVE	
OTHER	
TOTAL ASSETS:	

WARNING: Some assets are more difficult to estimate than others. It may be easy for a man experienced in business to hide assets from his wife, who may not be knowledgeable concerning business affairs, particularly if he has had practice in minimizing his income for tax purposes. You may wish to consult an accountant if you feel your husband is trying to minimize or hide assets. If you think your husband is selling assets, such as a car that has been paid for, or is accumulating liabilities, such as a new car that has not been paid for, you will want to keep records and consult with your attorney.

Now draw up a list of your liabilities. Which of the following liabilities do you have?

LIABILITIES

—*bank loans*
—*debts to friends*
—*debts to business associates*
—*lease commitments (cars, buildings, office equipment, etc.)*
—*sales contracts (encyclopedia companies, dinnerware, book and record companies, enrichment programs)*
—*loans obtained on life insurance policies*
—*income tax payable for the current year (federal, state, and city)*
—*unpaid income taxes for prior years*
—*income tax interest or penalties*
—*real estate taxes*
—*real estate assessments*
—*real estate bonds*
—*interest due on loans*
—*credit card purchases*
—*charge accounts*
—*interest due on revolving charge accounts*
—*legal fees*
—*medical bills*
—*dental bills*
—*contingent liabilities (money you may have to pay if you lose a lawsuit, purchase of property you have agreed to buy, etc.)*
—*other*

Summarize your liabilities by completing a chart similar to the one below.

PAYEE	ORIGINAL AMOUNT	PAYMENT SCHEDULE	PRESENT AMOUNT OUTSTANDING
TOTAL LIABILITIES			

Now complete your balance sheet.

FINANCIAL SUMMARY

TOTAL ASSETS:	
TOTAL LIABILITIES:	
NET WORTH:	

SEPARATE PROPERTY

Separate property is property brought into a marriage by either party and kept separate after the marriage. Sometimes disputes arise concerning whether property is separate or joint property. In a marriage, it is wise to keep property owned before the marriage as separate property after the marriage, even if it means that you may have to file a separate income tax return for it. If you owned property before the marriage and added your husband's name to the title for tax purposes or for other reasons, you may now wish to claim the right to this property, even though, legally, the property may be in both names. Check the laws concerning separate property in your state if separate property is an issue for you.

Make a list of separate property if you have any. Differentiate between the property owned by you and by your husband.

SEPARATE PROPERTY OF WIFE

—item
—date of purchase
—market value

SEPARATE PROPERTY OF HUSBAND

—item
—date of purchase
—market value

COLLECTING SALARY INFORMATION

To gather information concerning how much you and your husband earn, draw charts similar to the ones that follow for your husband's income and then one for your income.

It helps if you have a record of your husband's income for at least the last three years. The purpose of this is to indicate a stable work record and yearly salary increases. If you do not have copies of tax returns, you may get a copy of a joint return by having your husband and yourself sign a form to obtain copies. If your husband refuses to provide you with information concerning his income, speak to your lawyer; the information may then be obtained by means of a deposition or a subpoena. If you feel your husband is hiding income, such as bonuses and commissions, speak to your lawyer and/or accountant. You can obtain a rough idea of your husband's income from the deposit column of your bank statements.

HUSBAND'S INCOME

	GROSS INCOME	NET INCOME	ADDITIONAL SOURCES OF INCOME *	TOTAL INCOME
PRESENT YEAR				
PREVIOUS YEAR 1				
PREVIOUS YEAR 2				

MY INCOME

	GROSS INCOME	NET INCOME	ADDITIONAL SOURCES OF INCOME *	TOTAL INCOME
PRESENT YEAR				
PREVIOUS YEAR 1				
PREVIOUS YEAR 2				

* Additional sources of income include funds matched in company thrift plans, stock options, commissions, bonuses, and so on.

How much money does your husband earn per month? What is his take-home pay?

How much do you earn per month? What is your take-home pay?

When considering your husband's income and income you may receive in child support and/or alimony, be sure to compare your husband's gross income (before taxes) with your gross income, or his net income (after taxes) with your net income. If you are receiving alimony payments, comparing your husband's net income to your gross income would not be a valid comparison. Since you will have to pay taxes on alimony, you should deduct the taxes you will have to pay to arrive at your net income.

WHAT ARE YOUR EXPENSES?

To obtain an accurate account of your expenses for the past year, gather all the financial data you have that indicate what it has cost you to live for the last several years. This includes bills, canceled checks, bank statements, credit card statements, and so on. If you pay most of your bills by check and have access to your canceled checks, you can work primarily from this source. Remember, you want to document how much it costs you to live per year. You may also want to note your expenses for previous years. Although it is more work, documenting your expenses for the past several years sometimes gives you a more accurate picture of your expenses and how they have increased.

Sort your canceled checks and/or documents by year and then by the months in each year. Then sort each month's documents into the expense categories listed on the following pages. Be sure that bills paid by check are marked with a check number, check date, and dollar amount so that you do not duplicate cash and check payments. Be sure your checkbooks are up-to-date by noting the bills paid by check in the checkbooks. Accurately describe items paid by check. Reconcile your checkbooks with the bank statements.

If you pay all bills by check and have notations on your checks concerning what the checks are for, you will not need to check your bills against your checks. If you have bills that do not match canceled checks, these bills were probably paid by cash. Be sure to add up checks made out to "cash" in order to approximate how much money you spent on cash items such as magazines, meals, gifts, and so on. If you are in the habit of cashing checks you receive for cash, add these amounts to the cash figure and assign estimated expenditures for items on the expense categories you usually pay by cash.

A list of categories of expenses follows. Look at each category and make a list of the expenses that apply to you.

1. **SHELTER**
   a. Rent/mortgage/condominium maintenance
   b. Taxes
   c. Insurance—fire, liability, homeowner's, theft
   d. Water, sewer, improvement bonds, assessments
   e. Other

2. **HOUSE OPERATION**
   a. Gas
   b. Heat
   c. Electricity
   d. Phone
   e. Water/sewer
   f. Garbage pickup
   g. Household supplies
   h. Cleaning expenses
   i. Soft water service
   j. Gardening service
   k. Home maintenance—painting, plumbing, electrical, and so on
   l. Home improvements
   m. Appliance repair
   n. Major purchases—furniture, rugs, appliances
   o. Other

3. **FOOD**
   a. Groceries
   b. Dairy
   c. Lunches—school/work
   d. Meals out
   e. Cleaning supplies
   f. Liquor
   g. Other

4. **PERSONAL**
   a. Cash for pocket money and minor expenses
   b. Clothing
   c. Cleaning/laundry
   d. Cosmetics/beauty
   e. Entertainment/hobbies
   f. Vacations
   g. Education
   h. Dues and membership fees
   i. Charity
   j. Gifts
   k. Other

5. **CHILDREN'S EXPENSES**
   a. Tuition
   b. Travel to and from school
   c. Room and board at school

d. School uniforms

e. Summer camp—equipment, clothing, travel

f. Lessons—music, singing, dancing, etc.

g. Clothing

h. Allowance

i. Entertainment

j. Child care/baby-sitting

k. Other

If your children are young, you will need to consider how expenses will increase for child care, housing, food, education, and so on.

6. MEDICAL

a. Drugs

b. Lab fees

c. Doctors

d. Dentists

e. Psychiatrists/psychologists

f. Other

It might be a good idea to distinguish between normal medical expenses, those occurring normally on a year-to-year basis, and unusual medical expenses. *Unusual expenses* are nonre-curring items, such as orthodontia, accident, surgery, and so on.

7. CAR/TRANSPORTATION

a. Car payments

b. Car lease

c. Car insurance

d. Gas/oil

e. Tires

f. Repairs, maintenance, tune-ups

g. Carfare

h. Other

8. INSURANCE

a. Life

b. Accident/health

c. Other

Look at the expenses that apply to you and then make up expense sheets. Use a system that works for you. You may want to follow one of the example formats provided here.

EXAMPLE 1

You may want to put each category on a separate page. Items in each category would be listed across the top of the page and the months would go down the left-hand side of the page. The sample chart on page 94 will give you a model to follow. The more accurate you can be, the better.

EXAMPLE 1 HOUSING EXPENSES

YEAR	MORTGAGE	TAXES	HOME INSUR-ANCE	ELEC-TRICITY	WATER, SEWER, ETC.	GAS, OIL	HOME MAINTENANCE IMPROVE-MENTS	OTHER	TOTAL
JAN.									
FEB.									
MARCH									
APRIL									
MAY									
JUNE									
JULY									
AUG.									
SEPT.									
OCT.									
NOV.									
DEC.									
TOTAL									

EXAMPLE 2

If you follow example 2, you would make up a separate sheet for each month. Each month's sheet would list every category that applies to you. The charts on pages 94–95 can be used as a model. If you have expenses that do not fall into the listed categories, add these categories to your chart.

At the end of the year you would make up a summary sheet of expenses that might look like the one on page 95.

Once you figure your individual monthly expenses, compute your yearly expenses and divide by twelve to arrive at your average monthly expenses.

Since alimony and child support are usually computed on a monthly basis, it is important to know what your average monthly expenses are. If you do not average your expenses, you may forget to consider expenses that you have once or twice a year such as insurance premiums and property taxes. Some months your expenses will be higher than others.

Once you have finished with your canceled checks, bills, and other documents, place them in a file folder on a year-by-year basis, ordered by month. This will allow you almost immediate access to any document. Since you may be asked for canceled checks and/or bills to prove your expenses, you should have them readily available.

WHAT KIND OF SETTLEMENT CAN YOU EXPECT?

You have been asked to compile records concerning your assets and liabilities, your income(s), and your expenses. These will have to be divided in some way. Generally, alimony and child support are awarded on the basis of the living expenses for the last year or two. Another guideline is that one-third of the earning partner's income is paid as alimony and child support. Factors that determine alimony and child support payments are:

- The husband's ability to pay
- The person judged to be the wrongdoer— in states that take fault into consideration

---

EXAMPLE 2 MONTH:_____

SHELTER			PERSONAL (cont.)		
Rent/mortgage	$_____		Vacations	_____	
Taxes	_____		Gifts	_____	
Insurance	_____		Other	_____	TOTAL_____
Water, sewer, bonds, etc	_____		**CHILDREN'S EXPENSES**		
Other	_____	TOTAL_____	Clothing	_____	
HOUSE OPERATION			Allowance	_____	
Gas	_____		Child care/baby-sitting	_____	
Heat	_____		Lessons	_____	
Electricity	_____		Summer camp	_____	
Phone	_____		Other	_____	TOTAL_____
Water/sewer	_____		**MEDICAL**		
Garbage pickup	_____		Drugs	_____	
Household supplies	_____		Doctors	_____	
Maintenance/improvements	_____		Dentists	_____	
Other	_____	TOTAL_____	Other	_____	TOTAL_____
FOOD			**CAR/TRANSPORTATION**		
Groceries	_____		Car payment	_____	
Dairy	_____		Insurance	_____	
Lunches	_____		Gas/oil	_____	
Meals out	_____		Maintenance	_____	TOTAL_____
Other	_____	TOTAL_____	**INSURANCE**		
PERSONAL			Life	_____	
Cash	_____		Health	_____	
Clothing	_____		Other	_____	TOTAL_____
Cleaning/laundry	_____				
Cosmetics/beauty	_____				
Entertainment	_____		**TOTAL MONTHLY EXPENSES**_____		

- The wife's ability to work
- The wife's educational level
- The wife's age—the older she is, the more difficult it is for her to obtain employment
- The number of years married. (In some areas, the formula for alimony is: the number of years married divided by two or three. For example, if you had been married for ten years, you would receive from three to five years of alimony.)
- The number and ages of the children (If there are young children of preschool age, the court will generally consider the woman as unable to work.)

The manner in which the property is divided often varies. In some areas, a woman who has young children is almost always awarded the house. In other areas, property is divided equally between husband and wife. Knowing the kind of awards that are made in your area will help you be realistic in assessing the probability of getting what you want. You *can* gather information concerning settlements made in your geographic area.

Consider your position in regard to the factors listed as affecting alimony and child-support pay-ments. Ask your lawyer the following questions if they apply to you:

1. How much child support is commonly awarded to a woman in my situation?
2. Is alimony awarded to a woman in my situation? For what period of time?
3. In a situation such as mine, who gets the house?
4. Which judges are known to award the house and generous alimony and child-support awards?
5. Which judges should I avoid?

Lawyers may hesitate to answer these questions but there are generally discernible tendencies and trends in given locations when it comes to divorce settlements. Your lawyer should be able to advise you in that he or she has seen what other clients have won. Of course, every case is different but your lawyer should be able to give you a rough idea. You may have asked these questions of other lawyers initially when you were deciding who would represent you. It might be worth paying for a phone call or two at this time to compare the responses of several lawyers in your area.

A second way to learn about the awards in

SUMMARY SHEET OF EXPENSES

YEAR	SHELTER	HOUSE OPERA-TIONS	FOOD	PER-SONAL	CHILDREN	MEDICAL	CAR/TRANSPOR-TATION	INSUR-ANCE	TOTAL
JAN.									
FEB.									
MARCH									
APRIL									
MAY									
JUNE									
JULY									
AUG.									
SEPT.									
OCT.									
NOV.									
DEC.									
TOTAL									

your particular area is to check the divorce decrees on file at your local courthouse. The information you will get from looking at decrees will be incomplete; although you will be able to see what the woman gets in child support and alimony payments, whether alimony is permanent or time limited, how the property was divided, who the lawyer was, and what judge presided. You will not be able to tell what factors affected the settlement—the husband's salary, the separate property each party brought to the marriage, the woman's ability to support herself, and so on. You can call the woman involved, tell her you are in the process of a divorce, and ask her if she would mind answering some general questions concerning awards made in your area. She may be able to give you names of other women in the area to whom you can talk. Women who have been through a divorce are often sympathetic and willing to provide helpful information to other women in the process of going through a divorce.

A third way to gather information concerning what you can expect in terms of an award is to talk to as many women as possible. Ask women who are divorced for names of other women who may have been in a situation similar to yours. Women's groups and groups for single parents are also excellent sources of names of divorced women. You may want to ask women you contact the same questions you asked your lawyer about what you can expect in terms of a settlement. If you state your questions in general terms, for example, "Approximately what percentage of your husband's salary did you receive in child support and alimony payments?" you will probably find the woman willing to answer your question. Many women are more than willing to share the particulars of their situation.

Other questions you may want to ask are:

1. Did you get the house?
2. Did you receive alimony? For how long?
3. Did you have to pay your own legal fees?

The most important questions to ask women are:

4. Is there anything you neglected to include in your divorce decree?
5. If you had to go through the legal process again, is there anything you would do differently?

Many women are painfully aware of oversights or things they neglected to include in a decree that caused them problems after they were divorced. While it may be too late for them to correct their mistakes, they are often willing to advise other women who can then avoid making similar mistakes.

Although situations vary, you will probably be able to get a rough idea of what you can reasonably expect to get in a divorce settlement if you talk to four or five women. The women to whom you talk may not have the legal insight that your lawyer has, but neither do they have anything at stake in what you decide to ask for in terms of a divorce settlement. Your lawyer may

1. Discourage you from asking for what you think is rightfully yours—perhaps your case has dragged on and he or she wants to wind it up in order to have more time to deal with cases that are more lucrative.
2. Encourage you to ask for everything even though this may be unrealistic if he or she feels that a court trial will be to his or her financial advantage.

Hopefully, the lawyer you have selected will encourage you to be reasonable and realistic and will have your best interests in mind.

DO YOU WANT TO ASK FOR ALIMONY?

If you are considering asking for alimony, decide which of these statements apply to you:

1. I have preschool children.
2. I have been married for more than ten years.
3. I have health problems that would make it difficult for me to support myself.
4. I worked to send my husband through school.
5. I am over age forty.
6. I have never held a job during my marriage.
7. I worked many years in the home as a mother and housewife.
8. I have no education.
9. I need retraining before I will be able to support myself.
10. I have no job skills.
11. I couldn't earn enough money to even

come close to my present standard of living.

12. I have been married less than ten years, am not eligible for my husband's Social Security benefits, and have not worked myself.

13. I feel I am entitled to alimony.

If any of these statements apply to you, you may be entitled to limited or permanent alimony, depending upon your situation. While some people may argue on principle against alimony, stating that age and sex discrimination laws enable a woman to be self-supporting, age and sex discrimination do exist, which, in practice, may make it difficult for you to adequately support yourself. Consider the realities of your situation and make the decision that you feel is fair and best for you.

If a woman needs training or several years to adjust economically to her single status, the trend is toward awarding alimony that is time limited for the purpose of "rehabilitation." It is good to consider the training, education, or experience you will need, its cost, and the length of time required so you can demonstrate the financial help necessary to enable you ultimately to support yourself.

EXAMPLE
Betty married John when she was twenty; they were married for eight years. During that period, she worked as a secretary (a job she hated) in order to help her husband through medical school. They decided not to have children until John was established in his own practice. Their efforts were just beginning to pay off. John was beginning to earn a good salary in his own practice. During the last few years, Betty and John had been having problems—they no longer had as much in common as they once had. John fell in love with his nurse—he had more in common with her and wanted to marry her.

John argued that since there were no children and since Betty had been working all along and was capable of supporting herself she was not entitled to alimony. Betty argued that she was entitled to alimony for several years so that she could return to school in order to prepare herself for a career she really wanted.

Do you think Betty is entitled to alimony? What are your reasons?

HOW TO NEGOTIATE

Most divorces are negotiated divorces, that is, there is no court battle and people reach agreements concerning support payments and property divisions with the help of their lawyers. The process usually goes something like this. Both parties decide what they want, one party makes a proposal of what he or she wants and the other party decides if he or she will accept or refuse the proposal. If the second party refuses the proposal, he or she offers a counterproposal listing what they want. After a number of proposals are exchanged, a compromise is usually reached whereby each person is required to give in on some of the terms he and she originally wanted.

The thing for a woman to keep in mind during the negotiating process is that she has a right to state what she wants, as much right as her husband has to state what he wants. Some women, who have been in marriages where the husband always stated and got what he wanted, continue this mind-set into the negotiation process. Consider these statements.

—*"My husband won't give me the house."*
—*"George would never agree to my getting the children as dependents for tax purposes."*
—*"I'm waiting to see what Frank is willing to give me and then I'll decide what to do."*
—*"John would go crazy if he had to pay for my lawyer."*

What is missing in the above statements is a sense of what these women want in a divorce settlement and the belief that they have an equal right to state what they want and to go after it. Men have many advantages in the negotiation process; be sure you do not create additional advantages for your husband by failing to state what you want and standing up for it. The women who made the statements above seem to continue to defer to the wishes of their husbands. If you know you have a tendency to do this, share this knowledge with your lawyer and ask him or her to protect you from yourself. If you know you are greatly influenced by your husband and have the tendency to give in to him, it would be wise not to discuss the negotiations concerning the divorce settlement with him.

WARNING 1: In negotiating, it is important to take an active, rather than a passive, stance. Don't react to what your husband wants, act according to what you want. The woman who knows what she wants and is willing to fight for it usually ends up with more than the woman who doesn't expect much.

WARNING 2: Don't worry about whether your husband will feel your proposal is fair. Your major concern is not what he will think of you, but to get the best settlement for yourself.

WARNING 3: If your lawyer becomes impatient and indicates that you may be taking more time than he or she wishes, remember that he or she is your employee and that you are paying for this time. Think of yourself first; don't allow yourself to be pressured by what your lawyer or husband will think of you.

WARNING 4: If the settlement agreement is not quite what you want or if it is not specific enough, don't go along with it on the grounds that you can go back to court after the divorce and have it changed. Postdecree matters are expensive to work out. You may discover you don't have the money to pay for a lawyer and court costs. You may also find that the judge will honor the original contract. Get what you want the first time around!

WARNING 5: Don't trust your husband to be fair, generous, or to take care of you. While you may feel you know him, he is going through trying times and may act in ways that you don't expect. Your best protection is to look out for yourself; your husband will be looking out for himself.

Know what you want before the process of negotiating a divorce settlement begins. If you have done your homework, you will know what income and property there are to share and will be aware of the kinds of awards that are made in your geographic area. The aim is to be realistic and reasonable. You do not want to make a proposal that is so demanding that you will give your husband little choice but to go to court, or a proposal that will be so low that it will affect you adversely for years to come.

As a general rule in negotiations, the individual who states what he or she wants first, usually does not do as well. Giving the initial proposal informs the other person of what is wanted and it allows time for reaction. If, for example, a husband offers generous settlement terms due to guilt, his wife will benefit since she might have agreed to less had she been the person who offered her proposal first. For this reason, it is usually wise to learn what your husband wants first so that you will have time to consider a counteroffer.

Each person usually has at least three proposals in mind:

1. A proposal that is on the high end—one that would be of optimum advantage to you (which you may not expect to get), but would provide room for negotiation.
2. A proposal that is fair and realistic.
3. A proposal that is the minimum you would accept because of your financial needs or in the interest of fairness.

The rationale for having three proposals is that it is very unusual to get everything you want in a divorce settlement. Negotiation means that there will be some give-and-take. If the first proposal you make is what you want or the minimum you will accept, you may find yourself faced with the choice of accepting a settlement that is less than you need to cover even your fixed expenses, or of going to court because you can't agree.

To decide how to negotiate effectively in your case, answer these questions about the three proposals.

PROPOSAL 1

1. What do you want in terms of a monthly net payment (after taxes) so that you can live as you have been living for the past few years?
2. How would you like the property to be divided?

PROPOSAL 2

1. Considering the available income and the reality that both you and your husband will end up with less income than you had when you were married, what do you need in terms of a monthly net payment to live in reasonable comfort?
2. What would you consider a desirable and reasonable division of the property?

PROPOSAL 3

1. Considering the available income, what is the minimum net monthly payment that you feel you could accept?
2. What is the minimum you would accept in terms of property before you would take the matter to court?

WARNING 1: You cannot get more money from your husband than he is presently making. If your husband's income or your combined incomes are not meeting your financial needs now, your financial needs will not be met after the divorce. Somehow adjustments will have to be made by both of you—property will have to be sold, you may have to go to work, your life-style will have to change.

You and your husband have certain fixed expenses that will still have to be met. Perhaps you will both have to find ways to reduce your fixed expenses. If your husband cannot afford to live, he will not have an incentive to work.

You may be fortunate enough to get everything you want in a divorce settlement, but collecting it is another matter. A man who feels that the divorce settlement is grossly unfair may appeal the case and another judge may be more sympathetic to his case. Men have also handled settlements they consider unfair by leaving the state, refusing to pay, paying late every month, missing payments, quitting jobs, and so on.

WARNING 2: Some couples become involved in legal battles that can last for years and result in thousands of dollars' worth of lawyers' fees and court costs. If you feel that your spouse will not agree to any settlement and would rather end up with nothing rather than give you anything, you may want to assess the financial and emotional costs of a prolonged, contested divorce. It is possible to "win" the settlement you want, only to pay it out to courts and lawyers. As one woman stated, "I would have been ahead of the game financially and emotionally if I had just given him what he wanted in the first place. I should have considered that I was buying my freedom."

WARNING 3: Some women who feel guilty because they want the divorce are willing to give up everything to their husbands to avoid a court battle. Remember that you are not solely responsible for the divorce, under any circumstances. Being willing to fight for what is your fair share may be best in the long run. Women who give in often regret their decision later. They may blame themselves for allowing themselves to be victimized and may take a much longer period to resolve their anger toward their ex-husband.

PROPOSAL ALTERNATIVES

Rarely does a woman get everything she wants in a divorce settlement. A negotiated divorce means that the needs and desires of both parties are considered and an agreement is reached wherein each party gets some of the things he or she wants. In the last activity, you were asked to prepare three proposals. One of the proposals was to consist of the minimum amount you would accept in terms of property and monthly payments. You may find it helpful to think in terms of items you consider negotiable and not negotiable as you formulate your proposals.

For example, if there is a family house, some women may consider this as a nonnegotiable item for them. They want the house and will fight for it if necessary. Other women would be willing to take half of the profits from the sale of the house, particularly if they are compensated in terms of alimony, other property, and so on. Most women will consider child support a nonnegotiable item but will consider negotiating when it comes to alimony payments.

Decide which items are negotiable for you. Draw up alternative proposals and analyze the advantages and disadvantages of each alternative. The list that follows contains items you may have to consider. Make up a list of your own based on this list—differentiate between those items that are and are not negotiable for you.

—*child support*
—*alimony*
—*lump-sum payment in lieu of alimony*
—*home*
—*family car*
—*furniture*
—*recreational vehicles*
—*family heirlooms*
—*art/collections*
—*antiques*
—*jewelry*
—*vacation home*

—*business property*
—*major appliances*
—*stock*
—*cash in checking and savings accounts*
—*children as income tax deductions*
—*income tax refunds*
—*pension funds*
—*future income*

Don't forget that negotiable items may also be items you would rather not pay such as debts, bills, lawyers' fees, and so on.

Now look at the items you designated as negotiable. What alternatives are you able to identify that would be satisfactory to you? For each alternative, list also the nonnegotiable items. Use the negotiable items to generate alternative proposals. Be sure to list a total value for each alternative so that you have a financial basis for comparison. Rank each proposal according to your order of preference.

EXAMPLE

The only nonnegotiable item Sally had was child support. She wanted $800 a month for two children. Every other item was negotiable. She was able to generate three alternatives.

ALTERNATIVE 1

Child support—$800 a month (nonnegotiable)
Alimony—$500 a month for three years (total: $18,000)
Family car—$5,000
Savings account—$3,000
　　　Total value—$26,000

ALTERNATIVE 2

Child support—$800 a month (nonnegotiable)
Home—husband's investment $18,000
Major appliances—$2,000
Furniture—$4,000
　　　Total value—$24,000

ALTERNATIVE 3

Child support—$800 a month (nonnegotiable)
Stock—$10,000
Antique clock—$3,000
Piano—$2,000
Furniture—$4,000
Income tax refund—$3,000
　　　Total value—$22,000

Total values do not include child support which remains constant.

Sally's first choice was alternative 2 because she wanted to stay in her home for one year. Her second choice was alternative 1 because she felt it was most beneficial to her financially. Her third choice was alternative 3 because she felt it was least beneficial to her financially.

What are the alternative proposals that make sense in your situation? Compare your alternatives. Be sure you know which alternative is best for you and why. In considering risks and disadvantages as well as benefits and advantages, remember to consider how well you know your husband. Surveys available indicate that many men default on alimony and child support payments, even in the first year after the divorce. Even if you are sure you can trust him to send payments regularly, he may change, feel less committed, remarry and start another family, or move away. While you can take legal action if he fails to send you the payments you are due, lawyers are expensive and payments may be difficult to collect. Under other circumstances, such as losing a job, he will not be expected to pay you money he doesn't have. Therefore, if you have a choice between getting property now that can be converted to cash or of collecting alimony payments in the future, it may be wise to decide in favor of the "sure thing."

NEGOTIATING A DECREE

Rarely are a husband and wife evenly matched when they begin negotiating. When stating and standing up for what you want, it helps to analyze the points that are in your husband's favor and those that are in your favor.

To analyze your strengths and weaknesses, as well as those of your husband, answer the following questions:

1. What factors in your situation work in your favor in terms of getting what you want?
2. What factors in your situation work against your getting the terms you want?
3. What factors work in your husband's favor for getting the terms he wants?
4. What factors work against your husband's getting the terms he wants?
5. Is there anything you can do to minimize the factors working against you and maximize those in your favor?

The following categories list factors that can work to a person's advantage when it comes to getting what is wanted in a divorce settlement. Make a list of those factors you think are in your favor, those in your husband's favor, and those favorable to both of you. Ignore those factors that do not apply to your situation.

FINANCIAL FACTORS

1. Money to retain a good lawyer
2. Money to retain the services of private detectives, accountants, and other people to work on your behalf
3. Money to use in influencing others
4. Money to support yourself while waiting to get a desired settlement
5. Money to appeal a court decision if it doesn't go your way

Although many people do not have money to use in these ways, in cases involving considerable amounts of money or a large estate, it is usually the husband who has control of the money. This puts the wife at a practical and a psychological disadvantage.

INFORMATION

1. Information concerning the total assets of the couple
2. Information concerning the ins and outs of the court and legal system of your area
3. Information concerning the minimum a spouse will accept (often the woman) or the maximum a spouse will offer (often the man) before going to court
4. Information concerning a spouse that he or she does not want divulged (e.g., income tax evasion) that can be used to exert pressure on that spouse to accept certain terms
5. Information and/or proof concerning "misconduct" of a spouse in states or areas where "fault" is taken into consideration in divorce settlements.
6. Information concerning future plans of a spouse (e.g., remarriage) that can be used to anticipate the terms that spouse will accept or to determine how long that spouse is willing to wait it out.
7. Information concerning the psychological makeup of one's spouse

EXPERTISE

1. Negotiating skills
2. Financial knowledge and skills
3. Legal knowledge
4. Tax knowledge
5. Logical thinking and logical approaches to decision making

EMOTIONAL FACTORS

1. A personal support system and the feeling that people are on your side
2. The conviction that divorce is the best solution and that you are entitled to the settlement you want
3. The feeling that you tried your best to make the marriage work
4. Absence of guilt
5. A feeling of personal worth and self-confidence
6. A sense of personal strength and power and refusal to be intimidated
7. A sense of who you are and what you want
8. The ability to wait it out (staying power, stamina, and endurance) until you are able to arrive at terms that are acceptable to you
9. The ability to remain calm and to withstand verbal and emotional abuse
10. The ability to act (rather than react) in a rational fashion to protect your best interests
11. Outside interests that can provide some diversion and perspective if the divorce becomes a long-drawn-out process
12. Future plans, goals, and a sense of purpose (the conviction that life does go on after divorce and that it will be worth living)
13. Mental and physical health
14. A sense of humor

If you listed certain factors as being in your husband's favor rather than yours, what can you do to improve your position? If, for example, your husband has money and is using it in his favor, you might consider hiring an excellent lawyer and making it clear that a nonnegotiable item for you is that your husband will pay for legal fees, or that you will pay the lawyer on a contingency basis.

Information often means power. If you feel your husband has information concerning his assets or the court system that puts him at an advantage, you might consider hiring an attorney or an accountant who has or will be able to get the information you don't have in these areas. Husbands and wives often have access to private information concerning each other that one partner does not want divulged. While blackmail is not a pretty concept, husbands and wives have been known to exert pressure upon one another in this way. Be careful about the information you divulge to your husband and watch your phone conversations. One husband tapped his home phone and learned the minimum his wife would accept as a settlement; this saved him thousands of dollars. Keep your plans concerning the future, including remarriage, to yourself. Your husband may feel he is not obligated to give you as much support if he thinks you are getting married soon. After all, your plans may change—leaving you in an unfavorable position. Some women have been so used to approval seeking and checking things out with their husbands that they divulge information concerning their future plans and divorce strategy that should be kept to themselves. Remember, no matter how fair, decent, and ethical you feel your husband to be, don't volunteer any information that could be used against you. The unfortunate reality about divorce is that it can turn into a situation where everyone is out for themselves!

If you feel there are areas of expertise that your husband has that put him in a more favorable position than you, decide what you can do to get the expertise you need. It may not be realistic for you to think that you can turn yourself into a tax expert overnight, but you could begin to learn about the areas you will need to know about as a single person and consider hiring an expert accountant in the tax field.

If you feel your husband has emotional factors in his favor and you don't, or if you would like to develop emotional assets that would be helpful to you now and in the future, consider ways to develop them. Ideally, you should have listed every factor in the emotional category as being in your favor. Unfortunately, unhappy relationships often have a negative effect on one's self-confidence and feelings of self-worth. If you have been told for years that you are worthless, you may need help in developing positive feelings about yourself. New friends, support groups, and counseling can often help (you may want to refer to chapter 1).

STRATEGIES AND TACTICS

Many women may not be experienced in calmly assessing their strategies and tactics and those of an opponent. While you may not want to think in these terms, you may find yourself unprepared and at a great disadvantage if you do not. Women are brought up to believe that thinking in these terms is ruthless and calculating; men are brought up to believe that thinking in these terms is shrewd and simply taking care of themselves. Because men have had more opportunities to think in terms of strategy in competitive sports and the business world, they may be at an advantage at the bargaining table. Some women discover after their divorce is over that tactics were being used against them that they were not aware of at the time. Others realize that they expected their husbands to be fair, ethical, and even chivalrous in their behavior, and were stunned when their husbands used certain tactics against them.

The best policy is to be prepared! If you recognize or anticipate that certain tactics may be used against you, you will be in a better position to hold out for what you want. Consider the strategies and tactics that your husband may use against you, how you can block them, and the tactics and strategies you can use yourself. To help prepare you for this, answer the following questions:

1. Do you think your husband has a plan (strategy) for getting the divorce settlement he wants? If so, what is his plan?
2. What does your husband do (what tactics does he use) to get what he wants?
3. Do you have a plan for getting the divorce settlement you want? If yes, what is your plan?
4. What do you do to get what you want?

If you think about it, you may realize that your husband does certain things and that you do certain things to get what you want in a divorce settlement. This is one reason why divorce can become so bitter—some people will stop at nothing to get what they want. When one person uses a tactic that the other thinks is dirty or underhanded, the other party may retaliate, thus escalating the conflict. Tactics can be overt—such as hiring the best possible lawyer—or they can be subtle—such as playing upon a partner's sense of guilt to get as much as one can. The tactics you decide to use depend on many factors: your values, your partner's tactics, how desperate you are, your level of anger, your desire for revenge, and so on.

The following are examples of tactics that can be used by one partner against the other. List those you feel you use, then list those you feel your husband uses. Now make a list of those you both use.

1. Hiring the best possible lawyer
2. Hiring accountants, detectives, and other people who can help with divorce
3. Using information one has against his or her spouse to get what one wants
4. Withholding as much money as possible from a spouse to create a state of financial crisis
5. Using the fault system of divorce to punish spouse for wrongdoings by getting the best possible settlement
6. Physical abuse or threats of physical abuse against one's spouse
7. Using the children to get what you want from your spouse
8. Playing upon your spouse's sense of guilt to get what you want
9. Playing upon your spouse's sense of responsibility or feelings of pity by appearing helpless, incompetent, incapable, and so on
10. Doing everything you can to wear your spouse down emotionally so he or she will give up

What other tactics could you add to your list?

Reread the list and decide which tactics you would not want to use because of your values.

Look at your lists. How can you block or counteract tactics used by your husband against you? What tactics are you using or allowing to be used against yourself?

Two tactics women often use against themselves or allow others to use against them are playing upon a sense of guilt and playing upon a sense of responsibility. Women are often raised to feel that it is their responsibility to make a

marriage work, to keep a husband satisfied, to be a good wife, to be a good mother, to live according to the *Better Homes and Gardens* image, and so on. When a marriage fails, many women feel guilty and responsible. Do you feel guilty because your marriage did not work?

Do you feel responsible for your husband's happiness? Your children's happiness? Do you feel you "failed them" or "let them down"?

Are you afraid of what others think of you? Do you feel so guilty and responsible for what went wrong that you find yourself willing to give in and make concessions?

If you answered yes to any of these questions, you may want to reconsider your position. Some feelings of guilt involving divorce are normal; many people wish they had done things differently. If, however, your sense of guilt is overwhelming, you may discover that it will work against you—not only when it comes to a divorce settlement but also in adjusting to a single life. While it is possible to learn from hindsight and feelings of regret, overwhelming guilt serves no purpose and is dysfunctional. If you feel that guilt is getting in your way, you might consider ways of helping yourself, such as counseling or participating in a women's group.

In most cases, there is something you can do to block tactics your husband may use against you. The first step is to be aware of the tactics that are being used. Some tactics may be fair, such as hiring a good lawyer. Others may be downright cruel, such as physical or mental abuse. There is no reason to put up with certain tactics. Recently, increased attention has been given to women who are physically abused by their husbands. Often, women in this position have been beaten down emotionally for so long that they find they have no energy left to even defend themselves. If you are in this position, get the help you need to physically protect yourself and to develop your self-respect so that such a situation will not reoccur. You may have to call the police repeatedly and/or go to a crisis center for women to get the protection you need. Although it may be difficult to get help, it is not impossible. The first thing you have to do is decide that you will not put up with any more abuse; then you must act on the decision.

EXAMPLE

Mary wanted a divorce from John. She felt she had nothing in common with him—they hadn't clicked for years, if ever. There was nothing for which she could blame her husband—he didn't drink, he didn't have affairs, and he was a good provider. Mary just wanted to go her own way. John accused her of being selfish, of taking the children away, of breaking up their family. Every time the subject of a settlement came up, John reminded Mary that the divorce was her idea, she had no real grounds for divorce, and if it weren't for her their children would have two parents and a real homelife. Mary was ready to give John everything, to the point of causing financial hardship for herself and her children.

What tactic did John use against Mary to get what he wanted? Why did Mary allow John to use this tactic against her? What could Mary do to block John's tactic?

INCOME TAX RAMIFICATIONS

To consider the income tax ramifications of your divorce settlement, answer the following questions:

1. Do you have minor children who can be claimed as dependents on your income tax?
2. If you claimed your children as dependents, approximately how much money could you save in taxes each year?
3. If your husband claims your children as dependents, approximately how much money is he saving in taxes each year?
4. If you receive monthly alimony payments, how much money will you have to pay in taxes on that money?
5. How much money will your husband save on taxes if the monthly payments are termed *alimony*?
6. If you receive the family home in a divorce settlement and decide to sell it without reinvesting the money in another home, how much will you have to pay in capital gains taxes?
7. If you receive the family home in a divorce settlement, sell it, and buy a cheaper home, how much will you have to pay in capital gains taxes?
8. Are you entitled to a "head of household" deduction on your income tax?
9. How much money do you save each year in income tax because of deductions you are entitled to as a homeowner—deductions for property tax, mortgage interest, and so on?
10. Will you be filing a joint income tax return for the last year you were married? If so,
    a. What taxes will be owed?
    b. Who will owe them?
    c. Will you get a tax refund?
    d. Who will get that refund?
11. If you are filing a separate income tax return, who will receive credit for real estate taxes paid, declare children as deductions, and so on?
12. If you were married for part of a tax year and are filing separate returns, who is getting the deductions for real estate taxes and mortgage interest on a home you both owned?
13. How much of your legal expenses are tax deductible?

How many of these questions could you answer? Many women go through a divorce without being aware of income tax ramifications of a divorce settlement. You should be able to answer the questions listed above if they pertain to your situation. Income tax concerns can be an important part of a divorce settlement. You cannot afford to remain ignorant concerning the way income tax agreements in a divorce settlement can affect your pocketbook. If you are unable to give dollar and cents answers to these questions, you will need to get that information. You can get that information by

1. Figuring out your taxes—you can follow the directions provided by the Internal Revenue Service and/or buy guides that help people to complete their tax returns
2. Asking your lawyer to figure out income tax angles of your divorce settlement
3. Asking an accountant or tax expert to calculate the income tax ramifications of your divorce settlement
4. Visiting the nearest Internal Revenue Office and asking its employees how much you will have to pay in situation A, situation B, and so on.

If you ask your lawyer how certain aspects of your divorce agreement will affect your tax situation, get a specific answer—one stated in dollars and cents. If a lawyer says, "You won't have to pay much," he or she may be saying, "I don't want to take the time to figure it out." What is *much* to your lawyer may be *too much* for you. A woman who is awarded the family home and sells it, moves into an apartment, does not have the children as deductions, and has part or all of her monthly payments termed alimony, may find that her financial situation is not what she expected it to be when income tax time comes around. It is your responsibility to get the specific tax information you need. Tax considerations may become negotiable items. You will want to know how they affect you in order to negotiate intelligently.

A key factor to keep in mind when negotiating a divorce settlement is to compare and strive to achieve equity in the net incomes of a husband and wife. Unfortunately, most courts will not uphold the right of a woman to have the same income as her husband, and fail to take into consideration the years she was out of the labor force when she worked as a wife and mother. A woman can, however, be informed concerning the manner in which income tax ramifications affect the net incomes of both parties and can make decisions that are in her best interests.

Lawyers often compare the gross income a woman receives with the net income a man is left with after deducting taxes, alimony, child support, and other expenses. This makes their relative economic positions look much more equitable than they really are and may lead the woman to ask for less. Because alimony is taxable for the woman, some lawyers suggest that husbands disguise part of the child support payments as alimony. You should be wary of this tactic for several reasons.

1. You know how much money you need each month to support your children. It is wise to receive an amount termed *child support* that you can use for that purpose.
2. You must pay taxes on alimony.
3. Alimony ceases upon remarriage.

Sometimes a woman will receive alimony for a limited period of time while she trains herself for a career. In this case, her lawyer may suggest that she receive a higher portion of the monthly settlement as alimony as a tax benefit for her husband who may then be able to pay her more. She should calculate the taxes she will have to pay and make some provision for a higher payment to compensate her for those taxes or get her husband to agree to pay the taxes. She should also be sure that the decree states when alimony will cease and when child support, and what amount, will begin.

THINGS TO REMEMBER

1. Alimony is taxable for the woman.
2. Child support is not taxable for the woman.
3. Alimony usually ends if the woman remarries.
4. Child support continues if the woman remarries.
5. In most cases, the parent who has custody of the child for the greater part of the year can take the child as an exemption. The parent who does not have custody may take the child as an exemption if that parent contributed over half of the child's support during the year or the divorce or separate maintenance decree states that he or she can take the exemption. If the noncustodial parent claims a child as an exemption, the custodial parent must complete and sign IRS form no. 8332.

    Stating who gets the children as deductions for income tax purposes in the decree can save time and arguments after the decree. If your husband is given the children as deductions in the decree and fails to pay child support, you can claim your children as deductions. The matter then becomes the concern of the Internal Revenue Service. If you both claim the children as deductions, you will both be required to prove who provides the majority of support for the children in question.
6. If you owned a joint business and are filing separate returns, how will profits, losses, and business expenses be divided?
7. If you receive the family home as part of the divorce settlement, sell it, and make a profit, you will have to pay capital gains taxes on your profit. Remember, you can deduct the money you spent for home improvements from your profit. You will not have to pay taxes if you reinvest the money in another home that

costs as much or more. The time limit for reinvesting money obtained from the sale of a home is two years.

8. If a home was owned jointly the year before your divorce and you are filing separate returns, who will receive credit for mortgage interest and real estate taxes?

9. As of 1976, certain payments made for child care can be claimed as a credit against your taxes. Employment-related expenses for household services, such as a maid, may also be claimed as a tax credit.

10. A "head of household" pays lower taxes than other single persons in the same income bracket. In order to qualify, you have to be unmarried or legally separated under a decree of divorce or separate maintenance and must have furnished over half the cost of maintaining a household for at least one relative during the tax year. Your children do not have to be your dependents in order to qualify.

11. You *cannot* deduct education expenses for education you need to meet the minimum educational requirements of your job, trade, or business. Nor can you deduct education expenses that are part of a course of study that will lead to your entering a new trade or business.

12. You *can* deduct education expenses if the education helps you keep up or improve skills you must have in your present job, trade, or business. You can also deduct these expenses if your employer, laws, or regulations require you to have the education to keep your present salary or job.

13. The portion of a lawyer's fees spent for tax advice to produce taxable income can be deducted.

WHAT NAME DO YOU WANT?

When Juliet learned that Romeo's last name was Montague, she uttered the famous lines, "What's in a name? That which we call a rose by any other name would smell as sweet." Many feminists would not agree with Juliet; they would stress that a name symbolizes a person's identity and,

thus, is very important. Lawyers often assume, particularly if you have minor children, that you will continue using your married name. Be aware that you do have a choice concerning the name you use—even though this choice may not be mentioned and even though you may be pressured into continuing to use your married name.

To decide upon the name you want to use as a single person, answer these questions:

1. Imagine that there would be no difficulties whatsoever in choosing a name you would like. What name would you select and why?
2. Did you select
   a. Your married name?
   b. Your maiden name?
   c. A name from a previous marriage?
   d. A name you created?
3. What, if any, would be the advantages and disadvantages of using the name you prefer? Be sure to include the emotional as well as the practical advantages and disadvantages.
4. To what extent are you allowing others (children, parents, ex-husband, lawyers, society) to influence the name you decide to use as a single person?
5. Have you discussed the name you would like to use with the people you care about? What is their reaction?
6. If you decide to use a name other than the one you would prefer to use, what are your reasons for this decision?
7. What are the laws concerning name changes in your state?

In most states, a woman who wishes to change her name can state so in a divorce decree. If you do not change your name in your divorce decree and decide to do so later, you can use any name you choose under common law or go through a state's formal name-change procedure. Several states require that a formal name-change procedure be completed. There are also advantages to obtaining a legal document stating a legal surname when dealing with banks, department stores, employers, and so on.

DECREE CHECKLIST

The items listed here should either be included in your divorce decree or have been considered and not included for a definite reason. Check to see which apply to you.

1. A provision concerning who pays legal fees.
2. A provision requiring the husband to pay for legal fees and court costs if the woman must take him to court for non-support or for not complying with the divorce decree. Consider interest charges on default payments.
3. A provision enabling a woman to ask for alimony at a later date, even if she does not request it at the time of the divorce.
4. A provision for alimony, particularly if the woman has not worked and/or needs to pay for educational expenses to qualify her for a career. The amount and duration of alimony should be stated.
5. A provision for child support; the amount of child support and how long it will continue should be stated.
6. A provision stipulating whether or not the father will be required to continue paying child support when the children are visiting him for an extended period of time.
7. A provision stating whether the father is required to continue paying child support if the children are in college and he is paying their college expenses.
8. A provision stating who will pay for the children's education (college, graduate school, trade school) and related expenses (room and board, books, transportation to and from school, etc.).
9. A provision stating who has custody of the children.
10. A provision stating visitation rights.
11. A provision stating who will see the children on the major holidays.
12. A provision stating who will pay for the cost of transportation to see the parent who does not have custody.
13. A provision stating who is responsible for medical and dental expenses—routine and major expenses.
14. A provision stating who will pay for special lessons, camps, and so on for the children.
15. A provision stating who will provide medical insurance for the children.
16. A provision requiring life insurance to cover alimony and child support if the husband should die (husband can give wife incidents of ownership on the policy so that the policy cannot be used as security for a loan or the beneficiaries be changed) or additional alimony may be provided so that the wife may make the premium payments herself. It is possible to have yourself or your children named as irrevocable beneficiaries on life insurance carried by your husband. Check with an insurance agent to learn how this can be arranged.
17. A provision stating how pensions or rights to future earnings will be handled.
18. A provision stating when payments are to be made and to whom; ex-husbands can be required to send child-support payments to the court. In such cases, the court sends the payment on to the woman after recording that the payment has been made. The advantage of this system is that the court has a record of payment or nonpayment of support and will take action when an ex-husband fails to pay. Some men may be more conscientious about sending their payments to a court than they would be about sending them to an ex-wife.
19. A provision stating if the woman wishes to use her maiden name.
20. A provision stating who will receive the children as tax deductions and any other relevant tax considerations.

DARE TO BE CREATIVE
IN YOUR DIVORCE SETTLEMENT

Some women have the courage to include new things or try something that usually "is not done" in a divorce settlement. Frequently, when women suggest a novel approach, lawyers will say "It can't be done," "That is not possible," "It's never been done before," or "Your husband will never go for it."

Do not be discouraged by these remarks. Your lawyer may be very conservative, lack imagination, not want to spend the extra time your suggestions require, or not want to risk being considered "different" by other professionals of the legal system.

Listen to the objections your lawyer has. If they do not seem rational or logical to you, insist that your lawyer follow your instructions. You are paying your lawyer to work for you and to consider what will benefit you.

EXAMPLE

Beth's husband was a very successful neurologist. She had worked hard as an executive secretary, putting her own career on hold in order to pay her husband's way through medical school. They were busy years for Beth—working full time, returning to work soon after the birth of their two children, and taking the major part of the responsibility for rearing the children and managing the home to give her husband the time he needed to study.

Once her husband got on the staff of a major university hospital he was busy developing his practice, teaching and doing research. He had no time for Beth and the children as he was developing his career. This was supposed to be the key to both their futures. He kept assuring Beth that someday their sacrifices would pay off. Beth complained that their children needed their father now.

Beth was shattered when her husband left her for a nurse in his office. She became angry and bitter, feeling that she and her children deserved part of his income since they had sacrificed to help him earn it. Beth resented that he had spent so little time with them and so much time developing his career. She insisted that her lawyers pursue a yearly increase for child support that was a healthy percentage of the increase in her husband's salary. Her husband's W2 forms would be furnished to document his yearly earnings. Beth also asked for the family home and six years of alimony so she could complete undergraduate and graduate degrees. After all, she had put her own career on hold in order to put her husband through six years of medical school.

Beth's lawyers agreed to her request for the house and six years of alimony. However, they balked at the yearly increase in child support based upon the increase in her husband's earnings. They said that "it couldn't be done; that there wasn't a precedent for it." Beth insisted that it could be done and that she would establish the precedent. She informed her lawyers that if they weren't willing to fight for what she wanted she would find lawyers who would.

Beth's husband agreed to her proposal. Because of his guilt and hectic schedule, he didn't want to spend time and emotional energy on lawyers and a court battle.

MORAL: What is never asked for is never gained.

DO YOU WANT TO GO TO COURT?

As mentioned, most divorces are negotiated—that is, husbands and wives, with the help of their lawyers, agree on a divorce settlement. The court appearance is a formality during which the judge signs the decree. Most couples try to avoid a full-scale trial because of legal fees and the emotional trauma involved when a private controversy is made public. Court battles usually end with bitterness and hostility. This makes any future dealings a couple may have concerning children much more difficult. Sometimes, however, a woman will decide to go to court. If a husband will not agree to a divorce, will not negotiate, is totally unreasonable, and the woman feels she is not getting the financial arrangements that are fair, it may be in her best interests to go to court.

To decide if it might be to your advantage to go to court, answer the following questions:

1. Why are you considering taking your case to court?
2. What do you hope to gain in terms of money or a property settlement by going to court?
3. Is your hope realistic? (Your lawyer should be able to give you some idea about the chances you have of getting a court decision favorable to you.)
4. How much will your lawyer charge per hour for preparing and representing you in a court case? What court costs are involved? Approximately how many days will the trial take? What is the likelihood that you will have to pay the court and legal fees?
5. What would be the emotional cost of a trial to you? To your children?
6. Make up a chart for your situation similar to the one on the next page.

	NEGOTIATED SETTLEMENT (ONE YOUR HUSBAND WILL ACCEPT)	COURT TRIAL SETTLEMENT
PREDICTED OUTCOME		
RISKS/ DISADVANTAGES		
BENEFITS/ ADVANTAGES		

It is important that you consider your real motives for going to court. Are you going to court to get a fair settlement? Or, are you going to court to continue to fight with your spouse? While a court trial can serve as a catharsis, divorce counseling may be less expensive and more effective. Some individuals use a court fight to continue the emotional involvement they have with their spouse.

How will you feel about yourself if you accept the terms your husband offers you? If you will feel you have allowed yourself to be cheated without fighting to protect yourself, a court trial might be in your best emotional interests. If you feel there is a possibility you may gain little from a trial except increased legal fees and bitterness toward your husband, you may decide that a court trial is not for you.

DECISIONS CONCERNING CHILDREN

The hardest part about being divorced for me is having the major responsibility for my children. I don't have someone I can turn to and say, "You take them for a while." It really becomes wearing at times. But on occasion, when one of my children does something that is adorable, or says something that is beautiful, I know that I'd miss my children terribly if I didn't have them with me.

When I was married, I expected to meet all my children's emotional and physical needs myself. When I divorced, I was forced to examine how realistic this expectation of myself was. My responsibilities so increased that it was no longer possible for me to do all the things I did for my children when I was married. To my surprise, my children did not suffer from this—they grumbled a bit but became more independent, more responsible for themselves and each other, and benefited from the other people I brought into their lives.

If most divorced mothers are honest, there are times when you feel that you simply can't cope with it all. You feel like you can't get out of bed to face another day, you start to cry and can't stop, you find yourself yelling uncontrollably at your children, or you find that you hit them when you really didn't want to. At this point, it helps to have friends who will take your kids for a few hours or who will give you a cup of coffee and an understanding ear, until you can pull yourself together.

Divorce raises many issues concerning children. These include telling the children you are getting a divorce, deciding who should have custody of them, and learning to cope with the problems of single parenthood. This chapter will deal with decisions involving children that divorced women must face.

TELLING THE CHILDREN

Sooner or later, you will have to tell your children you plan to divorce. Some parents put this off; they may have a difficult time facing the decisions themselves and feel they can't handle the additional burden of their children's emotional response to divorce. There are several good reasons *not* to put off telling your children about your decision to divorce.

First, your children may have been experiencing anxiety simply because they do not know what your marital status is or will become. Being told about your decision to divorce will eliminate some of their anxiety even though, in many cases, they may not want to hear about your decision to divorce. Second, your children deserve to be told by their parents who love them, rather than to hear it through neighborhood gossip or from other children who can be cruel. If they hear about the decision from you, you are there to assure them that you love them and to answer any questions they may have. Third, if your decision to divorce is definite, the sooner your children are told the truth the sooner they can begin to work through the grief process that is necessary for them to adjust to divorce.

Your children probably know you are having marital difficulties. They may have asked you if you will get a divorce. This is often an awkward question if you have not made a decision. A wise response, if you are in this situation, is an honest one. You might say something like, "As you probably know, your daddy and I are having trouble getting along. We are doing our best to work out our problems. A divorce might be the best for all of us. We both love you very much and will let you know when we reach a decision. I know this is a difficult time for you, it is a difficult time for us, too."

You may have made the decision to divorce but have not decided how to tell your children. It is best if you give some thought to how you are going to tell your children and what you are going to say. If they ask you if you are going to get a divorce and you are not ready to discuss the subject with them at that moment, tell them that you understand their need to know what is happening and arrange a time in the near future when it will be good for all of you to discuss your decision. Consider the timing of such a discussion. It is best not to discuss the decision just before their bedtime, before an important event such as an exam, or before they leave for camp.

The ideal way for you to tell your children about your decision to divorce is with your husband. If this is possible, you may want to ask your husband to work through this activity with you. If you and your husband decide to tell your children about your decision together, there are certain guidelines you should follow.

1. If possible, provide a united front. You may disagree on everything, but this isn't the time to wage a full-scale battle in front of your children.

2. State briefly your reason for your divorce, such as, "Although we have tried, we find it difficult to live with each other." Don't burden your children with the intimate details of your marital problems.

3. Stress the fact that you both still love and care for them. If your children see that one parent is leaving because you no longer love each other, they may fear that you may stop loving them and leave them, too.

4. Stress the fact that your children were in no way responsible for your decision to divorce. It also helps if you indicate that the decision is a final one (be sure if you say this, that it is) and that the children will not be able to do anything to change your minds.

5. If possible, know what the custody and visitation arrangements will be. It helps if children can be given information concerning what will be happening to them.

6. Once the decision has been made, it helps the children to accept the finality of the decision if you can act upon it as soon as possible. Telling your children that you are getting divorced and then continuing to live together for the next six months only creates confusion and uncertainty for them.

To decide how you and your husband will tell your children about your decision to divorce, write a brief and simple summary of how you have agreed to tell them.

If you are not able to tell your children about your decision to divorce with your husband and must tell them alone, follow the same guidelines. Keep in mind the following additional guidelines.

1. Try to speak only for yourself. If you try to speak for your husband, you may be misrepresenting him.
2. Try to keep your relationship with your husband separate from the relationship that your husband has with your children. Your husband may not be a good husband for you, but he may be a very good father for your children.
3. Don't downgrade or blame your husband. This will only cost you respect and put your children in an uncomfortable position. If your husband is the rat you think he is, your children will discover this soon enough. If they don't, they may need the illusion that their father is a good guy.
4. In the event that your husband has disappointed you and your children by his actions and you and your children are angry, it is best to acknowledge that anger. You may say, "I know you are angry that your father left and that it is hard for you to accept. It is hard for me to accept and I am angry, too. His leaving had nothing to do with you or anything you did."
5. If you know your husband loves and cares for the children, do not withhold that information. Children need to continue their relationships with both parents if this is possible.
6. If your husband is not able to have a healthy relationship with your children at the present time due to his absence, alcoholism, emotional problems, and so on, keep in mind that this is the present situation and that it may change. Try to deal with your children's feelings of disappointment and anger and with the situation as honestly as possible. You may say, "It must really hurt that because of your father's problems you are unable to have the relationship you would like to

have with him right now." There have been cases where parents have developed close relationships with their children years later, after they have changed and situations have changed. If this is a possibility, do not stand in the way of this happening. Some women are secure when their ex-husbands are unable to have close relationships with the children; this makes them right and their ex-husbands wrong. When the situation begins to change, they feel insecure or are thrown off balance. It is best for your children if they can continue a relationship with both parents.

7. Don't attempt to glorify your husband or to protect him. After all, you are getting a divorce and your children won't trust your sincerity if you paint nothing but glowing pictures. If you continue to protect your husband, you may become a martyr; this is not good for you or your children.
8. Watch how you express your anger. If you express your anger, try to stick to "I" statements. For example, "I am angry that your father isn't sending us money. It really makes things difficult." This is better than, "Your father is irresponsible; he never could keep a job and he always drank every penny he earned."

Both statements express anger, but the first statement may be easier for your children to accept. Remember, your children are your husband's too. If you downgrade your husband, it may have a negative effect on how your children feel about themselves.

At this point it might help you to write a brief and simple summary of how you will tell your children about your divorce if you are telling them by yourself.

Most parents find the job of telling their children about their decision to divorce difficult. Try to select a time when you feel calmer or more positive about the divorce so that you will be emotionally available to your children. While it is honest to express your pain and the emotional turmoil you are feeling, you don't want your children to feel that they are not free to express their feelings or that they must meet your needs when they need to take care of their own.

Children react in different ways to the news

that their parents have decided to divorce. How do you think your children will react? Among the common reactions are anger, tears, denial, and relief. How would you handle each reaction?

It is wise to simply allow your children to express the feelings they have about your divorce. Do not tell them that their feelings are wrong, that they shouldn't have them, or that they are not rational. Just try to accept your children's right to their own feelings.

DO YOU WANT CUSTODY?

It is usually assumed that a mother will want custody of the children. Most women don't even allow themselves to think of alternatives to their having custody. There are several dangers in assuming that a mother will want custody of the children. First, a woman may ask for custody because of social pressure due to the social stigma she will feel if she doesn't have her children. Second, a woman may not want custody or may not be the logical parent to have custody of the children. Third, a woman may not seriously consider the alternatives involved with the decision of who should be given custody. When she does not see child custody as a matter of choice, she may feel victimized and act as a martyr because she is granted the custody and responsibility of the children.

Listed below are several alternatives to the decision of who should have custody of the children.

1. Mother has custody.
2. Father has custody.
3. Parents are given joint or split custody—children spend half the year with one parent and then half the year with the other, or three days with one parent and four days with the other.
4. Children are divided—boys go with father, girls go with mother.
5. Neither parent has custody—child/children live with relatives, foster home, and so on.

Which alternatives are possible in your situation? What are the advantages and disadvantages of each alternative for you?

Which custody alternative would be best for you? Why? Which custody alternative would be best for your children? Why?

If you want custody of the children, what are your reasons? Do you want custody because your identity is gained through your role as a mother? Do you want custody because you would fear the criticism you would receive if your husband had custody? In making your decision, it is important not to let what other people think totally influence your decision. In a decision involving child custody, the woman who decides her husband is the best one to have custody of the children often faces criticism and the suggestion that she is somehow "less of a woman" or selfish because she has made such a decision. If you think your husband should have custody of the children, how do you feel about the decision? How will you handle any adverse criticism you may receive?

Remember that usually the decision that is best for you will also be best for your children. If you decide, for example, to keep custody of your children when that is not what you really want, it is likely that your children will sense this.

EXAMPLE

Julie tried to be the all-American wife and mother portrayed in the women's magazines. While she was able to achieve the outward appearance of a woman who was happy to stay at home as a housewife and mother, she knew she wasn't happy. After joining a women's group, she decided to go to college, something she had always wanted to do but had been financially unable to do as the oldest of eight children from a poor family. While her husband, George, didn't object to her going to college, he wasn't overly enthusiastic. Julie realized that although her husband had a college education, she had more drive and ambition than he did. She wanted to finish college and go to law school. Gradually, they drifted apart.

When they decided to divorce, they both discussed the question of who would have custody of their sons, Peter, age ten, and John, age eight. George had always done many things with his sons and had a good relationship with them. Essentially, he was the more nurturing parent. It took Julie awhile to admit this, but she knew it was true. She did not care for the daily chores connected with child rearing. She did love her sons and enjoyed doing educational and special things with them. Her husband had often helped with the chores while Julie was going to college. She knew that her main ambition to be a lawyer would be difficult to achieve if she had custody and the major responsibility for the boys.

After much consideration, she decided to agree to joint custody and have her husband stay in the house and take care of their sons during the week. She got a room near the law school she was attending. Her sons brought their sleeping bags and spent frequent weekends with her. The custody arrangement worked out to be best for all concerned.

WHO HAS CUSTODY—
WHEN SHOULD CHILDREN DECIDE?

Asking children which parent they would prefer to live with is a very difficult decision for a child to make. Hopefully, when children are very young, parents have the maturity to act in the best interests of the child. But divorce cases where custody issues are contested can cause bitterness and put the child in the middle. When a couple fights over a child because each parent wants custody, they are not considering the harmful effects this has on the child.

While women usually get custody of the children, it is becoming more common for fathers to have custody or mothers to admit that children would benefit from living with their father for a variety of reasons. The deciding factor should always be "What is in the best interest of my child?"

Occasionally, one parent may try to get custody from the other when he or she feels the child is not properly cared for; there is mental or physical abuse, extreme neglect, a question of incest, or inappropriate influences in the home. Some of these concerns are easier to prove than others. Where there is a question, a psychologist or judge may consult with a young child in an attempt to gather information to make the best decision concerning a child's welfare.

When a child is older (frequently around adolescence), he or she may express a desire to live with the other parent. While this may hurt a mother if she has custody, the child's desire should be listened to and considered. Sometimes what a mother fears most is that her children want to live with their father. Children need both parents. If a child has had an opportunity to develop a relationship with you, he or she may feel the need to get to know his or her father

through living with him. We do not own our children. They are on loan to us for the period of time it takes for them to become self-sufficient and independent. Your ultimate objective should be to have your children leave home to establish an independent, meaningful life.

Sometimes children threaten a mother that they will go to live with their father. Such threats are emotional blackmail, used to make the mother feel various forms of fear and guilt. They should not be tolerated. While children are important and provide one's life with meaning, a woman should have other interests and an identity other than her role as a mother. Otherwise she will not be prepared for the time when her children will leave home.

If your child expresses a desire to live with his or her father, ask yourself the following questions:

1. Am I listening to my child and trying to keep the channels of communication open? Or, am I so defensive and hurt that I am not hearing what is behind my child's request?
2. Why does my child want to live with his or her father?
   a. Is it to have an opportunity to get to know him better?
   b. Is it due to any problems my child and I are having with our relationship?
   c. Is it because my child is not happy with his peer group or school situation and would profit from another environment?
   d. Are there things either material or nonmaterial that my ex-husband can give my child that I can't give or find difficult to give?
3. Are there contributions my husband can make because of his sex? (Sometimes daughters need to learn about men through knowing their fathers; sons need to learn how to be a man through knowing their fathers.)

When a child is older and custody issues arise, a judge will usually talk to the child to see which parent the child wants to live with and the reasons for the choice. The older the child, the more weight his or her feelings will carry in the judge's decision. If there is a question of custody of an older child, it is best if the parents can agree without going to court. Professionals such as counselors and mediators can assist parents to make the best decision for all parties involved.

EXAMPLE 1

When Gloria's daughter Jennifer turned thirteen, she started to choose friends who got in trouble, were not motivated to stay in school, and were generally poor influences. For two years, Gloria went with Jennifer for family counseling to deal with Jennifer's rebelliousness, her cutting school, and the friends she chose.

One summer, after Jennifer had been involved with some friends who had minor brushes with the law, Gloria decided that Jennifer needed a change of environment, a second chance. Aware of the harmful effects of peer pressure, Gloria doubted if her daughter would be able to turn over a new leaf in September when she returned to tenth grade. Since Gloria's ex-husband had always said he would love to have Jennifer live with him, Gloria decided to take him up on his offer. Since he lived in another state, it would enable Jennifer to make new friends and a fresh start. Gloria, her ex-husband, and his wife spent several sessions with the family counselor who provided insight and helped facilitate decisions that would benefit all parties. It was decided that Jennifer would live with her father. She was not given a choice. Jennifer was relieved that the decision was made for her and she could have an opportunity for a new beginning.

EXAMPLE 2

When Judy's son Andrew was thirteen, he expressed a desire to live with his father so he could get to know him. Judy and her ex-husband, John, had divorced when Andrew was an infant, leaving only summers and vacations as opportunities to develop a father-son relationship since John had moved to the East Coast. Judy and John decided that Andrew should have an opportunity to live with his dad and Andrew was delighted. Judy then relocated to the same city as her ex-husband and son so she could see Andrew on a regular basis.

Three years after Andrew moved to live with his father, John received an excellent career opportunity from his company which would involve a transfer to another state. Andrew loved his school, had made good friends, and was bene-fiting from a special program the school had for students who were gifted in dramatics. He expressed a strong preference for staying at his high school until he graduated.

Andrew's father, John, did not want to pass up an opportunity for advancement that he had been working toward for years. Judy decided to have Andrew live with her. She moved to a home in Andrew's school district so that he could continue going to the same high school.

NOTE: Even though you may think you have settled the custody issue once and for all when you divorce, parents, children, and situations change. It is not unusual for children to go to live with the other parent. It is wise to maintain a civil relationship with your ex-husband and to encourage your children to maintain a relationship with their father whenever it is possible. It is very wise to have options concerning where children could live.

VISITATION ARRANGEMENTS

In considering visitation arrangements, many factors must be considered—the age of the children, what is best for you, what is best for your ex-husband, where your ex-husband will live, and so on. Think about your situation and answer the following questions:1

1. Some people, for a variety of reasons, do not want their ex-husbands to have visitation rights. If you do not want your ex-husband to see your children, what are your reasons?

NOTE: You may have valid reasons for not wanting your ex-husband to have visitation rights. If, for example, your ex-husband is cruel to your children or refuses to return your children at the time that has been agreed upon, this is a matter for the court to consider. Seldom will a court deny a father or mother the right to see their children. The court may require a parent to have a chaperone or to post a performance bond if there are special problems regarding visitation. If your ex-husband has custody of the children, you should have visitation rights. If you waive visitation rights either through legal processes or through practice, consider if this is what you really want to do. Sometimes women feel guilty because they don't want custody or have not been model mothers and allow themselves to be convinced, or decide themselves, that they have no right to see their children.

2. If you do not want your ex-husband to see your children, consider the short-range and long-range advantages and disadvantages for you and your children. (If your ex-husband has custody and does not want you to have visitation rights, think about the advantages and disadvantages of your not seeing the children.)

   Sometimes a parent may interfere with an ex-spouse's right to see the children not because of the children's welfare but because of unfinished business between the parents. If you suspect the real issues behind your not wanting a spouse to have visitation rights are feelings concerning that spouse, is there any other way you can deal with those feelings?

3. How far away does your ex-husband live? How does this influence visitation alternatives?

4. How often does your ex-husband want to see the children? (Often, people may not be consistent in visitation arrangements when they first separate or divorce. The person who says it is inconvenient or too painful to see the children often changes his or her mind later on.)

5. How often do you want your ex-husband to see the children?

6. How often do you want and need time alone that you get when your children are with your ex-husband?

7. How old are your children? How does this influence visitation alternatives?

8. How often do your children want to see their father? Their mother?

9. Are long periods of visitation, such as summer vacations, or short and more frequent periods of visitation, such as weekends, or a combination of the two best for everyone concerned?

10. How does the presence of a stepparent (his wife, your husband) or a new relationship for either parent affect your feelings about visitation arrangements?

11. What arrangements do you want to make for visitation during the holidays and vacation periods?

12. What visitation arrangements are best considering your work schedule if you are working?

WARNING: Women have been conditioned by society to put the needs of others before their own. Guard against this when you make visitation agreements. Some common mistakes women who have custody of their children make when it comes to visitation agreements are:

1. Having an open-ended visitation agreement that results in your ex-husband's seeing the children at *his* convenience, never at yours. If you tend to put others first most of the time, you may need a more specific agreement to protect you against yourself.

2. Having an open-ended agreement that results in your ex-husband's dropping in to see the children, and you, when it is not convenient for you and when it makes emotional separation harder for both of you.

3. Always putting your children's schedules or feelings concerning visitation first so that you never have time to yourself when you need or want it.

4. Always deferring to your ex-husband's request concerning visitation because you feel that it is harder for a man to care for the children, arrange his work schedule, arrange for child care, and so on. If you have custody of the children, these are the responsibilities that you are required to meet. He is also capable of meeting them.

5. Having such a strict visitation agreement that those concerned cannot benefit from special occasions or opportunities that may occur because it is not the specified visitation day of that parent.

It is wise to arrange for a visitation agreement that is best for all concerned and to state this agreement in the divorce decree. Uusually, after a man and woman have adjusted to a divorce, they are able to agree upon visitation changes when they are needed without having to go through legal proceedings. For starters, however, it might be best to have a basic visitation agreement stated in legal terms.

GETTING QUALITY CHILD CARE

Most divorced women with custody of their children find it necessary to obtain child care. Unfortunately, in some cases quality child care is either unavailable or so expensive that women with preschool children decide, or are forced, to go on welfare. Some women who want to stay home with their preschool-aged children decide that this is the most sensible alternative. Other women are forced to depend on their parents or other relatives to provide child care when they must work. Depending upon the relationship a woman has with her parents, this can either be an arrangement that has great advantages or great disadvantages. Out of desperation and need, some women grasp the first child-care alternative that presents itself—a mother who offers to baby-sit, a neighbor who sits for extra money, a child-care center that is nearby. The more consideration you give to child-care alternatives, the greater your chances that the child care you select will be right for your child.

Considering the ages of your children, your finances, and your location, list the alternatives you have for child care. You can generate alternatives by asking other working mothers about child care, contacting local family-service agencies that may have lists of licensed sitters, looking in newspapers, placing an ad in a newspaper, calling colleges with child-development programs and asking for their recommendations, and consulting listings of nursery schools and other child-care agencies. Child-care alternatives used by divorced mothers include:

- Relatives
- Teenage baby-sitters
- Employee day care
- Nursery schools
- Baby-sitting exchanges or co-ops
- Federally funded programs, for example, Head Start
- Housekeepers
- Sharing home with student, family member, older person, or other single woman
- Doing part-time work at home
- Taking child to work

Consider each alternative; evaluate the information you have concerning that alternative. Can you answer the following questions:

1. How long has the individual or the center been baby-sitting or providing child care?
2. What qualifications, training, and/or licensing does the individual or center have? If the home or center is licensed in your state, what are the licensing requirements?
3. For how many children does the individual sit? What are their ages? What is the teacher/child ratio of the organization?
4. How many children does the individual have of her own?
5. What is the individual's or center's philosophy concerning discipline, child care, and child rearing?
6. What kinds of facilities are available for the children?

   a. Are there proper heating and ventilation?
   b. What are indoor and outdoor play areas like?
   c. Are outdoor areas fenced and away from traffic?
   d. Are the rooms safe? Well-lighted? In good repair?
   e. Are the facilities attractive?
   f. Is the home or center clean?
   g. Is the bathroom safe and in working order?
   h. Are there footstools so children can reach faucets and toilets?
   i. Is there a space for the child to keep his or her own things?
   j. Is there an area for the children to rest?
   k. Does each child have his or her own cot?
   l. Are there handrails on the stairs?
   m. Are there books and educational materials?

7. What kind of schedule does the individual or center follow concerning naps, meals, and playtime?
8. Do the children go outdoors?
9. What kind of meals are served?
10. How much does the individual or center charge?
11. What hours is the sitter or center available for child care?

12. What references can the individual or center provide?

    a. How do parents who have used the individual or center in the past feel about the quality of child care their child received?

    b. How do parents who presently use the individual or center feel about the quality of child care their child receives?

13. What feelings do you have about the individual or the staff members after meeting and talking with them?

14. Do the children seem happy and content?

One way you can answer these questions is to visit the home or center with your child while other children are there. Pay attention to how the day-care individual or staff members relate to the children. In evaluating child-care alternatives, you will have to be aware of your philosophy concerning child care.

1. What is your philosophy concerning discipline? Do you tend to be authoritarian? Permissive? Somewhere in between?

2. How important is it to you that your child follow a schedule? Do you want your child's time to be very structured or nonstructured?

3. How important are external appearances to you? Are you impressed by a center with sleek, shiny equipment or is this unimportant to you?

4. How much money can and will you spend for quality child care?

5. What do you feel would be the ideal child care for your child?

An ideal situation would be to locate child-care facilities before you get a job so that you will not be pressured into making a quick decision. After you have decided on child-care arrangements, your child will let you know if the situation is good for him or her. If you can answer yes to the following questions, it is likely that your child is receiving good care:

1. Does your child seem well cared for?

2. Does your child talk about what happened during the day?

3. Does your child talk favorably about the person(s) who cares for him or her?

4. Does your child seem willing to go to the home or center in the morning?

5. Does your child seem active and cheerful?

6. Does your child have the same eating, sleeping, and toilet habits?

7. Is your child eager to learn new things and go to new places?

8. Is your child free of such new habits as thumb sucking, bed-wetting, hair pulling, and so on?

If you suspect something is wrong, talk honestly to the sitter or personnel at the center. Not all sitters or centers meet the needs of every child. If you suspect that a sitter or organization may not be caring properly for your child and if your child is too young to tell you so, try arriving at the sitter's or center unexpectedly. It is important for everyone concerned that your child receive adequate care. This is one area where you owe it to yourself and to your child to be assertive about the care you want.

If you have a sitter in the home, it helps if you discuss your expectations clearly with the sitter. Making the assumption that a sitter will provide the care you want for your children will only create difficulties. When you have a sitter for the first time, do you explain the following:

1. The time you want the children to go to bed

2. The bedtime routine concerning baths, brushing teeth, stories, and so on to be followed

3. Your rules concerning food and snacks the children can have

4. Your rules concerning food the sitter can have

5. Your rules concerning the sitter's having friends in the house

6. The TV programs the children are allowed to watch

7. Special activities you would like the sitter to do with the children

8. What you expect the sitter to do in terms of cooking and cleaning up

9. What the sitter should do in case of an emergency—friends to call, emergency numbers, where you can be reached

10. What you expect to pay

The divorced mother often feels she is lucky if she is able to get a sitter and get out the door. Leaving specific instructions and making her expectations known to the sitter are something she may not get around to doing. Sitters who are selected carefully and informed of your expectations can make valuable contributions to children. The mother who expects nothing of sitters often finds that she gets nothing, or even worse, that she gets what she doesn't want. If you are paying for a sitter, it is your right to get quality child care.

GETTING EMOTIONAL SUPPORT FROM CHILDREN

Which of these feelings do you experience most often concerning your children?

—protective
—guilty
—supported
—resentful
—cared for
—burdened
—overwhelmed
—angry
—playful
—trapped
—dependent

—drained
—responsible
—proud
—unappreciated
—joyful
—loved
—manipulated
—appreciated
—respected
—refreshed
—happy

There are no right or wrong, good or bad answers. Most women have had each of these feelings at one time or another in connection with their children. How many of the feelings indicate that when it comes to your children you feel drained, overburdened, and alone? How many feelings indicate that when it comes to your children you feel energized, refreshed, and supported?

Many women do not realize that their children can provide emotional support. Have you tried to explain to your children how you feel and what you need without

1. Making them feel they are burdens and that they add to your problems?
2. Making them feel guilty, that in some way they are at fault?
3. Making them feel that they should do something to solve your problems?
4. Making your ex-husband seem like a culprit?

Try to avoid doing these things. You may be trying to get needed support from your children but trying to get it in a way that will benefit neither you nor them.

While it is good to expect and coach children to be supportive of you and other family members, guard against using children as your sole source of emotional support. In extreme cases, women may make the mistake of expecting their children to "parent" them. This role reversal is harmful for a child's development. Remember that you are the parent. If you need considerable support, do not burden your children who are struggling with their own issues. You may want to refer to chapter 1 which deals with where you can get emotional support.

Which of the following statements do you feel would be appropriate ways of telling your children what you need in the specific situations cited?

SITUATION: You are lonely and would like some affection.

1. "I am feeling lonely and would really like a hug."
2. "You never pay attention to me anymore."
3. "Why do you do nice things for your father but not for me?"
4. "You like your father more than you like me."

SITUATION: You feel overwhelmed with work and would like some help.

1. "If your father were here, I wouldn't have to do all this work myself."
2. "You never do anything around here. I'm the only one who does any of the work."
3. "You have no idea of what I am going through."
4. "I am really feeling overwhelmed and would like some help."

SITUATION: You feel scared and insecure and would like to hear some positive things about yourself.

1. "I can't do anything right."
2. "If your father hadn't left, I wouldn't have to do all this."
3. "I'm feeling a little nervous about things I have to do that I've never done before. It would really help if you could be supportive and tell me some things I do well."
4. "It isn't fair that I have to do all this!"

List one thing that you wanted from your children in the last few days. Were you aware of what you really wanted and needed from them at that point? What would be a good way, for both you and your children, for you to express that need?

When you find yourself screaming, nagging, blaming, name-calling, or accusing, ask yourself, "What do I need and want?" and, "What is the best way for me and my children to express what I want?" The purpose of these questions is to provide some time to allow you to *act* rather than *react*. It is very easy to react to your children, particularly when you are worried, tired, upset, and pressured. This does not mean that you should never get angry or express these feelings to the child. If a child is doing something you do not like, say so. Describe the behavior you don't like, the effects the behavior has on you, how you are feeling, and what you will do if the behavior continues. For example, "Constant criticism wears me down and leaves me feeling unappreciated. If it continues I'll simply let you do the cooking for yourself" rather than, "You ungrateful kid. You never think I do anything right. If it weren't for me you . . ."

When angry, it is best to use "I" statements rather than "you" statements. "I am angry" is better than, "You make me angry." Using "I" means you have some choice in how you feel and you may give yourself time to consider how you want to *act* rather than *react*. If you are used to expressing your feelings in terms of "you," you make other people responsible for your feelings and in the process, give them a lot of power. Learning how to express your feelings while considering the rights of the other person increases your chance of communicating with that person. The mother who loves herself and her children realizes that she and her children have certain rights. It is possible to express your feelings in a way that makes both you and your children feel like winners.

HOW DO YOUR CHILDREN FEEL ABOUT DIVORCE?

When divorce occurs, parents and children often go through a grief process simultaneously. Sometimes this enables parents to be sensitive to their children's emotional needs and vice versa. At other times, parents are so involved with their own grief, anger, and feelings of disorientation that they are not available for their children emotionally, even though they may want to be. If this is the case, it is a good idea to consider other people who could be available for your children emotionally. If you have been focusing on your reactions to the divorce, you may not know or be aware of how your children feel.

To help you examine your children's reactions to the divorce and to examine their emotional needs, answer the following questions:

1. How did each child feel about the divorce initially?
2. How does each child feel about the divorce now?
3. How does each child feel about you?
4. How does each child feel about his or her father?
5. How does each child feel about changes caused by the divorce, such as a new home, less money, your working, and so on?
6. How does each child feel about the custody and visitation agreement?
7. How is each child handling his or her grief concerning the divorce?
8. How does each child feel about stepparents or people their parents are dating?
9. How does each child handle the subject of their parents' divorce when it comes up with their friends or with strangers?
10. How does each child feel about, and handle, the transition from being with one parent for a visit and then returning to the parent who has custody?

How many of these questions were you able to answer?

Some children do not talk freely about their feelings. However, it may be possible to determine how they are feeling from their actions. If your child does not wish to discuss his or her feelings about your divorce, you can still let the child know you are available to discuss these feelings when he or she wants to do so. You may say, "I know you don't want to talk about things right now, they may hurt too much. I want you to know that I am here if you want to talk to me later."

Sometimes parents stifle communication and open discussion with children by acting in a certain way. Which of these behaviors apply to you?

—ordering
—questioning
—providing answers
—blaming
—criticizing
—directing
—warning
—disapproving

—diverting
—threatening
—moralizing
—persuading
—advising
—recommending
—name-calling
—judging

When a child is trying to express feelings, activities such as these on the part of the parents serve as roadblocks to open discussion. How do you think the following responses in the situation given would block or discourage a child from further sharing his or her feelings?

Child: I miss my daddy.
Mother: Why do you miss your daddy?
(*Questioning*)
If you say that again, I'll send you to your room!
(*Warning*)
Stop saying that!
(*Commanding*)
Why don't you go in your room and play with your toys?
(*Diverting*)
Think about happy things, not unhappy things!
(*Moralizing*)
Don't be a crybaby.
(*Name-calling*)

This does not mean that parents should never use these responses. But when a child has a problem and is trying to express feelings, such behavior may discourage a child from discussing feelings openly. Alternative responses that may enable the child to feel more free about expressing feelings are:

—*silence*
—*noncommittal responses such as "umm," "oh," and "I see"*
—*expressions that encourage the child to continue, such as, "I'd really like to hear about that"*
—*active listening*

Active listening is a learned skill that indicates through your words and actions that you want to listen and accept the child's feelings, even if they differ from yours. An example of an active listening response to a child's statement, "I miss my

daddy," would be, "You must feel sad about that." Such a response indicates that you are trying to understand and accept the child's feelings. If you are mistaken about the child's feelings, the child will correct you.

EXAMPLE

Child: I miss my daddy.
Mother: You must feel sad about that.
(*Active listening response*)
Child: No, I feel angry.
(*Corrects mother*)
Mother: Oh
(*Simply accepts child's response*)
Child: Why did you have to get a divorce, anyway?
(*Child is not really asking a question, the reasons have been explained in the past, but is expressing a feeling*)
Mother: It must really be difficult for you:
(*Mother responds to a possible feeling of the child's, not to the literal question*)
Child: It sure is. When I'm with dad, I want to be with you. When I'm with you, I want to be with dad.
(*Mother's response has encouraged child to continue*)
Mother: Sounds like you feel torn, not being able to be in two places at once
(*Active listening response*)
Child: Yeah.
(*Is apparently finished and feels mother has listened and has tried to understand*)

Note that the child's problem is not solved; most problems concerning feelings involving divorce do not lend themselves to easy solutions. The parent recognizes that the child has a problem, has feelings concerning a problem, and needs to be listened to. Active listening is a learned skill that may be called by different names in different books and courses involving communication and parenting. If you feel you are unable to communicate with your children, or if your present ways of communicating aren't working, you might try courses in parenting offered at churches, schools, adult-education centers, mental-health centers, or family-service agencies. One of the better known courses in parenting is Parent Effectiveness Training.

Before enrolling in a course on parenting, check the qualifications of the instructor who is teaching the course you are considering. Be sure to give the course a chance; the ideas that may be presented may seem strange at first or may not work immediately. A good course in parenting should deal with parent-child communication, encourage you to practice in class and at home, encourage you to share your experiences, and be supportive. The most beneficial courses do not push either permissive or authoritarian approaches to child rearing but offer ways to respect the child's rights as an individual and your own rights as well. The skills taught must be practiced and such courses are not cure-alls; they can, however, offer alternative behaviors for you to use with your children if you are not pleased with your present parent-child relationships.

ARE YOU TRYING TO BE "SUPER MOM"?

Many women are brought up to believe that they should be "Super Moms"; they are encouraged to take total responsibility for their children. When women divorce, they usually find that they cannot continue their "Super Mom" roles. If they try to "be everything" and "do everything" for their children, they soon find that they become exhausted, resentful, overwhelmed, and have no time for themselves. Usually, when women divorce and circumstances reduce the time they have for parenting, they are forced to evaluate what they value as parents. Often the things they thought were important concerning their children turn out to be not as important and receive less time or are eliminated entirely.

Examine what you do for your children. Write down everything you can think of that you do for your children; be sure to include things you do for them emotionally, such as listening to their problems, encouraging them, talking with them, as well as those things you do for them physically, such as grocery shopping, washing clothes, making beds, and so on.

Now take an honest look at your list.

1. Put an **X** in front of those things you do because they are important to you or primarily meet your values. For example, if you make your children's beds, are you doing it to meet your children's needs for neatness or your own?

2. Underline those things you do that are not absolutely necessary for the family to function. For example, if you are the only licensed driver, you will have to grocery shop if your family is going to eat. If you stop baking cookies, your family will continue to function.

3. Put a **C** in front of those things that your children can help you with or do for themselves.

4. Put an **O** in front of those things that other people can help you do for your children.

5. Circle those things that you do only because your children or other people expect you to do them.

6. List those things that you want to do because they are vital to your being the parent you want to be and/or because you feel they are necessary for your children's development.

7. Put a **1** in front of the things you do that you feel are most important, a **2** in front of those that are next important, a **3** in front of those that are least important.

Now look at your list again. Are there things you could eliminate? Do you want to spend more time doing some things and less time doing others? Do you want to delegate some of the things you do to other people?

8. List all the possible individuals who could contribute in some way to your children.

NOTE: You may have to look for people who can contribute to your children. People who can contribute might include:

—*your ex-husband*
—*stepparents*
—*family members*
—*teachers*
—*park-district leaders*
—*leaders of children's groups*
—*neighbors*
—*retired people*
—*counselors*
—*Sunday-school teachers*
—*Big Brother and Sister programs*
—*social workers*
—*your friends*
—*your children's friends*
—*parents of your children's friends*

—children's activities conducted by single-parent organizations
—baby-sitters

Which, if any, of these people do you think could contribute to your child?

Sometimes women discourage contributions others can make to their children because they are proud, believe that their children may inconvenience others, or feel that they should do everything for their children themselves. This not only limits benefits your children may get from others but it also produces unnecessary strain on you and may cause your children to become overly dependent upon you.

WHAT ARE YOUR EXPECTATIONS AS A MOTHER?

For many reasons, women find themselves emotionally vulnerable when the subject of children and divorce comes up. One reason is that women have been conditioned to base their identity on how well they perform the mother role, to take total responsibility for the individuals their children will become, and to take total responsibility for their children's happiness. These expectations, which society places on women, can be overwhelming under the best of circumstances. When a woman divorces and tries to live up to them, she may feel particularly burdened and overwhelmed.

Examine the expectations you have of yourself, your children, and those you have of each other. Make a list of the expectations you have of yourself as a parent. Do you feel that these expectations are reasonable and realistic? Look at the expectations you have listed and circle those that you feel you can accomplish.

Mothers often have the following expectations of themselves. Which do you share?

1. To need no other fulfillment than my children
2. To be the person who can care for them the best
3. To provide a happy childhood for my children
4. To always protect them
5. To compensate for the divorce
6. To be the "all-American" mother
7. To keep my children happy
8. To keep my children healthy
9. To spend all my spare time with my children
10. To always love my children
11. To be responsible for my children's intellectual development
12. To be responsible for my children's report cards
13. To be responsible for the way my children relate to others
14. To provide the "better things in life" for my children
15. To be responsible for the development of special talents my children may have
16. To be responsible for my children's manners
17. To always have my children under control
18. To be responsible for my children's mental health
19. To be responsible for my children's appearance at all times
20. To always know where my children are, regardless of their ages

The expectations you just read are unrealistic. First, there are many things over which you have no control. How can you be responsible for your child's appearing spotless when you are working and he or she is playing with finger paints at a day-care center? Second, some expectations require that you, rather than the child, take responsibility for actions that are up to him or her. Why should a child's report card be your responsibility? Unrealistic expectations of yourself as a parent lead to feelings of frustration and guilt.

Ask your children to list what they expect of you as a parent. Do your children's expectations agree or disagree with those you have of yourself?

Now list what you expect of your children.

Compare your lists. Do you think the expectations you have of each other are realistic? If they are not, you are only setting yourself up for disappointments. While parenthood does mean responsibility, you may be making that responsibility heavier than it need be if your expectations of yourself are unrealistic.

WHAT IS YOUR GUILT QUOTIENT?

It is important to determine whether guilt plays a part in your relationship with your children. To do so, answer the following questions with a yes or no.

1. Do you feel guilty because you were the one who wanted a divorce?
2. Do you feel guilty because your children no longer live with a father and a mother?
3. Do you feel guilty because you work and don't have as much time for your children as you once had?
4. Do you feel guilty because you have less money than you once had and can no longer afford the same life-style?
5. Do you feel guilty when you spend time doing things you want to do—dating, taking classes, seeing friends, and so on?
6. Do you tend to give in to your children more because they have been through a lot?
7. Do you feel guilty because your ex-husband may be able to give your children material things that you are not able to give them?
8. Do you feel guilty during the times you are tired, overwhelmed, and don't want to be with your children?
9. Do you usually put your children's needs, wishes, and desires before your own?
10. Do you try to compensate or make up for the fact that you are divorced?
11. Do you feel guilty because you are no longer able to present the *Better Homes and Gardens* nuclear family image to the world?
12. Do you feel guilty and somehow to blame if your ex-husband doesn't see the children or disappoints them?
13. Do you feel guilty because you leave your children at a day-care center or at a sitter's when you work?
14. Do you feel guilty because you aren't providing a perfect childhood for your children?

If you gave a number of yes responses, you are probably struggling with guilty feelings concerning your divorce that influence your relationship with your children. Feeling overwhelmed by the responsibilities of being a divorced parent is inevitable at times. However, allowing yourself to be drained by guilty feelings is something you can control. What purpose do your guilty feel-ings serve? Are they making your situation any better? Are they enhancing your relationship with your children? When divorced mothers are honest with themselves, they often realize that guilt feelings underlie their reluctance to be firm with their children. Some women may go so far as to believe that if they always put their children first, they will somehow make up for the pain the children have suffered due to the divorce. The best way for you to deal with your children's pain is to acknowledge it, get them to talk about it, and go about the business of living. Guilt feelings help no one!

QUALITY TIME VS. QUANTITY TIME

Examine a typical weekday. How much time do you spend with your children? Include the time you are together but not necessarily relating to one another.

Listed below are categories that describe activities mothers often participate in with their children or activities they perform while their children are present in the home. Estimate honestly the amount of time you spend on each activity. There may be activities on which you spend no time, on others you may spend a great deal of time. Add categories that apply to you and which are not listed.

- Eating meals with children
- Doing housework while children are in the home
- Preparing meals while children are in the home
- Giving children instructions—"Clean your room," "Do your homework," and so on
- Helping children with homework
- Playing games with children
- Talking with children
- Yelling at children
- Punishing children
- Talking on the phone
- Driving children places
- Reading stories to children
- Watching TV with children
- Being by yourself and doing things—sewing, reading, studying, watching TV—while children are in the house
- Spending time with children and guests who visit
- Spending time with guests without including children

Look at the list again; in which activities are you actually interacting with your children? For example, you are interacting with them when you are talking with them; you are not interacting with them when you are in a different room of the house. You may be interacting with your children when you talk with them at mealtimes, but you are not interacting with them if you read the morning paper at the breakfast table. What is the total amount of time per day that you spend interacting with your children?

The purpose of this activity is *not* to make a value judgment concerning how much or how little time you spend with your children, but to examine the quality of the time you spend with your children. Some women wail, "I spend all day with my children." That may be true, but there is a difference between being with your children and interacting with them. Some women who stay at home spend the entire day trying to escape from their children. You may have had days when you didn't feel like being with your children so you read a book, talked on the phone, spent time with a neighbor drinking coffee. Every woman needs and is entitled to time for herself. It is possible that you will honestly feel like interacting more with your children if you have time for yourself. The woman who has a stimulating career, for example, often *feels* like being with her children when she is with them. A woman who works may spend more quality time with her children than a woman who doesn't work. The object of the activity is to enable you to increase the quality of the time you spend with your children, not necessarily the quantity of the time you spend with them.

Look at the list of categories again. Is there any way in which you can improve the quality of time you spend with your children? For example, could you

1. Arrange to sit down to meals together rather than eating in front of the TV, reading the morning paper, or being the last person to sit down at the table and finding that your children have finished eating?
2. Arrange to prepare meals with your children—give one child the potatoes to peel, another the carrots to chop?
3. Do some household chores together—"You pick up, I'll vacuum?"
4. Turn off the car radio and talk with your children when you are with them in the car?
5. Talk about the TV program you watch together during the commercials and after the program?

Many women find that when they are with their children, they are not totally with them. They are thinking about something they have to do, that they really want ten minutes to themselves, and so on. When they are by themselves or with friends, they may be watching the clock knowing that they will soon have to go home to take care of the children or to pay a sitter. The end result is that they are never where they really want to be; they can never fully allow themselves to enjoy what they are doing at the moment. Therefore, the woman never truly feels that she has enough time for herself; her children feel they never have enough time with her.

SUGGESTION 1
If possible, try experiencing where you are at a given moment as fully as possible.

SUGGESTION 2
Some mothers have found that their children are much happier and more satisfied if they can arrange to spend a special time or fifteen minutes of uninterrupted time with each child. For this to work,

1. The child should know when his or her fifteen-minute period or special time will be each day. This period should be kept as consistent as possible.
2. This time should be uninterrupted—no phone calls, visitors, and so on.
3. Mother and child should discuss what they are going to do *together*—the mother should not say, "Here's what we are going to do."
4. The mother should show younger children when the special time will begin and when it will end on a clock. The child should know that this time will end so that this special time is different from other times.
5. The mother should focus on the child with complete attention so the child feels he or she is really being heard.
6. The child should know that this is a time

when it is okay to express anger, talk about what is upsetting him or her, or discuss a hidden fear or anxiety.

6. When a parent is busy and unable to give the child attention, she may remind the child that they will have their special time pretty soon.

Mothers rarely give their children their full attention. Mothers may glance at a child who calls "Watch me! Watch me!" and then go on with what they are doing. Children do not feel they have the mother's attention when it is given haphazardly and incompletely. The child who is able to act on his or her own is often the child who, at some point, feels that the mother is really there. Mothers often think in terms of spending a whole afternoon or a Saturday morning with their children. When they don't have an extended period of time to spend with children, they may find that they spend no time at all with them. For fifteen minutes a day, it is possible for a parent and child to focus their complete attention on each other.

EXAMPLE
Judy had two children, a part-time job, and was completing graduate school. She also was beginning to develop a relationship with a man she had been seeing. Judy wanted to be a "good mother" and to have a close relationship with her children. She felt pulled, however, in four different directions. When she was with her friend, she thought about the time she was not spending with her children. She also thought about the work she had to do for school. When she was at school or work, she thought about her children. When she was with her children, she thought about her friend or the work she had to do. At times her situation seemed so overwhelming she wanted to be with no one and to have some time to spend on herself. Everyone and everything seemed to be demanding more time than she had to give.

Judy resented the fact that her children didn't help her more with the housework. She found that when she was with them she was either giving them instructions or nagging. Whenever they asked for her attention, she was preoccupied and unable to focus totally on them. She began to discover that much of her children's misbehavior was an attempt to get her attention. She found that the more they misbehaved, the less she wanted to be with them; the less she wanted to be with them, the more they misbehaved.

Judy finally began to work on her time problem by focusing on what she was doing at that moment and without thinking about the other things she could or should be doing. She also recognized that she needed time just for herself and explained this to her friend and her children. She put a limit on the time she spent with her friend and found that her children became more accepting and less resentful of him. She tried to spend some time every day with each of her two children. When she needed help with the housework, she tried to work with her children rather than demand that they do the entire job themselves. She tried to break down the chores to be done so they could be done a little at a time and would not seem so overwhelming. She also realized that she had not planned any special times with her children. Once a month, she and her children planned to do something special together—go to the beach, to a children's play, the zoo, and so on. While her children's behavior changed gradually, she found it easier and more enjoyable to spend time with them. The children seemed happier, too. Although Judy still felt overwhelmed at times with the demands on her, she felt as though she was dealing with the problem in a more creative fashion than she had been by nagging or avoiding her children, behavior that had only increased her problems.

SINGLE PARENTING AND ADOLESCENCE

Very few parents are truly prepared for adolescence, which can be a very stormy period for parents and children. Some children progress through adolescence very smoothly, with few problems and conflicts. Others seem tormented and confused, struggle to have a sense of self, and are easily led by their peers. Even if you feel your relationship with your children has been excellent, adolescence is frequently a problem. As one mother stated, "When they turn thirteen or fourteen, I think the state should take them for around ten years."

Parenting adolescents may take a tremendous commitment to hang in there through some tough times. Adolescence is a period during which power and control issues surface. Your child may want power and insist you have no control; yet when they have the power, they may not want it nor know what to do with it. It is a period when they may feel adult one day and like a child the next, with intense mood swings which often may be attributed to changing hormones.

Adolescents whose parents are in the process of divorce often find that this change adds more stress to a time that is already difficult. What often complicates the situation is that parents undergoing divorce may also be experiencing a second adolescence marked by issues of power and control, dependence and independence. If a woman has not resolved some of the issues of her own adolescence, and if she married to avoid them, she may be experiencing the same developmental issues as her adolescent child. Thus, there may be several adolescents (of different generations!) in the family with no one truly in charge.

The issues generally raised during adolescence generate the query "Who am I," and other identity questions. How many of the following questions can you answer?

1. Who am I?
2. Who am I in relation to the important people in my life such as my parents, my siblings, and the people I care about?
3. Who am I in relation to my peers?
4. How independent am I?
5. Do I have the convictions, courage, and strength to stand alone when it means being different from my peers?
6. Am I willing to risk being ridiculed and perhaps ostracized by my peers to do what I know is best for me?
7. What *is* best for me?
8. What are my values? What do I believe in?
9. Who am I as a sexual being?
10. Do others find me attractive? Do I find myself attractive?
11. What do I want to do in the way of work? How will I support myself? Do I have the intelligence and ability to compete effectively to get what I want for myself?
12. What are my interests?
13. What are my responsibilities involving myself, my family, my country, and the world?
14. How much power do I exert in the universe?
15. Is there a God?

If you find some of these questions difficult to answer, consider how difficult they must be for your adolescent with half the life experience. The adolescent may know that he or she is confused, but they may *not* be able to articulate the questions they struggle with, nor be able to get the help they need in arriving at their own answers. This is why adolescents usually exist in groups. It helps them to know that others are dealing with similar issues, even if the issues are never made explicit.

NOTE: If you have always been very close to your child and suddenly find yourself rejected, be aware that this is a typical reaction many adolescents have toward their parents. It does not mean they do not love you. It does mean that they are confused, need to be with their own age group, are struggling with issues of dependency, and may need the illusion that they are independent from their parents. Individuals who are truly independent have come to terms with their parental relationships.

YOU AND YOUR EX-HUSBAND AS COOPERATIVE PARENTS

Listed below are a number of ways of behaving that consider the needs of the children you and your ex-husband have in common. On a separate sheet of paper, indicate which of these behaviors is generally true of you. Then indicate those true of your ex-husband.

1. Children do not hear one parent talk against the other.
2. Children are free to contact the parent they are not with when they wish to do so.
3. When one parent has a complaint against the other parent, it is discussed directly with the ex-spouse and not mentioned to the children.
4. Children are not questioned to get information about the ex-spouse.
5. When difficulties arise between a parent and child, the other parent generally allows the child and parent involved to work out their difficulties themselves, without interference.
6. Parents allow new mates and friends of

the ex-spouse to contribute to the children.

7. Children are not used as pawns or go-betweens by ex-spouses.

8. Visitation rules are upheld; the parent with custody respects the visitation rights of the other and the child is ready on time. The parent who has the visitation returns the child at the specified time.

9. Parents are reasonably supportive of each other. They don't encourage misbehavior when the child is with the ex-spouse or hold out the opportunity of "living with me" if you "don't like it there."

10. Parents cooperate with each other for the sake of the children when emergencies arise.

Ideally, each behavior pattern would have applied to both you and your ex-husband. If you were unable to indicate that a certain form of behavior applied to you, ask yourself

1. What do I gain when I do not exercise this behavior?
2. What do my children gain when I do not exercise this behavior?

Your actions are the only ones you can control. If your ex-husband acts in a way that you fear is harmful to your children, try to discuss it with him. If you approach the subject with statements about how you feel and how a given situation affects the children, you may have a better chance of being heard. For example, if you were to say, "It makes it very difficult for me and the children when the child-support payments don't arrive on time" rather than, "If you are late once more with your child-support payments, not only will I take you to court but you will not be allowed to see the children. You are totally irresponsible."

It may very well be that your ex-husband *is* irresponsible, and that you will have to go to court. If this is the case, it is a legal issue between you and your ex-husband. Don't put your children in the position of being child-support collectors.

Sometimes it is too much to expect a mother to keep her anger to herself. In cases where you feel unable to contain your anger, try to confine your statements to your feelings.

EXAMPLE

For example, you have not received a child-support payment for two months; this has added to your already tense financial situation. You have taken legal action but courts are slow and your ex-husband has been granted continuances. It is your son's birthday and your ex-husband arrives with a $200 train set. What do you do?

1. Push your ex-husband out the door and tell him to take the train set with him.
2. Yell at your ex-husband in front of your son that he only "comes through" on special occasions but doesn't love his son enough to send the child support regularly.
3. Tell your ex-husband how irresponsible he is and that this incident will be brought up in court.
4. Yell at your son that his father is trying to "buy his love," that if daddy *really* loved him he would send the child support regularly.
5. Say nothing and call your ex-husband later to discuss the matter.
6. Tell your ex-husband that you understand that he wanted to do something special for his son's birthday and that you are sure that your son will enjoy the train, but what you really need is the child-support payments to help with everyday expenses such as food, rent, and clothing. You tell him that you are very angry.
7. Murmur what a nice train it is and say nothing else.

In situations where you are trying your best and your ex-husband is continually irresponsible —refuses to send the child support, misses visitation days with the children—it is unreasonable to expect yourself to act as if nothing had happened. Try to deal with your ex-husband directly concerning the obligations he is not meeting. If you express anger when the children are present, try to express it in terms of your feelings and "I" statements.

A situation that divorced mothers may find particularly irritating is that no matter how hard they are trying to cope with the responsibilities of single parenthood and how irresponsible their ex-husband may be, the children continue to worship, adore, and seem to favor their father. Several assumptions may underlie the natural feelings of irritation you may feel in such a situation.

1. Your children should love you more because you are the responsible parent.
2. Your children should punish your ex-husband for his irresponsible behavior by not loving him as much.
3. Life, in general, should be fair—responsible individuals should be rewarded; irresponsible individuals should be punished.
4. Parenthood should have some rewards; children should realize that you are trying to be a good parent and should reward you with their love, respect, and loyalty.

If you are making any of these assumptions, you may be setting yourself up for disappointment. It would be nice if life operated according to these feelings about the way life *should* be, but it often does not. Your children may seem to favor their father because

1. You have shown that you can be trusted and they feel safe in taking their anger and frustration out on you.
2. They know their father is not consistent, responsible, or dependable and they feel responsible for his behavior. If they were good and loving enough, then he would come to see them; if he doesn't come to see them, then they weren't good and loving enough.
3. You have adopted the role of martyr and you are not much fun to be around.
4. Your ex-husband, who has decided not to be involved with parental responsibilities, can fully enjoy and be a "fun person" the infrequent times he is with your children.
5. Your children need to construct an ideal image of their father to protect themselves from the reality that their father cannot be counted on.

If your ex-husband is irresponsible, take the legal means necessary to correct the situation. Sometimes women find they have little or no control over their ex-husbands; they do not have the money to take the legal proceedings necessary, their ex-husband has disappeared, their ex-husband produces a check for part of the overdue child support so that the judge declares that the ex-husband is trying, and so on. The sad fact is, if an ex-husband wants to make life difficult for

an ex-wife, it is possible for him to do so, and vice versa. An ex-husband often withholds support money to make things difficult for an ex-wife; an ex-wife often uses the children to make things difficult for an ex-husband.

In cases where an ex-husband has moved away, or doesn't care about seeing his children, the ex-wife has little hold on him. Even if she manages to have her ex-husband jailed, this will not enable her to collect child support. If your case is an extreme one and you have exhausted all legal possibilities to get your ex-husband to fulfill his responsibilities with regard to your children, you may be forced to accept the fact that life is not fair and that your ex-husband is getting away with acting irresponsibly. There are women who allow themselves to become bitter because of an ex-husband's irresponsibility, blame their ex-husbands for any ill-luck that befalls them, use their ex-husbands as an excuse for their not making the most of themselves and their lives, and generally make life miserable for themselves and their children. If your husband refuses to accept his responsibility as a parent you can

1. Face the fact that you have been left with all of the parental responsibility. Try to deal with your justifiable anger and then go on to do the best job you can.
2. Realize that life and the judicial system are often neither just nor fair.
3. Deal with the reality in as matter-of-fact a way as possible with your children. You might say, "I realize that you are hurt and angry that your father has disappeared and makes no effort to see you or send money for your support. I am angry, too, and the situation is a difficult one. Unfortunately, life is not always fair. We will simply have to do the best we can on our own."
4. After you have exhausted all the possibilities for legal recourse, give yourself credit for trying your hardest. Refuse, however, to beat your head against a wall; it will only give you a headache. Don't make "getting your husband to pay" your sole cause in life. You can only control your own actions—not his.
5. Devote your time and energy to things that might make a difference—divorce law reform, more stringent laws concern-

ing husbands who refuse to pay support, NOW task forces dealing with the problems of divorced and single mothers, and so on.

6. Examine your relationships with men and people in general. Do you have a pattern of being associated with people who are irresponsible, who leave you holding the bag, or encourage you to become a victim?

7. Try to develop friendships with men and women who are responsible—not only for your benefit but to provide positive role models for your children.

8. Don't use your ex-husband's irresponsibility as an excuse for you not to get your life in order and take responsibility for yourself. You can counter the negative example which your ex-husband is setting your children by showing them that people can be responsible and independent, despite adversity.

HOW MUCH COMMUNICATION SHOULD YOU HAVE WITH YOUR EX-HUSBAND CONCERNING THE CHILDREN?

When a woman divorces, supposedly she becomes truly separate, emotionally and physically, from her ex-husband. This separation is the reason for the divorce in the first place. But the reality when children are involved is that there are times when you will be involved either directly or indirectly with your ex-husband.

The guideline for communication with your ex-husband concerning the children is as follows:

1. Are we communicating in an effective way?

2. Are we communicating because we want to serve the best interests of our children?

Sometimes, particularly when the children are older, there is no real reason for frequent communication between a woman and her ex-husband. Children who are older can make their own arrangements and are responsible for relationships with each parent.

If you felt you were responsible for your children's relationship with their father before your

divorce, you may continue to serve as a "coach" to inform your ex-husband how he should relate to his children, to explain to your children the dynamics of their father's personality, to explain to your ex-husband how the children really feel, to serve as a referee, and so on. While your actions are well intentioned, the reality is that your children and their father are responsible for their relationships and you have no control over them. Sometimes women expend useless energy trying to facilitate father-children relationships, keeping themselves tied to their ex-husband emotionally. If you find yourself involved this way, with a father-child relationship, ask yourself the following:

1. Is it really necessary for me to be involved?

2. Am I truly involved because of the interests of the child? Or, do I still want to maintain involvement with my ex-husband?

3. Am I involved because I am "hooked" by issues of power and control that existed during the marriage?

If your children talk to you about their father, it is best to respond to their feelings and not comment on their father's behavior since you cannot control it. It is also possible that you may have to ask your children not to talk about their father at all.

EXAMPLE 1
When Judy's daughter returned after spending college break with her alcoholic father, she told her mother how much her father was drinking and how he had deteriorated physically. Judy chose to respond to her daughter's feelings by saying, "It really must upset you to see your father hurt himself by his drinking when you love him so much." That way Judy supported her daughter but did not criticize her father or rehash the impact alcoholism had on Judy's former marriage and their family life.

EXAMPLE 2
Lynne's husband worked for a major corporation and did very well financially. Lynne felt that she had not gotten the settlement she deserved and resented the fact that her ex-husband and his

new wife had an affluent life-style while she struggled to make ends meet. Every time her teenage children returned from visiting their father, they brought back expensive gifts from him and told her about the new car, the fur coat their stepmother had been given for Christmas, the cruise their father had been on, and so on.

Lynne found that she began to dread the first few days when her children returned after their visits with their father. Their stories of his affluence stirred everything up for her—how life wasn't fair, how she wished she could afford a more affluent life-style, how she wished she could afford expensive gifts for her children, and so on. She felt more and more like a victim and more depressed each time they returned.

Lynne finally chose to respond by saying to her children, "I think it is great that you are given things that give you pleasure because I can't afford to give them to you. However, when you discuss your father's affluent life-style and his recent purchases, I become angry and upset because it reminds me of many things I feel are unfair. In the future when you return from visits with your dad, I'd appreciate your not discussing his life-style or recent purchases with me."

EXAMPLE 3

Mary's son, Ben, and his father did not have a good relationship. Ben showed his father a report card with Bs and a few Cs when he was visiting him. Ben's father flew off the handle, called him stupid, and said that he would never amount to anything anyway because he was "thick" just like his mother.

After his return to Mary, Ben relayed this incident with his father. Mary chose to respond by saying, "You must really have felt upset when your father said those things to you. I know how much you want your father's approval. Sometimes what we want from a person emotionally is simply not available. It has nothing to do with you. I think your report card was good, particularly since you are in honors classes and play sports, which take time from your academic studies. I think you are an intelligent, well-rounded kid and you will be very successful at whatever you want to do. I also happen to love you very much."

NOTE: Mary chose not to attack her ex-husband or become "hooked" when she was called "thick"

by him. She did her best to supply the support her son needed without getting involved. Sending messages back to her ex-husband through her son would only make things worse and ultimately hurt the child even more.

If you feel that your ex-husband is doing something that is truly harmful involving your children, you may want to talk to him directly. Consider how this would impact the situation. Mary might have chosen to call her husband and state, "Ben told me your reaction to his report card. He so wants to feel that you love him and admire him. When you are hard on him, he feels bad about himself and that doesn't help matters and give him the incentive he needs to get good grades."

In Mary's case, she knew her ex-husband would blame Ben for talking to her and was not likely to change his behavior. It would only make things worse for Ben in the long run if she called her ex-husband.

EXAMPLE 4

Coleen's husband George, on the other hand, really was working on his relationship with his children. He was going to therapy and realized how his workaholic tendencies contributed to his divorce and his emotional distance from his children. Even though it was too late to save his marriage, he genuinely wanted a good relationship with his kids.

After he had canceled special arrangements with his children for the third time, Coleen decided to call him. She chose to say, "I thought you would want to know how disappointed the kids were when you canceled plans with them three times in a row. They really look forward to being with you. Not only does it affect my plans when you cancel, but they take their anger and disappointment out on me."

Because the children didn't want to give their father the satisfaction of appearing disappointed, they had developed a defensive "I don't care" attitude when he canceled his plans with them, which was frequent. They didn't want to get their hopes up one more time, only to be disappointed. George really wasn't aware that the children cared as much as they did about his visits with them. His lack of awareness of others' feelings was one thing he was dealing with in therapy. He was genuinely glad that Coleen called him.

WHEN YOUR EX-HUSBAND REMARRIES:
YOU, YOUR CHILDREN,
AND THEIR STEPMOTHER

Women have various reactions when their husbands remarry. If a woman has adjusted to the divorce emotionally, she may take the remarriage in stride and even be happy that her ex-husband has found someone. If she did not want the divorce and is still in love with her ex-husband, she may be extremely upset by it. If a man marries a woman he had been involved with previous to the divorce, the situation may be a very difficult one for the first wife to handle.

Regardless of how you feel about your ex-husband's remarriage and his new wife, she may have a relationship with your children if your children are involved with their father. If your ex-husband and his new wife have children together, they will be your child's half sisters or brothers. Your children may feel loyal to you and may watch for your reaction concerning their father's remarriage, his new wife, and their family if they have children.

There are several things to consider:

1. Your children may feel uncomfortable with their stepmother.
2. Your children may feel they have to ignore or even hate their stepmother out of loyalty to you.
3. How your children get along with their stepmother will influence how often they want to see their father and their relationship with him.

Allow your children to form whatever relationship they want with their stepmother and any children that your husband may have from that marriage. Being a stepparent is not an easy job. She may feel she is resented and treated poorly when she has done nothing to deserve that treatment.

Your children may benefit greatly from having a good relationship with their stepmother and any children their father may have from his new marriage. The more adults with whom your children can have a special, caring relationship, the better it will be for their development. A mature woman tries to allow for what is best for her children—even though this may be a tall order!

EXAMPLE 1

Susannah had never really wanted to have children. Her main interest had always been science and she was an exceptionally gifted researcher. She was trying to develop a better relationship with her thirteen-year-old son, Todd. Being a mother never came naturally to her, and now that Todd was entering adolescence, things were even more difficult. Todd wasn't interested in science. He was more interested in art and music, so she didn't feel she had anything in common with him.

When her ex-husband Joel married Chris, an "earth mother type," Susannah was delighted. Chris loved to parent and had lived successfully through two adolescent children of her own. Chris hit it off with Todd from the start and could provide some of the nuturing that Todd needed. She had a "more mellow" temperament which Susannah felt allowed her to deal more effectively with adolescents and children in general. Todd's relationship with his stepmother was good for him and good for Susannah. His mother was relieved that he got what he needed, even if she wasn't the person to provide it.

EXAMPLE 2

Joyce, a woman in her sixties, watched as her daughter Holly developed a very close relationship through the years with the two children her ex-husband had after he remarried. As the years passed, her daughter (who was always lonely as an only child), developed a relationship with her half brother and sister that was closer than relationships most "full" brothers and sisters had. Holly was glad that her mother had never interfered with the relationship she developed with her stepmother and her half brother and sister. They were a very important part of her life and were her family. They did not detract from the very special and loving relationship she had with her mother. Joyce was secure enough in her relationship with Holly not to interfere or be jealous. She realized that Holly's relationship with her stepmother, half sister, and brother added a great deal to her daughter's life.

EXAMPLE 3

When Janet's husband, Mark, married Sally soon after their divorce and while their children were quite young, Janet tried her hardest to be fair and not say anything negative about Sally. Some of Sally's actions seemed immature and unfair, but Janet believed that they were due to Sally's insecurity as "the second wife." Janet was delighted to be divorced. She had married in her teens and learned after her marriage that she and her husband had nothing in common.

Through the years the children reported that Sally repeatedly said that Janet was no good, that she "bled" their father for more money than she was entitled to, and that she squandered the child support. Janet was mature and secure enough not to feel the need to defend herself. In fact, she even tried to explain Sally's insecurities and what might prompt her to say such things. She would address her children's feelings by stating, "It must upset you to hear me attacked and you might feel the need to defend me. That is not necessary. I know you don't believe what Sally says is true." But this response, while lessening the negative impact Sally's words might have on the children, did not take into account the children's need to have their perceptions validated.

Janet's children started to report consistently that Sally was saying demeaning things to them, trying to turn one child against the other, and telling things to their dad that were untrue to get them in trouble. Janet believed what her children were telling her, and even had evidence of several occasions which supported her children's reports.

Janet chose to change the way she responded to her children. Even though she had bent over backward over the years to be fair, she began to feel that her first responsibility was to her children. She decided that it was appropriate to address her children's feelings and perceptions. She simply said, "You are right, that is crazy-making behavior. I believe you when you say that Sally often lies and tries to create trouble. It must be a very difficult situation to deal with." When she responded this way, her children reported that during all the years that Janet had tried to be fair, they felt she was on Sally's side and had not really believed them. Janet was glad that she changed the way she responded. Her children's emotional security was more important than "fairness" to their stepmother.

Janet was in a difficult position. She knew if she confronted Sally directly it would not result in a mature, productive conversation. Janet had

tried this on one occasion with unfortunate results. She knew her ex-husband avoided anything that made him feel uncomfortable or put him in the middle. It would just make it more difficult for the children if Janet talked to her ex-husband and he talked to Sally. They both would feel that the children were "talking behind their backs." Janet felt that Sally would ultimately take it out on the children.

It is natural that you may be curious about the woman your ex-husband marries and their relationship together. However, try not to pump your children for information. It is up to them to decide what information they wish to share.

EXAMPLE 1

Joanne's children told her that their dad was drinking more than ever and that his new wife had crying spells where she either begged him to stop or blamed him for his drinking. While Joanne was sorry that her ex-husband had not come to terms with his alcoholism, she felt somehow vindicated and confirmed in her decision to get a divorce. Her husband had always blamed her for the fact that he drank too much. He had told her, "If you were more loving and understanding, I wouldn't have to drink."

Joanne simply said, "I know how upset you must feel when you see that your father has not come to terms with his alcoholism and that it is adversely affecting his marriage. It must remind you of the times you heard your dad and me fighting over his drinking. Unfortunately, alcoholism interferes with people's ability to love and be happy in marriages."

EXAMPLE 2

Betty's children came home and reported that their dad, John, was the athlete he always was: Saturdays and Sundays he played golf all day, Monday and Tuesday night he played basketball, Wednesday he bowled, and Thursday he worked out at the Y. Friday he either watched a sports event on cable or played poker with his buddies.

His second wife, Margaret, stayed home, read or watched TV, and ate. When John came home Margaret gave him the silent treatment. John in turn would taunt her with how fat she was and that she should go to the gym with him to burn off a few hundred pounds. Betty winced when her children told her this and said nothing. It was a replay of what her life had been before she had gotten a divorce.

If hearing about your ex-husband and his new wife upsets you, you may have to ask your children not to discuss their father. You may say, "I'm glad you have a relationship with your father. That is the way it should be. Your father and I divorced so that we could lead separate lives. I do not wish to hear about him unless you feel it is absolutely necessary." This is what Lynne chose to do when she informed her children that she preferred not to hear the details of the affluent life-style her ex-husband and his new wife enjoyed.

HOW TO HANDLE SPECIAL OCCASIONS

Decisions concerning special occasions involving children, such as bar and bat mitzvahs, confirmations, birthdays, graduations, and weddings can often be difficult. It is understandable that both parents want to attend. It may be particularly awkward if the relationship between a woman and her ex-husband is strained, if there are new spouses, siblings from a previous marriage, and so on. Many occasions that are meant to be enjoyable celebrations for both the parents and children turn out to be nightmares.

One principle should dominate in planning special occasions: it is a special occasion for the child and every attempt should be made to respect that. Try to avoid issues of power and control with your ex-husband if you are both involved with planning the arrangements. If disagreements arise, ask your child what he or she wants when it is practical to do so.

Parents should do their best to be civil and avoid confrontations. Arrangements should be made that are most comfortable for everyone involved. If relationships are strained between you and your ex-husband, do not feel that you need to be brave by sitting next to him at the table or interacting directly with him while in a receiving line.

If your ex-husband has remarried and you have not, you may decide to invite a male friend (even if you are not romantically involved) who will be supportive. Fortunately, ceremonies are less formal today and there seem to be more options available to divorced parents which allow them to feel more comfortable.

EXAMPLE 1

Special occasions shared with your ex-husband can actually be beneficial if both parties are mature individuals. Ellen returned to her hometown with her children to give a memorial service for her mother who had died the week before. Her ex-husband and his second wife lived in the same town. Because Ellen was involved in the service, she was not available to sit with the children. She was relieved and grateful to her ex-husband and his wife for attending the service so they could sit with the children and provide the support that they needed.

EXAMPLE 2

Clara reviewed her involvement in the celebration of her daughter Andrea's graduation and vowed that she would make different decisions when it came time for her son Adam to graduate.

Clara's ex-husband, Dan, had been remarried to Joyce for ten years. Clara and Adam arrived at the high-school auditorium at the same time Dan and Joyce arrived. They all sat in the same row to watch the graduation. During the ceremony Joyce couldn't help thinking that it wasn't supposed to turn out like this. She was watching her daughter graduate alone, while her ex-husband shared the event with his wife. Even though Clara had wanted the divorce, these moments were difficult for her.

After the ceremony, they all went to a restaurant where they had reserved a table for a celebration meal. Clara was tense, and realized that her ex-husband and his wife must have been, too. Dan insisted on ordering another bottle of wine, and everyone anesthetized themselves for an occasion that should have been joyful. The final straw came when Dan (who by now had had too much to drink) became argumentative and belittled the waitress because there was an error on the check. Clara, not wanting to add to an already tense situation, said nothing. She was only relieved that the whole event was over.

As for Adam's graduation, she decided she would sit with a special friend (if she was not involved with a man, she would ask her good friend, Susan) on another side of the auditorium. Adam could go to dinner with Dan and Joyce, and she could have her own special celebration dinner with him the next night.

DON'T PUT YOUR CHILD IN THE MIDDLE!

A cardinal rule for divorced parents is not to put your child in the middle. A child needs to have a good relationship with both parents. Asking a child either directly or subtly to choose which parent he or she likes the best simply isn't fair and is not in the best interest of the child. As children mature, they should be the ones to decide which parent they want to be with, and whose opinions they support. They should not be encouraged to feel guilty.

EXAMPLE
Judy, a college freshman, did not like to spend time with her father, who was a chronic gambler and always unemployed. It was painful being around her father. She preferred to spend vacations and semester breaks with her mother who lived in a different state. Judy's father became hurt and almost abusive when she chose to spend more time with her mother. Since her dad was paying for her education from a trust fund he was managing, Judy worried that her father might withhold her college funds or possibly even gamble with them if he became upset. Judy felt an obligation to spend time with him and realized how hurt he became when she chose to spend more time with her mother.

Judy chose to be political and make sure that the time she spent with her mother and father was totally equal. She looked for ways that she could live on her own during the summer by finding employment that included lodging and going on foreign study and travel programs. She looked forward to the day when she could freely choose how much time she really wanted to spend with each parent.

This situation put Judy in the middle, causing her unnecessary strain.

If your child feels torn between parents, try to follow these golden rules:

DO NOT:

1. Ask your children which parent they love the most.
2. Ask your children where they would prefer to live.
3. Act in manipulative ways that encourage a child to feel guilty if he or she wants to spend time with the other parent. Examples of manipulative behavior can be crying if you are going to be left alone, acting like a martyr, giving a child the "silent treatment," using anger to intimidate, and so on.
4. Criticize the other parent. This makes the child feel it is necessary to defend the parent that is not present
5. Put the child on the spot by asking him or her questions about your ex-spouse that are none of your business.

WHEN COPING BECOMES A PROBLEM

At times, divorced women find it difficult to cope, especially with their children. Make a list of the people and/or organizations you would feel free to call upon for help during a period when you felt you could no longer cope with the pressures and responsibilities of single parenting. List the kinds of help or support you feel each individual or group could give you.

Many women are reluctant to discuss their feelings of being unable to control their children, their inability to cope with family responsibilities, their fears that they are not "good mothers" or that their children are "not turning out right," their feelings of being trapped, their anger and resentment toward their children, and the weariness that comes with having all the responsibility; they feel that expressing such feelings would run contrary to the "perfect mother" myth. Most married women have these feelings at some time or other but are reluctant to discuss them with other women. When women divorce, they may be more willing to discuss their feelings concerning the problems they have as single parents particularly with other single mothers, because it is generally recognized that being a single parent isn't easy. The truth is, being a parent isn't easy.

The wise woman, regardless of her marital status, prepares in advance for crisis periods during which she may feel she can't cope with her children and responsibilities. She may decide on a reciprocal agreement with other single mothers who would be sympathetic to such a need. Your agreement with such a woman might be: "If I call you and tell you that I've had it, will you be able to take my children for a few hours so that I can get some time for myself? I won't take advantage of the agreement and will call you only when I really find it necessary. I will also be willing to do the same for you." Or, "If I call you, will you be willing to listen to me rant and rave so that I can get things off my chest? I will need you to listen and the assurance that what I say in desperation will not be held against me."

You may find that the people you would feel free to call for help are the same ones you listed as the ones you would turn to for support in chapter 1. You may also find that people who don't have children, or people who have not been married and divorced, are not as sympathetic. Possible people you could turn to include

- Women in a similar situation
- Family members
- Ex-husband—if you have a good relationship with him
- Male friends
- Counselors

The following are two accounts of divorced mothers who turned to family members for support when their parental responsibilities seemed too much for them to handle.

EXAMPLE 1
"I tried to talk once to my twenty-six-year-old sister who is single when I was fed up with the responsibilities of motherhood. We are both career women—the only difference is that she doesn't have children. I expected support and I guess some praise for my attempt to handle a full-time job plus motherhood. All I got was her response, 'Why don't you give the children to their father?' I knew that I had chosen the wrong person to complain to. While I realize that sending the kids to Frank is an option, I'd never give up my children. That wasn't what I needed to hear. All I needed was sympathy, not advice from a person who didn't even know what the ups and downs of motherhood—let alone single motherhood—are all about."

EXAMPLE 2
"My mother was really terrific when I first got divorced. Every so often, I'd call and tell her that I just couldn't take it anymore and I was bringing the children over to her. She'd say, 'Okay,' and I'd drive off—I was never coming back! I'd get as

far as the expressway, around twenty miles, and I'd realize I didn't mean it. By the time I'd returned to Mom's, I'd be calmed down. She would ask if I wanted her to keep the children overnight and I'd say, 'No,' that I had gotten things out of my system. She always took these episodes in her stride and never threw them up to me."

Support groups of divorced women who meet regularly for companionship and to give support to each other have been helpful to many single mothers. Such groups enable their members to realize that they are not alone—that other women are trying to cope with single parenthood, too. Other places you might turn to for help and support include:

- Courses in single parenting
- General courses in parenting, such as Parent Effectiveness Training
- Groups such as Parents Without Partners
- Family service organizations
- Counselors
- Social workers
- Ministers, priests, rabbis
- Crisis and rap lines
- Hot lines for parents under stress
- Child abuse groups
- Mental health centers
- Public health centers

Remember that there are services available for the parent who is unable to cope. One way to find out about the services that exist in your area is by calling your local mental health center or family service agency.

WOULD YOU BENEFIT FROM FAMILY COUNSELING?

Parents may hesitate to go for family counseling because they feel it is an admission that they can't handle things on their own, because they hope things will get better by themselves, or because they don't want to spend the money. There are times when single parents would benefit from family counseling. Family counseling works with the group that comprises the family unit. A family therapist deals with individuals, patterns of interaction, and how the family functions. A divorced mother may be helped by private counseling, but her children may need help, too. If parenting issues are her main concern, sessions where all family members are present may be extremely effective. The following are examples of women who found family counseling helpful.

Noreen: I was really shocked to learn that Julie, my daughter, was using drugs. It was particularly difficult for Joan, her twin sister. I was angry, upset, scared, and did not know how to offer the support Julie needed. I also needed to be there for Joan and my youngest child, Tom. My ex-husband, who is remarried and lives two thousand miles away, offered no emotional support. He just said if I were a better mother, Julie would not have used drugs in the first place. I felt guilty and overwhelmed. Family counseling helped us all deal with the problem, our feelings, and how to be supportive of Julie and each other.

Judy: I wished I had used family counseling when I first got divorced, when the children were five and two. I thought that since they were little they had few problems. Since my ex-husband left and moved across the country, the only person my five-year-old daughter could vent her anger on was me. She was angry with me for years. I wished I had approached the problem head-on with the help of a family counselor. Those years might have been happier for all of us.

Margaret: I have two very intelligent children. Several years ago I felt I had run out of energy—about the time they had reached early adolescence! They had more energy, were very manipulative, and I simply felt outnumbered. Going to family counseling enabled a counselor to observe their behavior and assure me I wasn't going crazy. I *was* outnumbered. The counselor gave me the support I needed and helped restore a balance of power. I felt better and the children felt more secure once I became more assertive and stood up for myself. Children don't really want to be in charge.

Sally: When my son Eric was twelve, he expressed a desire to live with his father. I had thought that Eric and I had a close relationship and I was terribly hurt. I wanted to do not only what was best for Eric but what was best for me, too. By going to a counselor, Eric was able to express that he wanted to live with his dad not because he didn't feel close to me, but because he had not had the opportunity to get to know his father. The counselor helped me adjust to the situation, realize that this is what Eric needed, and maintain my relationship with my son. Eric moved to live with his dad and it all worked out. I have a good relationship with Eric today.

The following are times you should strongly consider the support family counseling can provide:

1. If your child has a special problem (drug abuse, eating disorders, learning disabilities, physical or emotional disabilities, etc.).
2. If you feel your family is dysfunctional for any reason.
3. If you feel there is destructive sibling rivalry between your children.
4. If you feel overwhelmed, overpowered, and unable to cope with parenting responsibilities.
5. If you feel you may be abusive to your children either emotionally or physically.
6. If you feel that your children are abusive to you either emotionally or physically.
7. If you feel that your children are associating with peer groups that could be dangerous to their well-being and overall development.
8. If your children are having school or truancy problems.
9. If you are establishing a relationship with another person or planning to remarry.
10. If you feel there are unresolved issues

concerning your divorce that you feel adversely affect family members and the family's functioning.

11. If you feel a child is emotionally depressed or suicidal.

12. If you are unable to communicate effectively with your child.

NOTE: When parents have problems with their children, they may feel guilty and blame themselves. While it is positive to examine what you can do to improve the situation, it does not help to beat yourself and dwell on "where you went wrong." Divorced mothers may feel particularly vulnerable when special problems develop with children. If they have been playing the game of "Who is the best parent?" with their ex-husband, they may find it particularly difficult when a child has serious problems. A woman may feel that her child would have been fine if she hadn't divorced, or that she failed at parenting, or her husband would have done a better job, or that she was not strict enough, or she was too strict . . . the list is endless! To make matters worse, she may not be supported or may even be blamed by her ex-husband. It is very easy to sit in judgment of someone else's parenting.

There are several "truths" when it comes to parenting:

1. Parenting isn't easy.
2. There are no surefire techniques that work for every child in every situation.
3. Even children from two-parent families get in trouble.
4. Most parents try their hardest to do the best they can in raising their children.
5. Most parents are not "trained" to be parents and learn by experience.
6. At some point it becomes the child's "problem"—children must take responsibility for their own life and how they choose to live it.

If you find yourself consumed with guilt and unsupported when serious problems with children arise, don't take total responsibility for the problem. Get help from family therapy and from the numerous support groups that exist. There are support groups for parents of children with learning disabilities, severe behavior problems, emotional problems, and special conditions such as diabetes and anorexia. Be sure to get the support that you need. It is out there!

TEN

DECISIONS CONCERNING MONEY

When I realized after divorce how unfair my financial situation was, that I seemed to bear the brunt of the financial cost of divorce because I was a woman with preschool children who couldn't work, had no experience in the labor force, and could not get credit, I became very angry. I also realized how I had been protected from financial matters by my husband. I knew nothing about handling money. Not only was I angry with my husband for not sharing our financial concerns with me, I was angry with myself for not demanding that I be informed and for not insisting that I take an active part in managing the family's finances.

A positive aspect of my divorce was that I was forced to handle my own finances. Being financially responsible for myself gave me a sense of power and independence that I never had before. I learned that the world of finances is not impossible to understand—it is a world to which I had never been exposed. I learned that I was capable of making intelligent decisions concerning how to budget and invest my money which greatly increased my feelings of self-confidence.

After my divorce I invested some money from the sale of the family home in the stock market. I realized that giving instructions to my broker concerning what should be done with my money gave me a sense of power that I never had before. I had always believed that the stock market was for "men only"!

For many reasons, no matter how intelligent many women are, no matter how much education they have had, they may feel insecure when it comes to handling finances. If you feel threatened by the thought of taking the responsibility for paying the bills, if the idea of preparing your income tax makes you break out in hives, you are not alone. Most women are perfectly capable of managing their own or their family's financial affairs. Unfortunately, somewhere along the way to adulthood, women become brainwashed into believing they can't understand money or money management. If a woman can understand money management, she may feel she should underplay this ability because she won't be considered "feminine" or because she might undermine the male ego.

There are many aspects in the socialization process that encourage women to be financially dependent. A little girl may see that her father earns and has control over the money. She may also see that her mother, who doesn't work, must ask for money and use indirect ways to get it. She quickly comes to realize that money is power—men have that power, women do not. Because women do not have money, they are in a dependent position and must be taken care of by men.

As a divorced woman you will have two difficulties to overcome because you are a woman. First, you will probably have less money because you have to get it from your ex-husband and have less earning power. Second, you may be unprepared to handle money because you are inexperienced and insecure in this area. While it may be difficult to catch up with your ex-husband's financial status, it is possible to become financially independent and reap the emotional and monetary rewards that come with financial independence.

YOUR CURRENT ATTITUDES CONCERNING MONEY

Ask yourself these questions.

1. How confident are you in your present ability to handle financial matters for yourself and your family such as bills, income tax, decisions concerning insurance and investments? Not at all confident? Somewhat confident? Very confident?

2. What do you think is the reason(s) for your present level of confidence?

Many women will cite experience, or the lack of it, as the reason for their confidence level in handling financial matters. There are other reasons for your attitudes concerning managing money which are learned. Answer the following questions:

1. Who earned the money in your family when you were a child?
2. Who controlled the money in your family when you were a child?
3. How did your mother get money for herself?
4. What was the financial relationship between your parents?
   a. Each parent had own income
   b. Mother had own income but this amounted to less than father's
   c. Father gave money to mother and was generous
   d. Mother used "tricks" and cajoled father for money
   e. Parents were divorced and mother was dependent upon earnings and support payments
   f. other:
5. Briefly describe your financial situation as a child. Were you affluent? Comfortable? Was money tight? Was your father unemployed?
6. When a financial crisis arose or a financial decision had to be made, who made those decisions?
7. Who taught you about money and how to use it?
8. Did you receive an allowance? At what age? Who gave it to you, under what conditions?
9. If you had brothers, who taught them about money and how to use it?
10. With whom did you identify most when it came to handling money? Your mother? Father? Someone else?

Briefly summarize the effect your childhood experiences have had on your present attitudes concerning money and money management.

Another way women develop attitudes concerning money and money management is through their experiences as single women before marriage. How would you answer the following questions?

1. Did you have an opportunity to earn and manage your own money before your marriage?
2. Did you manage your financial affairs or ask someone else to do it for you?
3. How confident were you initially, as a single person, in your ability to handle your financial affairs? Not very confident? Somewhat confident? Very confident?
4. How would you rate your overall ability to handle money before marriage? Excellent? Adequate? Inadequate?

Try to summarize the effect your experiences as a single woman have had on your present attitudes concerning money and money management.

Women continue to develop attitudes concerning money and money management when they marry. Answer the following questions:

1. Who earned the money during your marriage—you, your husband, or both?
2. Who earned the most money during your marriage?
3. How did you get money for yourself during your marriage?
4. Who controlled the money in your marriage?
   a. Did you have your own checking account? If yes, was it mainly for household expenses?
   b. Did you have your own savings account?
   c. Did you have your own source of income?
   d. Did you have property and/or investments in your name?
   e. Did you have credit cards in your name?
5. Which of the following financial matters did you handle? Which did your ex-husband handle? Which responsibilities did you share?
   a. Buying groceries, children's clothing, small household items
   b. Saving money on minor and/or regular purchases through comparison shopping and bargain hunting
   c. Household budget
   d. Making small deposits in savings accounts
   e. Paying bills and balancing the checkbook
   f. The overall budget
   g. Investing money—making decisions concerning investment plans, stock purchases, insurance, and so on
   h. Deciding on major purchases such as a home, a car, appliances
   i. Preparing income tax returns
   j. Borrowing money and obtaining credit
   k. Making larger deposits in checking and savings accounts
   l. Handling negotiations concerning money

Financial matters a. through d. are concerned with everyday expenses and involve relatively little financial responsibility and risk taking. Items e. through l. involve handling larger amounts of money, more control over the money, and greater financial responsibility and risk taking. For which items were you responsible?

How would you rate the relationship you had with your ex-husband concerning financial matters? Who had greater financial control?

6. What were the advantages and disadvantages for you of the financial relationship you had with your husband? What were the advantages and disadvantages of that relationship for your husband?
7. What did you do (or not do) to cause the financial relationship you had with your husband?
8. How confident did you feel during your marriage about your ability to handle the financial matters for yourself and your family? Not at all confident? Somewhat confident? Very confident?
9. How would you rate your ability to handle money during your marriage? Inadequate? Adequate? Excellent?

Try to summarize the effect your experiences as a married woman have had on your present attitudes concerning money and money management.

Now reconsider all the questions you answered—those concerning your childhood, single, married, and present feelings concerning money and money management. Do you see any patterns in the development of your attitudes concerning money and money management? If yes, describe them. Were any periods of your life more influential in the development of your attitudes concerning money and money management? If so, can you explain why they were more influential?

Now that you have completed these questions, you may begin to see that your attitude concerning money and money management is neither inborn nor due to your being born female. Your confidence or lack of confidence concerning financial matters was learned. People often make assumptions about women's ability to manage money—"She can't save a cent," "She has no head for finances," "She can't balance a checkbook." Often women come to believe that they are truly incompetent when it comes to finances. Or, they are willing to transfer all responsibility for financial matters to a husband because it is easier, less trouble, less threatening, and involves no decisions and no responsibility. If you decide to turn the responsibility for your financial matters over to someone else, that is your decision. You may find that your lawyer, ex-husband, or a friend is willing to handle your finances. However, if you are tempted to turn over your financial responsibilities to someone else, answer the following questions:

1. What advantages will you get from turning your financial responsibilities over to someone else?
2. How will such a decision make you feel about yourself?
3. What risks are involved for you if you turn your financial responsibilities over to someone else?
4. How will the decision affect your relationship with the person who is taking care of your financial responsibilities?
5. How will the decision affect your total independence?

If you want to take responsibility for your financial matters yourself and gain financial independence, you are ready to complete the remaining activities in this chapter.

MONEY MYTHS

In the books, *How to Get Going When You Can Barely Get Out of Bed: Every Woman's Handbook for Dealing with Depression and Frustration* (Englewood Cliffs, N.J.: Prentice-Hall, 1984) by Linda J. Bailey, and *Money Is My Friend* (San Francisco, Calif.: Trinity Publica-

tions, 1979) by Phil Laut, myths that can prevent women from creating financial independence for themselves are examined. The following list represents a combination of ideas from various sources which can be harmful to a woman's goal of establishing financial independence. Which myths apply to you?

1. It is a man's job to support a woman.

This is simply not a reality in today's world. Women who are "taken care of" pay a price in loss of self-esteem, relationships that are not equal, and the insecurity of financial dependency.

2. Making money is unfeminine.

Everyone needs money to live. Making money is neither "masculine" nor "feminine." Traditionally in our society, men have been the ones to make the money. While our roles as men and women have changed, some men are threatened by women who are financially successful and independent. Some women in turn don't readily accept or feel comfortable with this newfound challenge of independence.

3. It is not right to be rich when others are poor.

While it may not be fair that some people have more money than others, it is your right to earn money. You are not the cause of others' poverty and being poor yourself will solve nothing.

4. One should only have the money that is needed to meet basic needs; extra money is decadent.

How much money a person "needs" is impossible to define since it varies from person to person, according to their values and perceptions. Having money after paying for your basic needs can provide delightful options!

5. Money is evil and corrupts.

Money is neither good nor evil. It is a necessary fact of life.

6. If I make a lot of money, I will become materialistic, selfish, and greedy.

An individual controls his or her own values and actions.

7. If I am educated and a professional, I will be wealthy.

While education may make it easier to obtain certain positions, it does not ensure financial success.

8. In order to make money, I must work long, hard hours at a job I hate.

It is possible to make money at a job you enjoy. It is also possible to work smarter rather than harder to earn money.

9. Rich people pay a price for being rich.

When bad things happen to rich people, it is not because they are rich. Bad things happen to poor people, too. Having money as a resource can make it easier to deal with bad times.

YOUR NET WORTH

In chapter 8, you were asked to compute a balance sheet for the purpose of establishing your assets, liabilities, and net worth as a married couple. Once you have agreed to a settlement or have obtained a divorce, you will want to repeat that process to determine what your net worth is.

Draw up an outline* like the one in column two for yourself. Add or delete items needed to describe your financial situation.

Look at the last line of your net worth statement. Do your liabilities exceed your assets?

If your answer is yes, you are in trouble and have some work to do. The activity on page 146 concerning getting out of debt will be particularly useful to you. Unless your financial situation changes drastically, it would be wise to compute your net worth once each year, preferably at the same time each year. Calculating your net worth provides you with

- A financial photograph
- A statement of your worth
- A statement of your weak areas
- A tool should you need a loan
- A basis of financial planning and goal setting
- A check to see if you have achieved your goals
- A tool for making insurance claims

It is also a good idea to have a visual inventory of your property through photographs or video tape. Keep all your financial information in a safe

* Format from the book *The Joy of Money.* Copyright © 1975 by Paula Nelson. Reprinted by permission of Stein and Day Publishers.

place. You may find it helpful to set up a special work area for dealing with financial matters. Set aside one day or evening a month to pay your bills, balance your checkbook, and complete other financial matters.

NET WORTH

ASSETS	
Cash on hand	$ _____
Checking accounts	_____
Savings accounts	_____
Corporate profit-sharing plans— money now due you	_____
Marketable stocks (cost or present market value whichever is lower)	_____
Money you have lent someone	_____
Life insurance (total cash surrender value)	_____
Bonds, including government	_____
Real estate:	
Home—at market value	_____
Investment properties	_____
Syndications	_____
Automobile (current market value)	_____
Furs, jewelry, antiques, paintings (market value)	_____
Total assets	_____

LIABILITIES	
Unpaid bills:	
Charge accounts	$ _____
Credit card accounts	_____
Taxes	_____
Insurance premiums	_____
Installment contracts	_____
Loans:	
Banks	_____
Savings and loans	_____
Insurance companies	_____
Credit unions	_____
Car loans	_____
Friends	_____
Mortgages	_____
Total liabilities	_____
NET WORTH (assets minus liabilities)	_____

DO YOU HAVE A WILL?

Many divorced women do not have a will because they feel they "don't own anything" or have "nothing to leave." If you wrote down anything in the assets column when you figured out your net worth, or have children, you should consider the importance of having a will—one that is current and workable.

If you already have a will, this activity will not be particularly helpful for you. If you don't have a will, why don't you? Do any of these reasons apply to you?

1. I haven't gotten around to changing my will since my divorce.
2. I don't feel I have anything to leave anyone.
3. I have no children so I do not have to worry about who their guardian would be in the event of my death.
4. I don't like to face the idea of my own death so avoid preparing a will.
5. I don't know how to go about preparing a will.
6. I don't know a lawyer to consult.
7. I don't have the money to pay a lawyer.
8. I don't care what percentage of my money goes to the state in which I live in the form of inheritance taxes.
9. I don't care how my assets are divided.
10. I don't care how long my estate is tied up because I have no will.

Should you decide that it would be in your best interest to draw up a will, the easiest way to go about it is to consult a lawyer. If your estate is a large one, you will want to see a lawyer experienced in estate planning; if your estate is very small, you might consider using the lawyer you used for your divorce (if you were satisfied with the work he or she did). You can get recommendations from your family lawyer, law firms that specialize in estate planning, your company's legal counsel, an accounting firm or an individual accountant you know and trust, an insurance company, a broker you know and trust, or the local bar association, which will give you the names of lawyers but will not provide any information concerning their competence.

Your estate lawyer will need an account of your assets and liabilities which you will have on hand once you have calculated your net worth. Use the following checklist as a reminder of the information you should have when you see a lawyer concerning a will.

ASSETS

- Bank accounts, stocks, bonds, saving certificates (identify by account and/or certificate number)
- Valuables (list and describe your most valuable possessions, including jewelry, antiques, books, paintings, and silver as well as how you want your possessions divided upon your death)
- All real estate you own (provide description, location, and market value of property)
- Insurance policies—both personal and through your employer (name beneficiaries, state face amount of policies, loans against policies, and premiums paid or due)
- Pension plans, stock options, profit sharing, retirement funds, and union benefits (give values and beneficiaries)

LIABILITIES

- Mortgages or leases
- Outstanding major debts (name creditor, amount owed, and date by which debt is to be paid)
- Taxes and other major commitments (provide a list of loans you have cosigned)

FAMILY INFORMATION

- Names and ages of children
- Relatives for whom you are responsible
- Name of guardian(s) for your children
- Conditions you want for your children (private school, camps, music lessons, etc.)

Remember, the more thorough you are in preparing the information a lawyer will need, the better your chances of getting a reasonable bill from your lawyer and the will that you want!

Although it is possible to write your own will—many books on the subject are available—the safest and easiest way to draw up a will that meets the requirements of the state in which you live is to consult a lawyer. If you cannot afford the services of a lawyer, contact the Legal Aid Society in your area.

YOUR MONTHLY BUDGET

To help you establish a monthly budget, complete a budget form like the one reproduced on page 145. You may want to make certain additions and deletions to make the form fit your situation. If you have payments that you make several times a year, add them up, divide by

MONTHLY BUDGET

MONTHLY INCOME

Alimony/child support — $ _____
Take-home pay — _____
Other: Specify — _____

Total monthly income: — $ _____

MONTHLY EXPENSES

Food
    Groceries — _____
    Lunches (school/work) — _____
    Meals out — _____
  Total: — $ _____

Shelter
    Rent/mortgage — _____
    Taxes — _____
    Maintenance/
      improvement — _____

Fire insurance
  Total: — $ _____

House operation
    Gas — _____
    Heat — _____
    Electricity — _____
    Phone — _____
    Water/sewer — _____
    Garbage — _____
    Other: Specify — _____
  Total: — $ _____

Children
    Baby-sitting — _____
    Education/tuition — _____
    Lessons — _____
    Medical expenses — _____
    Other: Specify — _____
  Total: — $ _____

Personal expenses
    Clothing — _____
    Education — _____
    Recreation/hobbies — _____
    Hair/cosmetics — _____
    Dues, membership fees — _____
    Vacation — _____
    Medical — _____
    Other: Specify — _____
  Total: — $ _____

Transportation
    Car payments — _____
    Car insurance — _____
    Repairs — _____
    Gas/oil — _____
    Carfare — _____
  Total: — $ _____

Insurance
    Life — _____
    Accident/health — _____
    Other: — _____
  Total: — $ _____

YOUR TOTAL MONTHLY EXPENSES — $ _____
YOUR TOTAL MONTHLY INCOME — $ _____

twelve, and enter the monthly average in the appropriate spaces.

Does your total monthly income equal your total monthly expenses? In other words, does the cash that comes in each month equal the cash that goes out? If possible, plan to have some income left over to deposit regularly in a savings account. It might be a good idea to include regular savings in your budget as an expense.

YOUR MONEY VALUES

The way you spend your money can be an indication of what you value. Use a circle to represent the amount of money you have available to spend each month. Estimate how much you spend on rent, food, entertainment, education, and so on. Draw slices in the circle to represent the portion of your money you spend on different categories. Your pie may look something like this one.

MONTHLY INCOME

_____

(net)

Look at the way you spend your money and answer the following questions.*

1. What represents the largest slice of your money pie?
2. What do the sizes of your money-pie slices tell you about your values?
3. Refer to the activity on page 40 asking

---

* This activity was adapted from Simon, Howe, and Kirschenbaum, *Values Clarification: A Handbook of Practical Strategies for Teachers and Students* (New York: Hart Publishing Co., 1972). By permission of A & W Publishers, Inc.

you to list your values. On which values do you spend money?

4. Is your money pie consistent with your values? For example, if you said education was an important value for you, do you spend a portion of your monthly income on education?

5. How do you think the slices of your pie have changed since your divorce (or will change when you become divorced)?

6. Are you satisfied with the way you sliced your money pie?

7. Are there any things on which you would like to spend your money that are not included in your pie?

8. Realistically, is there anything you can do to begin to change the size of some of your slices if you want to?

ELIMINATING YOUR DEBTS

If you have any debts, you realize how important it is to establish a plan to eliminate these debts. To help you draw up a debt-elimination plan, list all your debts and the amounts owed. Your list may look something like the example below.*

EXAMPLE

	AGE OF BILL		
DEBT OR BILL	30 DAYS	60 DAYS	90 DAYS OR MORE
Sears		$264.08	
Dr. Jones			$54.00

Look at the chart you have drawn up for your debts and decide which bill must be paid first. You may take into consideration a personal reason for paying off a particular debt (you owe money to a good friend), the length of time the debt has been owed, or the interest rates being charged. If your interest rates are very high, you may want to consider a bank loan at a lower interest rate to pay off your debts; this form of debt consolidation could be to your advantage.

List the order in which you plan to pay off your debts and the reasons for your decisions. Number your debts in the order you plan to pay them off. If you decide to pay off several debts at the same time, give these debts the same number.

Determine what portion of your income you can spare to pay off your debts on a monthly basis. Do this by consulting the budget you made up earlier. Does your monthly income exceed your monthly expenses? If your answer is yes, you can use that money to pay your debts. Be sure to deduct 10 percent of that amount for savings. This may seem strange, but it will get you into the habit of saving and will give you money for emergencies.

If your monthly expenses and income are equal, or if your expenses exceed your income, you are going to have to cut back. Look at your budget. Which expenses are fixed and cannot be reduced? Which expenses could you eliminate altogether?

Are there any other ways you can get money to pay off your debts? Do you have anything you could sell or any loans you can call in? Could you get a part-time job?

How much money are you able to come up with per month for repayment of debts? Now, take 10 percent of that amount and put it in a savings account to develop self-discipline, a savings habit, and to provide for emergencies.

Your next step is to contact your creditors by letter. You may have been avoiding or evading them but you cannot continue to do this. Your letter should:

- Outline your situation—you may wish to state that you have just been through a divorce, that you wanted to see who would be responsible for the debts, and that you are now in a position to pay off your obligations.
- Inform them how you will pay them.
- Tell them the amount you will send them every month.
- Tell them the date by which you will begin payments—it might help to include a check with your letter.

Your creditors will probably respect your frankness, the fact that you confronted the situation, and that you are willing to propose a payment plan. Creditors are human and appreciate knowing if and when they will be paid, even if the monthly payment is small. Receiving small monthly payments is better than receiving nothing at all. As one administrator of a pediatric clinic stated, "People don't realize that we understand financial problems. If they pay only a

---

* Adapted from *The Joy of Money.* Copyright © 1975 by Paula Nelson. Reprinted with permission of Stein and Day Publishers.

couple of dollars a month and we know they intend to pay their bill, we won't turn their account over to a collection agency—we lose money that way. People only get into more trouble when they try to avoid us and their bills. If they discuss the situation with us, it is possible to work out a solution that benefits both of us."

WARNING: Once you have notified your creditors and they have agreed to the payment schedule you proposed, stick to it. This system will only work once. If you propose a payoff rate that won't cripple you, you should be able to pay off your debts, provided you don't lose your job or suffer severe financial setbacks.

If you need help getting out of debt, contact your local bank; many banks offer debt counseling. Some family service agencies also offer financial counseling and/or referrals to agencies that do. There are over 150 consumer credit counseling services that offer help to overextended families. For the address of the service nearest you, write:

National Foundation for Consumer Credit
1819 H Street
Washington, D.C. 20006

Other sources of help include churches, labor unions, community services counselors, and employers' personnel departments. The army and navy also maintain debt counseling services to assist service personnel and their families.

If you feel your financial situation is absolutely hopeless, contact a lawyer. An attorney can inform you about last-resort alternatives such as the Chapter 13 method of debt reorganization or voluntary bankruptcy.

STAYING OUT OF DEBT

Once you are out of debt you will want to stay out of debt. Which of the following statements apply to you?

1. My monthly income equals or exceeds my monthly expenses.
2. I have a savings plan I follow regularly.
3. I have money set aside to use in case of an emergency.
4. I never use credit cards unless I have money to pay for my purchases or know from where the money will come.
5. I carefully consider my budget before taking on additional financial obligations such as loans, payments, and so on.

6. I am aware of interest rates and how much it costs me to have unpaid balances and to get a loan.
7. I compare interest rates when shopping for a loan.
8. I take advantage of savings plans at work by having money deducted from my salary.
9. I compare interest rates when considering where to have my savings account.
10. I think carefully about my budget when I make major purchases and try to avoid impulse buying.

Ideally, every statement should apply.

One of the easiest ways to get into debt is through the use of credit. If you know you are an impulse buyer—buying when you are down to boost your spirits and forgetting that when you hand someone a credit card you aren't *paying* for a purchase—the best thing to do is to destroy your credit cards. When you borrow money for major purchases—home, car, appliances—make sure you shop around for the interest terms that are best for you. For example, it may make more sense to get a short-term loan from the bank than to pay high interest rates on unpaid balances or charge accounts. The trick is to get credit to work in your favor by comparing interest rates. You may find that it is to your advantage to borrow money if the interest rate you pay on a loan is lower than the interest you are getting on money that is invested.

It is important to have a regular savings plan. A rule of thumb for the amount you should have in savings is to save an amount equal to five times your monthly salary. Before you open a savings account at a bank or savings and loan association, you will want to shop for the best interest rate.

To make the best decisions, you may want the following information about the institutions you are considering. Which of these questions* are important to you?

1. What are the hours of business?
2. Is there drive-up teller service?
3. What is the interest rate paid on savings accounts?
4. Are there rules concerning withdrawals?
5. What is the cost per check on various kinds of accounts?

* Adapted from *The Joy of Money.* Copyright © 1975 by Paula Nelson. Reprinted with permission of Stein and Day Publishers.

6. What is the monthly cost, if any, for a checking account? Are free checking accounts available?

7. Is there an overdraw account available to new customers? What interest rates are charged for this service?

8. What is the cost for printed or personalized checks?

9. What other costs are involved in a checking account?

10. How are bounced checks handled? What charges apply?

11. What is the procedure to stop payment on a check?

12. How much do traveler's checks cost?

13. Are safe-deposit boxes available?

14. How much do cashier's checks cost?

15. How much do certified checks cost?

16. Is a notary public service available to customers? What is the charge for this service?

17. Does the bank belong to an automated teller machine network? What charges are there for withdrawals using this system?

18. What other services are offered?

You may decide, because of interest rates, to have a savings account at one bank and a checking account at another. This way you may not be as tempted to make withdrawals from your savings account and transfer them into your checking account. Or you may decide, for convenience, to do all your banking at one bank.

It is often advisable to make regular deposits in a savings account at a neighborhood bank so you can establish a savings record and show that you have financial stability. If you have a savings account at a bank, it is more likely to consider giving you a loan should you need one.

If you, like most people, find it impossible to have money left over at the end of each month, you may want to consider saving the "painless way" by having your employer deduct a certain amount each month for a company-sponsored savings plan. You may also want to consider taking the minimum number of deductions possible on your W2 form so that the federal government will owe you money instead of you owing it money at income tax time.

ESTABLISHING CREDIT IN YOUR NAME

What kind of a credit rating do you have? To help determine your current credit status, answer these questions:

1. Do you have a checking account in your name?

2. Do you have a savings account and make regular deposits?

3. Are you known at a local bank where you do your banking?

4. Do you bank at the main branch or an important branch of the bank where you do business?

5. Do you know the name and title of the branch manager?

6. Have you introduced yourself to the branch manager?

7. Do you pay your bills regularly?

8. Do you have charge accounts with local merchants?

9. If you have other charge accounts, do you make purchases regularly and pay your bills?

10. Are you careful not to exceed your credit limit?

The more questions you answered yes, the better for you. Women have found it difficult, particularly if they are divorced, to get credit in their own names. Thanks to laws such as the Equal Credit Opportunity Act, it is easier for women to obtain credit today than it was a number of years ago. Institutions granting credit may no longer discriminate against women because they are divorced; in fact, they may no longer ask for your marital status. Nor may they ask what portion of your income comes from alimony and/or child support. For this reason, it is a good idea to establish a credit rating whether you need it or not; then if you do need credit you will be able to get it. One way to establish a credit rating is to buy something on an installment loan such as a TV, dishwasher, or car, or to borrow money from an institution with which you do business. You may find it wise to borrow from the bank where you have a savings account. Credit cards are another quick and easy way of establishing yourself as a worthwhile credit risk. You may want to apply for one of the following:

- Gasoline credit cards
- Department store credit cards
- Major credit cards—MasterCard, Visa, and so on.

THE CREDIT QUIZ

Institutions often consider these factors in deciding whether or not to give an individual credit:

marital status, dependents, age, residence, job status, monthly obligations, occupation, and bank accounts. How do you rate?*

- If you are married, give yourself one point.
- If you have one to three dependents, add two points; four or more, add one point.
- If you are aged 21–25 or over 65, give yourself one point; 26–64, give yourself two points.
- If you have lived at the same residence for more than five years, give yourself one point.
- If you lived at your previous address for more than five years, add one point.
- If you have held your present job less than a year, add no points; one to three years, add one point; four to six years, two points; seven to ten years, three points; more then ten years, four points.
- If you owe less than $400 a month, add one point; over $400 a month, add no points.
- If you are a professional, an executive, or foreman, add three points; skilled worker, add two points; blue-collar worker, one point; anything else, no points.
- If you have a checking or savings account at the bank where you are applying for credit, add two points.
- If you have a telephone listed in your name, add two points.

If your point total came to more than eleven, you would probably be considered a good credit risk.

Because the bank where you do business will be the primary source of reference concerning your character and your ability to handle credit, it is a good idea to know and be known by your banker. You should be known by at least one official of the bank—a vice president at least, and preferably the vice president in charge of loans. If you want to apply for credit

1. Learn who the manager of the bank is from the switchboard operator
2. Make an appointment with the manager
3. Introduce yourself to the manager
4. Plan what you want to say in a concise manner

* Quiz taken from the book *The Joy of Money.* Copyright © 1975 by Paula Nelson. Reprinted by permission of Stein and Day Publishers.

EXAMPLE

"Hello, Mr. Jones. My name is Susan Smith. I need a four-thousand-dollar loan repayable over twenty-four months to help pay for a 1988 Ford Tempo automobile I want to buy. I am a teacher, earn twenty-five thousand dollars annually, and can pay a hundred dollars a month toward the loan. The balance sheet I prepared will show you my assets and liabilities. I have a fine credit record at Marshall's Department Store here in town and have had checking and savings accounts with your bank for five years."

Now write the speech *you* would give if you were asking a bank manager for credit. Be sure to include the following in your speech:

- Amount you want
- Repayment period
- Your occupation
- Your salary
- The amount of money you can set aside each month
- Your credit record—at local stores, former loans you have paid off
- Your net worth—have a personal balance sheet prepared

When filling out credit references, it is wise to avoid filling them out at the bank or credit institution. Complete them at your office or home and make a copy of the credit applications and any additional forms you may fill out for your records.

A FINAL NOTE ABOUT CREDIT

Do you know your rights under the Fair Credit Reporting Act and the Fair Credit Billing Act?

If you are turned down for a loan or a credit card, find out why immediately. Under the Fair Credit Reporting Act of 1971, the law requires that

1. If you suspect you've been turned down for a loan, a job, or charged a higher rate on your insurance because of a bad credit rating, you may ask the institution that turned you down for the source of the rating. It must give you the name and address of the source of the report and of the credit reporting bureau that has this record of you on file.
2. You have a right to call or go to the bu-

reau and insist it tell you the substance of the report and the sources of the information.

3. The credit bureau must tell you the names of everyone who received an employment report about you within the last two years, plus the names of anyone else who got reports about you within the last six months.

4. If you find that the material is outdated or untrue, you have the right to insist that the bureau go over its records and prove that their records are accurate.

5. You have the right to insist that the correction on your file be sent to all employers or prospective employers who received the incorrect report during the last two years. You can also insist that the cedit bureau send this information to anyone else who has received a report about you in the previous six months.

If you contact the credit bureau within thirty days after receiving a report of a credit refusal, there is no charge for telling you what is in the file. If you are curious about your credit rating, or your credit file, you can get that information for a nominal fee. One credit firm that functions nationwide is TRW; it probably has a credit file on you.

The Fair Credit Billing Act requires that

1. Inquiries about your bills must be answered within thirty days, and the question in the inquiry resolved in no more than ninety days.

2. No dunning letters or threats to give you an adverse credit report can be sent or other collection action taken until your inquiry is resolved.

3. A creditor cannot send an adverse report to a credit agency on an amount you are questioning or disputing unless you, the customer, also get such a report and unless the credit reporting agency is told there is a dispute concerning the amount of the charge.

4. Your monthly bills must have an address to which you can write concerning handling billing disputes, and you must be reminded periodically of your rights.

5. You can withhold payment on merchandise you think was misrepresented or defective if you bought it with a bank credit

card on the same basis as you can withhold cash payment from a store. This protects the credit card buyer from stores that go out of business, leaving the customer holding the bill with no one to correct what went wrong or to return the money.

INCOME TAX

How do you feel about preparing your income tax return? It is important that you know something about income tax and where to get help with your tax return.

If you look upon preparing your tax returns as an unpleasant chore, your response is not unusual. Perhaps you feel a bit intimidated because you have never before prepared a tax return—your husband always took care of it. Although income tax forms may seem confusing initially, they are possible to master. You will probably discover, after you have gotten used to handling your tax matters, that there is a certain satisfaction and confidence that comes with being able to handle this aspect of your financial affairs.

You should know about income tax and be able to complete a 1040 form for several reasons.

1. If you know something about income tax, it will be easier for you to save tax money.

2. You will be familiar with the information you must save for income tax purposes.

3. You are liable for the statements in your tax return, even if a paid professional makes them for you.

4. You will be able to ask intelligent questions and prepare the necessary information needed by a professional to prepare your return.

5. It is a necessary part of learning to be financially responsible for yourself.

The following checklist presents the information you should collect, in an orderly fashion, for income tax purposes. Even if you don't think you will itemize your deductions, it is wise to keep this information in case you change your mind or discover it is to your advantage to do so.

INFORMATION PERTAINING TO INCOME

- Alimony
- Salary information—paycheck stubs and withholding statements, particularly those sent at the end of the year
- Savings account statements giving interest earned throughout the year
- Investment statements giving dividend and interest information
- Work-related expenses—travel, education, entertainment, union dues

INTEREST EXPENSES

- Mortgage interest
- Loan interest
- Interest paid on unpaid balance of charge accounts

WORK-RELATED CHILD-CARE AND HOUSEHOLD EXPENSES

- Sitters' fees—names, addresses, Social Security numbers of sitters
- Child-care institutions, nursery schools

You may deduct up to $2,400 for child care from your taxable income of you have one child; up to $4,800 if you have two or more children.

It is wise to consult income tax guides or someone at your local Internal Revenue Service Office to see if a given item is deductible. For example, educational expenses necessary to keep or advance in your present job are tax deductible, whereas educational expenses to enter a new field or to prepare you for employment are not. Fees to an employment agency are deductible if you get a new job in a field in which you have been working; if you change fields, employment agency fees are not deductible.

ALL INFORMATION CONCERNING BUYING AND SELLING PROPERTY, STOCKS, BONDS

- Records of purchase of stocks and bonds—when purchased, number of shares, price per share, broker's fees
- Records of sale of stocks and bonds—when sold, how many shares, price per share, broker's fees
- Records concerning buying of property—when bought, price
- Records concerning selling of property—when sold, price, selling expenses
- Records concerning improvements and costs of improvements made on investments—home and property improvements

MEDICAL DEDUCTIONS

- Cost of medicine and drugs
- Doctor's fees
- Hearing aids, dentures, eyeglasses
- Transportation expenses for medical purposes
- Medical insurance premiums
- Psychiatrist's/psychologist's fees
- Special food prescribed for illness
- X-ray services
- Ambulance hire
- Hospital care
- Laboratory services
- Nursing services

INFORMATION CONCERNING SAVINGS AND TAX DEFERMENT PLANS

- IRAs (Individual Retirement Accounts)
- Keough Plans
- 401 K Plans

MISCELLANEOUS DEDUCTIONS

- Contributions to charity
- Car use for volunteer work
- Losses due to casualty or theft
- Legal fees for tax advice or to produce taxable income
- Alimony paid
- Fees for income tax preparation
- Cost of income tax guides—part of cost of calculator if used for tax purposes
- Job hunting expenses

ALL TAXES YOU PAID

- Estimated tax payments
- Federal income tax withheld
- State and local income taxes
- State and local gasoline taxes
- Sales tax paid on large items
- Personal property tax

The following sources may be useful in providing background information about taxes:

- Paperback guides published annually—explain how to prepare your taxes and discuss new tax laws.
- Free publications available from the Internal Revenue Service such as
    Yearly instructional booklet sent with tax forms
    Publication 503—child care and disabled dependent care

Publication 504—tax information for divorced or separated individuals
- Courses offered through adult-education programs on preparing your tax return.
- The Internal Revenue Service's toll-free telephone service—the number is in your tax booklet and in your local telephone directory under the heading "United States Government—Internal Revenue Service."
- Your local IRS office; it would be wise to call and check on hours and busy times, particularly when April 15 approaches. IRS employees will not fill out your forms for you but they will answer questions and will review your finished form for completeness, allowable deductions, and correct computations before you file it.

Tax helps available for a fee include

- Lawyers, certified public accountants, and "enrolled agents" (former IRS agents with five or more years experience). Remember, not all lawyers and accountants specialize in the tax field; you want someone who knows tax laws and is a tax expert.
- Tax preparation companies.
- Individuals who prepare taxes.

Tax preparation companies and individuals can represent you before the IRS if you are audited. Remember, however, that you are ultimately responsible for your return. If a company completes your return incorrectly, it may pay the interest and penalties incurred. You will be required to pay the additional tax monies owed.

The fee for preparing your return will depend upon its complexity, the length of time needed to complete its preparation, and the expertise of the person you consult. Questions you should ask if you are considering paying to have your income tax prepared for you are:

1. Will the service be able to represent you in the event of an audit?
2. What kind of training does the person who will prepare your return have that qualifies him or her to prepare returns?
3. What do they do the remainder of the year? Will they be around if IRS questions your return?
4. How long has the service been in business?
5. What background and training have their employees had?
6. What kinds of guarantees and/or references can they give?
7. How much do they charge? What is the fee per hour? How many hours will it take to prepare your return?
8. What is their procedure if, because of an error they make, you are called to an IRS office? Will they assume responsibilities for any penalties or interest you would be required to pay?

Also remember that if it is legally possible for you to file a joint income tax return, it is to your advantage to do so. You may want to schedule your divorce after January 1 to get the advantage of an extra year of filing a joint tax return.

YOUR INSURANCE NEEDS

To determine your insurance needs, make a list of the kind(s) of insurance you presently have. What does each policy you have do for you? Are you protected by the following types of insurance?

- AUTOMOBILE INSURANCE: Liability insurance—protects you and any family members who drive against personal injuries and destruction of property resulting from automobile accidents. Collision, theft, vandalism insurance—if the car is an old one, you may decide to lower your insurance premium by not insuring your car against damage.
- HOMEOWNER'S INSURANCE: Covers your home or apartment for hazards such as fire, theft, and liability, including an injury to someone who trips on your living-room rug.
- HEALTH INSURANCE: Basic medical—takes care of initial hospitalization, surgery, and other services that might be needed. This kind of policy puts some limit on the length of time covered and pays a specified amount for room and board and the services required. Major medical—supplements the basic plan by covering more of your costs when you are out of the hospital or when you have used up your basic coverage.

These two kinds of medical insurance may be combined in one policy called comprehensive major medical.

Under federal law, health and life coverage provided by your spouse's employer may be continued at group rates for up to thirty-six months after a divorce, regardless of whether you or your spouse pays for it. The law does not apply if you are covered by another group plan, no matter how inadequate it might be.

- **LIFE INSURANCE:** Term insurance—provides temporary protection. The amount of the policy is paid only if the insured dies within the period of time covered by the policy. Term insurance does not build up a cash value. This type of insurance may be a good idea for a divorced woman who is dependent upon her ex-husband for support money; the coverage should be for him. Term insurance is also good for people who have a tight budget, since it provides the maximum amount of insurance for the minimum number of premium dollars. Lifetime policy—provides protection for the lifetime of the person insured. The value of the policy is paid to a beneficiary at the death of the insured. Endowment policy—enables a woman to save a sum of money that becomes available to her at the maturity date named in the policy. If the insured dies before the maturity date, the sum is paid to a beneficiary.

The advantage of life insurance as an investment is that you make one purchase and then forget about it except for the annual premiums you pay. Insurance protects you from yourself; it allows the cash value to accumulate without your being able to spend it. In addition to an investment, you also have protection for your family in the event of your death.

In looking for an insurance agent, recommendations from friends, bankers, and professional people may be helpful. Most insurance agents are willing to spend their time talking to you about your insurance needs. You may find it wise to talk to several agents before you decide on an agent and an insurance company.

- **COVERAGE FOR CATASTROPHIC ILLNESSES** such as cancer, severe and prolonged mental illness, open-heart surgery—the best kind of insurance would probably be membership in a prepaid group practice program through your employer. If you leave your place of employment, you have the option to pay to continue your insurance through your company's plan for 18 months.

If you are not employed, you may continue your insurance through your ex-husband's employer for a thirty-six month period after your divorce. You will need to decide with your husband who will pay your premiums. If this is not available to you, the next best thing is to join a group plan that offers a comprehensive policy. If you are not a member of a group, you may have no alternative but to buy individual health insurance. If you are not covered under a company policy where you work, you will find the cost of an individual policy more expensive. Be sure that your children are covered under either your ex-husband's medical insurance or your own.

If you must buy an individual policy, questions you should ask include:

1. How can the policy be renewed? (The best provision is "guaranteed renewability" for the rest of your life or until you reach sixty-five, as long as you pay the premium.)
2. What is the maximum coverage? (For each illness? For each family member? For the whole family?)
3. What is excluded? (Watch for exclusions for treatment in a mental hospital, alcoholism, drug addiction.)
4. What are the deductibles? (What amount do you have to pay? Does the deductible apply to each illness or to a calendar year? Does the company pay the entire cost above the deductible or a given percentage? If a percentage, what percentage?)
5. When does the coverage start?
6. Is the company licensed to do business in your state?

- **DISABILITY INSURANCE:** Protects you against times when sickness or injury takes you off the job and cuts off your income. Some employers provide company-paid disability. This type of insurance covers short-term, long-term, and permanent disabilities. If you are the only means of support for your family, you would be wise to consider this coverage.

Questions you should ask concerning disability insurance are:

1. How flexible is the definition of *disability*?
2. If you can't return to your regular job,

how long will the policy pay? (This can range from two years to until age sixty-five.)

3. If you can go back to some other kind of work, will the policy continue to hold?
4. What special benefits does this policy offer?
5. Will the income benefits be paid in full if you are totally disabled?
6. What kinds of disability are not covered?
7. Is it noncancelable?
8. Is the policy guaranteed renewable? (The company guarantees to renew it but not at the same rate.)
9. Does the policy cover you for a sickness that began but was not diagnosed before the policy was bought?
10. Are you required to be homebound in order to collect payments?

Before you buy insurance from an agent, you may want to ask:

1. How long have you been selling insurance?
2. How much insurance did you sell last year?
3. How long has your company been in business?
4. Why do you sell insurance for your particular company?
5. How does your company compare with other companies?
6. Can you give me the names of three people who use you as their insurance agent?*

YOUR FINANCIAL GOALS

In chapter 4, you were asked to dream about your future and set goals for yourself. One activity asked you to describe the financial status you would ideally like to have. Another asked you to state your goals and the resources, such as money, you would need to achieve these goals. Women often think in terms of "making do" with the money they have. They are seldom encouraged to think in terms of getting the money they need to accomplish their goals and to provide them with the life-style they want. Many women limit themselves in terms of their financial thinking. They may have learned that talking about

* This exercise was adapted from *A Woman's Book of Money* by Sylvia Auerbach. Copyright © 1976 by Sylvia Auerbach. Reprinted by permission of Doubleday & Company, Inc.

money is all right for men, but is unfeminine in women. Because women have traditionally been dependent upon men for their financial support, they have tended to be passive rather than assertive in terms of financial planning and goal setting. Since it is unlikely that many women will receive enough money from support payments to provide the life-style they want or are accustomed to having, women must change from a passive to an active stance in terms of deciding how much money they want and how they are going to get it.

People want different life-styles. Briefly describe the life-style you decided you wanted in chapter 4. You may be tempted to set your sights high, but be realistic. Do you want a subsistence type of life-style? A comfortable life-style, one in which you will be able to have some luxuries? How much will your desired life-style cost you each year?

Now figure out how much money you receive in child support and/or alimony payments. How much additional money must you provide in order to have the life-style you want?

To achieve the life-style you want, you will probably have to earn some money; it is unlikely that you will get more money than you want and need from your support payments. Women solve this problem in different ways. Some solve the problem by lowering the standards for their style of life; others go to work for the first time in their lives. Some decide to lower their life-style standards for a period of time while they focus on a goal that will ultimately enable them to have a means to earn the money they need and want. What alternatives do you have in your situation? What will be the *immediate* and *long-range* outcomes of each of your alternatives? What are the costs and benefits of each alternative? Which alternative is best for you? Why? Do you think this alternative is consistent with the values you decided were important to you in chapter 3 and the goals you set for yourself in chapter 4?

Begin to think in terms of your goals and how much they will cost. Your goal may be to finish your education, which will increase your earning power, or to save money to make a down payment on a home. Posting your financial goals where you can see them will serve as a reminder and create energy that you can direct toward achieving these goals. You may want to refer to chapter 4 to help you complete a chart similar to the one outlined on the next page.

FINANCIAL GOALS

GOAL	COST	DATE BEGUN	ACHIEVEMENT DATE

INVESTING YOUR MONEY

Most people have a hierarchy of financial needs. For example, the basics such as food, shelter, and clothing must be paid for first. If there is money left over, these basics might be upgraded; the family might move to a nicer apartment or buy a better quality of clothing. Perhaps the family would splurge and take a vacation. If there is any additional money, the family might think in terms of fairly safe investments—buying a home or insurance. Once these investments have been made, a woman might think in terms of investments that involve more risk but offer a higher return on the money invested. Hopefully, there will be a time when you will be able to afford your basic needs and also be in a position of putting your money to work for you. Since your savings account at 5½ percent interest cannot keep up with inflation, it is wise to think in terms of investments that will.

To consider possible investments and ways of putting your money to work for you, answer the following questions.

1. Are you able to afford your basic needs?
2. Have you reached the point where you have money left over that could be invested?

The ideal investment program is a careful balance of low-risk investments, which produce a lower income, and more aggressive, high-risk holdings. The investment plan you have depends upon your financial status. A woman who can barely meet her basic needs will not have money to invest. One who does not have a savings account or life insurance would not want to take great risks with her money by speculating in the stock market. The pyramid* on page 156 dem-

* From the book *The Joy of Money.* Copyright © 1975 by Paula Nelson. Reprinted by permission of Stein and Day Publishers.

onstrates the comparative risks and opportunities associated with various forms of investment.

In which, if any, blocks of the financial triangle have you invested? In terms of your financial goals, which blocks of the triangle would you want to complete first?

Some people enjoy risk taking, others do not. Some are willing to risk their lives but not their money. Women have been stereotyped as being conservative in money matters, while men have been pictured as being greater financial risk takers. The decisions you make concerning investments will be determined in part by your risk-taking behavior. Where would you place yourself on the financial risk-taking scale?

FINANCIAL RISK-TAKING SCALE

CONSERVATIVE	MODERATE	ALL OR NOTHING
become nervous at the thought of taking risks, sleep with my money under a mattress in case the banks fail	*carefully study the possible risks involved, am willing to take some risks but only if I can afford to do so*	*love to take risks, particularly when I could win big money*

The following are opportunities for investment on a rising scale of risk. Which do you think you would like to investigate?

- Standard savings account: Low interest, very low risk
- Long-term (time deposit) or investment savings accounts: Pay a higher rate of interest but commit you to leaving your money on deposit for a certain period of time (usually from one to four years). If you have to withdraw your money before the term is up, you pay a heavy penalty.
- U.S. Savings Bonds: Low interest, high degree of security. To obtain normal interest rates you must hold them for five years. Can be purchased in small denominations, starting at $25 through your bank or company's payroll deduction plan.
- Treasury bills: Offer high degree of security. Sold in minimum lots of $10,000; interest often higher than savings accounts can offer. They mature in three, six, or twelve months and may be purchased for a nominal fee through banks or stockbrokerages, or without a fee directly from a Federal Reserve Bank.

- Treasury bonds: Sold in $1,000 minimum lots. The major risk is the possibility that you may have to sell the bonds before their maturity date, at which time they may be selling for less than you paid.
- Government agency bonds: Issued by governmental institutions such as the Federal Land Bank. They pay high interest rates but carry a higher risk as they are not direct government obligations.
- Certificates of deposit: IOUs issued by commercial banks. Certificates may be obtained for a variety of periods. Usually the longer the certificate is held, the higher the interest. Penalties may result from premature redemption. Amounts that must be deposited vary from bank to bank. Interest rates vary with the amount invested.
- Money market funds: Allow for more ready access to funds invested. Specific conditions for withdrawal and privileges vary according to the institution. Interest rates for money market funds are usually somewhat lower than for certificates of deposit.
- IRA and Keough plans: These plans allow a person to defer payment of income tax until later years when income may be reduced, resulting in a lower tax bracket.
- 401 K plans: Many companies have plans which employees may elect to participate in, allowing them to deduct percentages of their income for the purpose of savings and tax deferment.
- Bonds

—corporate bonds: issued by business firms
—municipal bonds: issued by local and state governments
—U.S. Government bonds: issued by federal government and are direct obligations of the U.S. Treasury

FINANCIAL PLANNING PYRAMID

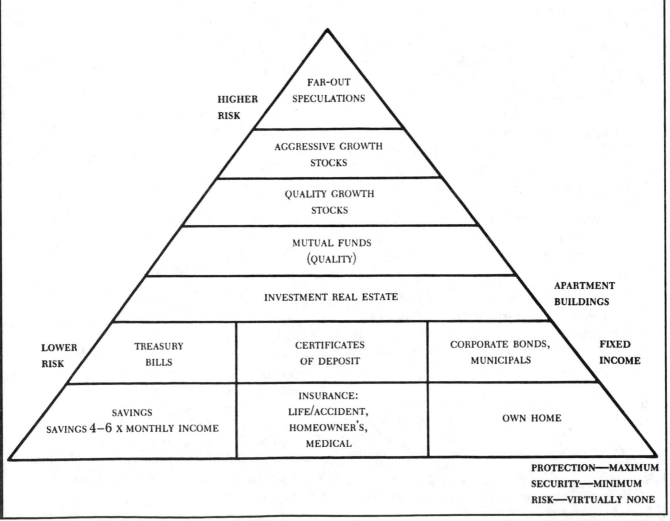

156

Bonds are issued to raise money for certain purposes. A bondholder is a creditor of the company whose investment is usually secured by a specific asset. While bonds tend to be secure investments, their after-tax investment value may not keep pace with inflation. There is no federal tax on municipal bonds nor is state income tax payable on bonds issued in the state where you reside.

- Real estate: Many people do not consider the fact that owning one's own home is an investment. No more than one-fourth of your annual income should be spent on property; this includes monthly payments, taxes, insurance, and upkeep. In looking for a home or for real estate for investment purposes, set yourself an absolute dollar limit. Consider the importance of location and look only at property you can afford.
- Mutual funds: A professionally managed portfolio of many different stocks and/or bonds. This tends to be a safe type of investment since risks are spread over a wide range of companies and industries. A downturn in one industry will not greatly harm the owner of mutual fund shares. The advantage of mutual funds is that professionals handle your money for you; the disadvantage is that there is a loading charge, generally 8 percent of the investment. Large, successful funds have difficulty in buying and selling large blocks of stocks without affecting the market price unfavorably. Having professionals manage your money is no guarantee that you will be shielded from the ups and downs of the market. If you are interested in the stock market and have the time and interest to become informed, you may be able to do better financially by investing on your own. While many people—particularly small investors—invested in mutual funds in the 1960s, the sharp decline in the market in the 1970s resulted in some disillusionment with this particular type of investment.
- Stocks: risk can vary with the type of stock bought.

  —quality growth or blue chip stocks: Have good earnings performance in bad times as well as in good, a long history of cash dividend payments, recognition as an estab-lished industry, and a clear prospect for continued earnings growth.
  —growth stocks: Stocks that have gone up in price and will probably continue to do so. The stock may belong to a company that dominates its market, is a leader in a fast-growing field, or is developing new concepts in an established field.
  —far-out speculations: Stock on which you're likely to make a profit as a result of a new or impending specific and unusual development within the company or in the outside environment affecting the company. The danger is that you may not be able to analyze the new development or be reasonably sure of all its ramifications. If you are unable to do these two things, the investment is speculative. Expected environmental changes often fail to produce the expected outcome.

A new trend in investing is developing; this consists of paying a professional management company to make decisions concerning your investments. Such firms charge an annual fee based on a small percentage of your portfolio's overall total value each year. Therefore, it is to the firm's advantage to invest your money wisely.

Many people hire financial planners who are paid by commission, fee, or a combination of the two. A financial planner usually represents a range of financial products and will help you select those that suit your needs. For advice on how to select a financial planner, consult Venita Van Caspel's *Money Dynamics for the 1990s* (New York: Simon and Schuster, 1988).

What is your "investment temperament"? Will a slight decline in the stock market upset you? Do you want to take the time to become informed about the stock market? Can you refrain from acting on the basis of tips or rumors no matter how intriguing they are?

What is your overall investment plan? Do you have funds allotted to different types of investments such as real estate, stocks, bonds, life insurance, and savings accounts?

How much money can you afford to lose if you decide to speculate or take high risks in your investments?

If you decide to invest in the stock market you will have to select a stockbroker who is right for you. One way of doing this is to call three or four brokerage firms in your area and talk to the managers about your investment goals and the amount of money you can invest. Ask the firm for its recommendations of investments and for research reports on the companies suggested. After comparing forms, you can ask the firm you select to assign a broker who will be right for you. The following questions will serve as a checklist in selecting a stockbroker. Note those that can be answered "yes."

1. Do the stockbroker's financial philosophy and objectives agree with yours?
2. Will the stockbroker take an interest in your investments, no matter how large or small?
3. Will the stockbroker take the time to answer questions and educate you concerning the stock market?
4. Is the stockbroker with a firm that is a member of the New York Stock Exchange?
5. Was the stockbroker recommended by friends, business acquaintances, your banker, or a person whose judgment you trust?
6. Do you feel comfortable discussing your financial situation honestly with the broker?
7. Was the broker recommended by the manager of a firm that you compared with at least two other firms?
8. Is the broker a member of a large firm with many local branch offices geared to the smaller investor?
9. Does the broker give you factual information in a concise manner?
10. Is the broker willing to let you make your own decisions?
11. Has the broker had a number of years of experience?
12. Has the broker had experience in both rising and falling markets?
13. Is the broker willing to give you names of clients he or she has served?

The more questions you can answer "yes," the better.

Collecting information is a vital part of making decisions concerning investments. The following sources of information can be consulted for specific details:

- *The Wall Street Journal*
- *The New York Times* financial pages
- Publications such as *Barrons, Forbes, Business Week*
- Guides that rate investments such as *Moody's, Standard and Poor*
- A firm's annual report
- The 10K report companies are required to submit to the Securities and Exchange Commission; available from the SEC
- Annual stockholders' meetings
- Public relations departments of companies
- Professional investment management firms
- Investment clubs
- Stockbrokers
- Adult education courses on investing

Before you consult professionals in the financial field, know your investment objectives. How would you answer the following questions: What are your investment objectives? Long-term growth? Current income? Maximum security?

Beware of brokers who plug one stock and refuse to sell you anything else, promise a quick and sure profit, claim to have "tips" and "inside information," try to pressure you into quick action, or are unwilling to provide references.

Remember, even though you may not be presently interested, do not dismiss this investment possibility simply because you feel Wall Street is a man's territory. More women are beginning to learn about, invest in, and earn money from the stock market. If you have felt intimidated by the stock market, you owe it to yourself to understand how it operates even though you may never own a single share of stock. The more you know about investment alternatives, the more competent you will feel about managing your money.

ELEVEN

DECISIONS CONCERNING CAREERS

The final step for me in becoming a fully functioning, independent person who felt good about herself, was to get a job with career potential and to be able to support myself.

It took me awhile to admit that I wanted to have a job that involved leadership, gave me power, and paid an excellent salary. These goals were never considered "suitable" for girls to have. Now that I know what I want, I go after it without apologizing.

When I explained my financial needs and told my boss I wanted to be paid the same salary as the former office manager who was a man, he looked at me and told me I should get married again. I then knew that I had no career future with that organization and started looking for another job.

An important decision for the divorced woman to make is what she wants to do in terms of a job or a career. Most divorced women find that it becomes necessary for them to earn an income. No matter how much money you have, no matter how good your divorce settlement is, it is wise to think in terms of how you can support yourself.

Women are often dismayed to learn that there is no guaranteed income other than the income they can earn for themselves. Little boys were brought up knowing that they will have to earn a living. Unfortunately, many little girls were brought up to believe that their job is to find a husband who will support them and that their lives will consist of being a wife and mother. No one warns them that husbands die or lose their jobs, and that people get divorced. Nor that they will have approximately twenty productive years after their children are grown, or that they may want to have their own career goals in addition to being a wife and mother. If married women do work, it is often for spending money, to supplement their husband's income, or to buy extras for the family. Women usually have jobs rather than careers. They work at a job to bring in money rather than at a career that brings money and personal development. There is almost an unwritten rule that it is all right for a married woman to work for extra money—but not too much extra money—but not all right to become involved and to derive fulfillment from a career. The latter could interfere with the role of wife and mother.

One reason divorce is so traumatic for many women is that they are suddenly faced with the responsibility of supporting themselves when they are totally unprepared to do so. Being able to support yourself and having a job you enjoy is a vital part of being an independent woman who is in charge of her own life. Every woman should be able to support herself, whether or not she chooses to do so. Even if you don't plan to work for the next few years, it would still be wise to go through the process of considering careers.

There are things you can do at home or on a part-time basis that can give you a head start if the time ever comes when you must work. For example, if you think you might be interested in the field of medicine, you could read books about medicine, take a biology course, or work as a volunteer at a local hospital for several hours each week.

In order to make career decisions it is necessary to gather information, information about yourself as well as prospective careers. This chapter will help you get started but it can only scratch the surface when it comes to helping you make career decisions. Continue your investigation by consulting books on careers; those listed in the bibliography might be a start. Also investigate courses concerning career decisions—offered through junior colleges, adult education courses, YWCAs, women's groups—and career counseling services in your area.

WHAT'S YOUR CAREER MOTIVATION?

Which of the following statements is true for you? There are no right or wrong answers.

1. I don't really care much what kind of work I do.
2. I'd never be able to get a job I'd like so I don't want to bother looking for one.
3. I don't think it is worth the trouble to really think about careers.
4. I want a job that requires a minimum of work and effort.
5. I'm just working until I find a man.
6. If I don't like a job I can always quit.
7. I don't want to invest my time and/or money in education and job training.
8. I just want to earn enough to cover my living expenses.
9. I am not interested in career advancement and achievement.
10. I don't plan on getting my personal needs and goals met through my job.

Evaluate your career motivation by choosing the appropriate point on the scale below.

DON'T WANT TO DEVOTE MUCH TIME AND ENERGY	WANT TO DEVOTE SOME TIME AND ENERGY	WANT TO DEVOTE ALL MY TIME AND ENERGY

If five or more of these statements applied to you and if you placed yourself on the left end of the motivation scale, this chapter may not interest you. There are some people who are passive, rather than active, when it comes to making career decisions. They may select a job by sheer chance, according to what is offered them at a particular time. It may not occur to them that they have any control over what they decide to do for a living. Some people do not see work as a means of fulfillment, nor are they work motivated. If you choose to take a passive, rather than an active stance when it comes to choosing a career, recognize this as a decision you have made.

Some people who would like to have a fulfilling job, earn a good living, and have opportunities for advancement just feel discouraged, overwhelmed, and lost when it comes to starting. If you are one of these people, you will probably find this chapter helpful. Finding a satisfying, financially rewarding job is not easy, particularly for the divorced woman who is untrained and who has been out of the job market for some time. It is possible, however, to find a career that is right for you. Your chances of finding the job for you depend upon your knowledge of yourself, career opportunities, and job-hunting skills. The activities that follow will help you develop the knowledge you need for making the right career decision.

HOW DO YOU DEFINE SUCCESS?

People usually feel good about themselves when they are able to do things that are consistent with their values, interests, and skills. Too often, the jobs people have do not meet their needs or make them feel good about themselves. These people may put in an eight-hour day and do the things that make them feel successful when they get home. Or, they may find that they are too tired after a dull and unfulfilling eight-hour workday to do anything.

It is particularly necessary for the divorced woman who works to have a job that is energy-producing rather than energy-draining. No one is waiting for her after a hard day's work with dinner warming in the oven and a sympathetic ear. Usually she returns to children who have their special needs. The divorced woman who has the responsibility for a family and works is bound to be tired. There is a difference, however, between being tired after working hard at a job you hate and being tired after working hard at a job you enjoy. The ideal solution is to know what makes you feel good about yourself and then do it for a living!

To examine what makes you feel good, positive, and successful about yourself, divide your life into three major time periods beginning with age five. For example, if you are 30, the time periods would be 5–12, 13–22, and 23–30; if you are 45, they would be 5–18, 19–31, and 32–45. Just subtract 5 from your age and divide by three to get the approximate number of years to include in each period. You don't have to be exact. On the left-hand side of a sheet of paper, list three major successes for each time period; on the right-hand side, list the reason or reasons why each was a success or an achievement for you. Try to be as detailed as possible. You can list any success that made you feel good, useful, important, or special. The items you list need not be considered successes by others—just by you. If you can't remember one period in your life, skip on to the next period and return to the one you passed over at a later time.

Look at your list. What do you think was your most successful experience? Which of the successes do you consider least successful? What key words appear with your most fulfilling success? Are any themes or patterns expressed in your list?

Now look at the following success patterns.* Which are important to you according to the list you drew up?

INTELLECTUAL
—need to learn
—need for academic degree
—need to communicate through writing and speaking
—need to excel
—need to use special talents and skills

EMOTIONAL
—need for approval from peers
—need for recognition: awards, promotions, raises, fame
—need for pleasure
—need for independence
—need for emotional growth-awareness

SOCIAL
—need to be with people
—need to nurture, help others grow
—need for acceptance and popularity
—need for intimacy and closeness
—need to travel

POWER
—need to compete and win
—need to be in charge
—need to influence others
—need to overcome difficult obstacles
—need to do things on my own
—need to organize

RELIGIOUS
—need to be in harmony with God
—need to work for a religious organization

AESTHETIC
—need for beauty
—need to create
—need for nature

PHYSICAL
—need to have a beautiful body
—need to master a sport

ECONOMIC
—need for material things: status, money, nice clothes, luxurious home, expensive car
—need to sell things for a profit

ATTITUDINAL
—need to be special
—need for security and stable relationships
—need for new experiences

Think about the patterns your choices reveal. Write your definition of success by including the patterns and the descriptions that your choices indicated were important to you.

What are your major area(s) of success? Consider your definition of success. Is it consistent with the values you indicated as important to you when you completed the activity on page 40?

Do you spend time doing things that make you feel successful? Have your past jobs enabled you to achieve your definition of success? What careers come to mind that might enable you to achieve your definition of success?

WHAT ARE YOUR INTERESTS?

Which things listed* below interest you most?

—help others directly
—deal with ideas

---

* Success chart and patterns taken from Lila Swell, *Success: You Can Make It Happen*, copyright © 1976. Reprinted by permission of Simon & Schuster, a division of Gulf & Western Corporation.

* Listed items from James I. Briggs, Career Development Seminar, Director of Career Planning and Placement, Georgetown University, Washington, D.C., July 14, 1976.

—use and work with mathematics
—be free to come and go as I please
—think creatively
—compete with others
—read and study
—get outdoors often
—use physical strength
—travel
—manage and handle money
—work by myself
—feel I'm serving society
—see the results of my efforts
—work at a fast pace
—face challenge
—deal with things: tools or equipment
—make my own decisions
—feel secure
—be in control of a situation
—plan events and activities
—work with children
—work with animals
—keep accurate and complete records
—use my artistic ability
—listen carefully
—organize programs and people
—motivate others
—teach
—make policy decisions
—hold responsibility
—write
—participate in sports
—meet the public
—create
—work precisely
—sell
—other

List your five favorite interests in order of their importance to you; you may wish to refer to your responses to the activity on page 40. Which interests would you like to use in a career? Can you think of a career where you could use these interests?

WHAT ARE YOUR SKILLS?

What is your definition of *career*? A career can be thought of in several different ways. First, one can think of it in terms of an organization in which one advances by climbing the organizational ladder. This concept of career was very prevalent in the past, when people spent most of their working lives in the employ of one organi-

zation. Second, a career can be thought of in terms of a profession or a field such as being a doctor or working in the field of medicine. Third, it can be thought of in terms of skills that can be taken from one organization to another, from one profession to another, or from one field to another. Because current career trends indicate that people will have several careers during their working years and that midlife career changes will occur more frequently in the future, you may find it helpful to consider your career in terms of the skills you have and enjoy using.

The woman who is in the process of divorce may have little confidence in her skills and abilities. She may have had little emotional support from her spouse and believe that she is stupid, incompetent, and unable to do anything correctly. If you have been a homemaker, you may think you have no marketable skills or abilities. Women are often taught to downplay their abilities and intelligence. Many women find themselves playing this game and losing in the long run. The danger is that if the game is played too long, a woman may forget that it is a game. She may believe that she has few skills and that she must depend on her husband's skills for financial support.

Faced with divorce, women must often reassess the skills they have. If this task seems frightening or hopeless, reassure yourself that you do have skills and abilities. Even if you haven't worked for a paycheck in a job outside your home, you have done things within your home, in your community, or with your children, that demonstrate your skills and abilities. Give yourself credit for the things you can do. You may want to review chapters 1 and 2, which encourage you to seek support from others and to be supportive of yourself.

To examine your skills you must think positively, have the help of several supportive friends, and take time to complete the task.

First, list your educational experiences. Don't forget to list nondegree courses or training you have had. List all special honors, offices, activities, or organizations in which you participated.

Second, list all your interests. You may want to refer to pages 161–162 where you were asked to list your interests.

Third, list your life achievements. Refer to page 161, on which you were asked to list major successes. List *all* your achievements, not just those others might consider important.

SAMPLE CHART

EXPERIENCES	SKILLS/ABILITIES/TRAITS
1. EDUCATION	
2. INTERESTS	
3. LIFE ACHIEVEMENTS	
4. ROLES	
5. SIGNIFICANT LIFE EXPERIENCES	

SAMPLE ENTRY

EXPERIENCES		SKILLS/ABILITIES/TRAITS
3. LIFE ACHIEVE-MENTS	Sewing a dress	Sewing (hand and machine) Measuring Estimating Comparing (shopping) Coordinating Patience Sense of humor Working well under pressure Color sense Fashion awareness Fitting Manual dexterity

Fourth, list the roles you play or have played (mother, friend, community leader, Girl Scout leader, saleswoman, secretary).

Fifth, list any significant life experiences you have had that are not included in the first four categories (travel, coping with a crisis, adventures, work experiences).

Try to list as many experiences as you can in each category. Don't minimize or undervalue your experiences. If something comes to mind, it is worth listing.

If possible, sit down with several friends. Look at the things you have listed in your categories and, as *quickly as possible*, list any skill, ability or character trait you used or developed during each experience. Don't stop to question whether or not you really have a particular skill or are using it presently. The purpose of this activity is to brainstorm—to list all the skills, abilities, and traits you have that may have made the experience possible.

NOTE: If you find you can list only a few skills, abilities, and traits for each experience, you may be overlooking the skills involved or may be taking them for granted. Try writing or describing the experience as if you were explaining it to a five-year-old child. Then look at the experience again to determine the skills, abilities, and traits involved.

The following are examples* of skills you may have used in your experiences. They are functional skills that may be used in a variety of contexts. You may have used some skills more than once. Make a list of the skills you have used.

The purpose of the list presented here is to provide examples; don't let it limit you. There are literally hundreds of skills. If you have used skills not on this list, add them to your personal skill list.

ADMINISTER-ING	a group of people, programs, a specific activity
ADVISING	giving financial advice, counseling in an educational setting
ANALYZING	social situations, quantitative data, statistical data
ANTICIPATING	recognizing early signs of a specific problem that may be developing, being able to sense what will be popular in consumer goods
APPRAISING	evaluating programs or services, judging the value of property, evaluating the performance of individuals
ASSEMBLING	technical equipment, information items to form a coherent overview
BUDGETING	using money efficiently and economically, outlining costs of a proposed project
CALCULATING	performing mathematical computations, assessing the risks of a proposed project
CLASSIFYING	sorting information into categories
COACHING	guiding activities of an athletic team, tutoring on a one-to-one basis

* This list was adapted from James I. Briggs, Career Development Seminar, Director of Career Planning and Placement, Georgetown University, Washington, D.C., July 14, 1976.

COMPILING	*gathering financial data, accumulating facts on a given topic*
CONSTRUCTING	*building physical objects such as furniture, assembling mechanical apparatus, working from a pattern*
COORDINATING	*events involving groups of people, activities in various locations*
CORRESPONDING	*answering inquiries, communicating clearly, asking for information*
CREATING	*new ways of solving problems, visual presentations, inventing new apparatus*
DEALING WITH PRESSURE	*working with a deadline to finish a particular project, handling complaints*
DECIDING	*making decisions about use of money, comparing alternatives and choosing from among them*
DELEGATING	*having others complete specific tasks, giving responsibility to others*
DESIGNING	*physical interiors of rooms, plans involving processing of information, a new process for completing a task*
DISPLAYING	*items in a pleasing manner, ideas in an easily understood manner*
EVALUATING	*assessing a proposed program to determine its probable success, judging the performance of a specific individual*
EXPLAINING	*clarifying vague concepts or ideas for others, justifying your actions to others*
GROUP FACILITATING	*managing the positive interaction of members in a group*
INTERPRETING	*other languages, meaning of technical material*
INVESTIGATING	*looking for the underlying causes of a problem, seeking information not readily available to the public*
KEEPING RECORDS	*setting up and maintaining a filing system, keeping an account book, keeping a work or travel log*
LISTENING	*to a speaker to obtain information, to recording devices in a monotonous listening situation, to a person who has a problem*
MEDIATING	*acting as a liaison between competing interests, trying to make peace between conflicting parties*
MOTIVATING	*helping others to overcome inertia, helping others to achieve peak physical performance*
NEGOTIATING	*working to set up a financial contract, dealing with someone to settle a complaint*
OBSERVING	*physical phenomena with accuracy, social change, details that make up a larger whole, human beings*

OBTAINING INFORMATION	*from documents or other written sources, from an organization, from unwilling individuals*
ORGANIZING	*gathering information and presenting it in a clear, interpretable manner, bringing people together for certain tasks*
PERSUADING	*influencing others so that they see your point of view, influencing others so that they are willing to help you complete specific tasks*
PLANNING	*anticipating future needs, scheduling a sequence of events, setting up an itinerary or agenda*
PROGRAMMING	*writing a computer program, using a calculator to work up a monthly budget, planning an organized activity for a specific purpose*
READING	*to obtain information, a foreign language, proofreading*
RESEARCHING	*extracting information from written sources, obtaining information from people*
SELLING	*products to individuals, ideas through effective use of various media*
SPEAKING	*addressing a group in order to inform about a specific issue, using recording devices easily and effectively*
SUPERVISING	*overseeing the work of others, being responsible for the physical maintenance of a building*
TEACHING	*helping others learn in a classroom situation, could include tutoring individuals in specific subjects*
TROUBLESHOOTING	*identifying sources of trouble in personal relationships, detecting problem areas in proposed projects*
WRITING	*reporting an incident or event clearly and concisely, using language to persuade, creating a story or script*

For examples of character traits, you may want to review the list on pages 37 and 38.

Now look at your list of skills, abilities, and traits. Did you list some more than once? Put an asterisk (*) by those mentioned more than once. Which skills can be combined in major categories? For example, writing, speaking, and reading can be considered communication skills; budgeting, calculating, and planning can be considered financial skills.

Can you see any patterns in your list? Some skills used in experiences before your marriage may not have been used since that time. This does not mean you no longer have these skills.

Did you have more skills and abilities in one area and fewer in others?

Circle words in your list that represent traits (e.g., courage, patience, a sense of humor). Although you will not refer to traits directly in a résumé when you mention achievements and responsibilities, it is always good to know your major traits and personality characteristics. Most employers want to know if potential employees are responsible, flexible, polite, and so on, and will try to obtain such information from a job interview.

Now take a colored pencil and underline the skills, abilities, and traits you *enjoy* using. You may list many skills, abilities, and traits, but you will want to focus on some and not others.

Look at your list again. Can you list five skills that you want to use and develop in a career? Can you give at least one experience during which you use each skill?

Can you list five traits that you have that would be beneficial to an employer? Can you think of at least one example that shows you have each trait?

It is not enough to say that you have certain skills, abilities, and traits. It is important for you to *own* them. This happens when you can claim them as yours, experience pride in them, feel comfortable in telling others about them, and realize that they are a delightful part of your uniqueness.

If you have trouble believing in yourself and what you have to offer, practice completing the following lines; say them in front of a mirror:

Five skills and abilities I'm proud of are . . .

Three achievements I feel good about are . . .

Special traits which make me valuable to an employer are . . .

I have a lot to offer!

When you can complete these sentences and say them comfortably in front of a mirror, say them to a friend. Choose someone who is supportive and will realize the importance of what you are doing. Your tendency may be to laugh due to nervousness, insecurity, or inhibitions. Practice until you can sound confident. It is important to take yourself seriously.

Preferred skills, abilities, and traits can give you a sense of direction and a place to start. They will help you consider careers that would enable you to use your unique combination of talents. Knowing your skills and being able to provide examples of when you have used them will give you a head start for writing a résumé and being prepared for a job interview.

SALARY AND RESPONSIBILITY

When considering career possibilities, it helps to determine how much money you want and expect to earn and the level of responsibility you want. Usually, the more responsibility you have, the larger your paycheck. There is also the possibility of special achievements in your career field. Usually, the more significant the achievement, the greater your paycheck. For example, if you had writing skills and decided to be a reporter for a small-town paper, your earnings would be modest. Then, were you to decide to take a year off to write a novel, your earnings could diminish to nothing if you were unable to get it published or they could run into the thousands if it were published and became a bestseller. As an editorial trainee, your earnings would be modest; if you accepted increased responsibility and worked your way up to senior editor or president of your own publishing company, your salary would be much greater.

How would you answer the following questions dealing with the salary you would like to earn?

1. Indicate how important money is to you by noting the appropriate point on the scale below.

| NOT VERY | SOMEWHAT | VERY |
| IMPORTANT | IMPORTANT | IMPORTANT |

2. Describe what money means to you. Why is it important?
3. Money can provide the following things—which are important to you?

—*luxuries*   —*services that save time*
—*security*   —*career options*
—*living essentials* —*chance to help others*
—*status*   —*education*
—*options*

4. How much money would you like to earn annually right now? Would you be willing to do what was needed in order to earn that amount in terms of time, responsibility, and emotional energy?

5. How much money would you like to earn annually in five years? Would you be willing to do what was needed to earn that amount in terms of work, time, responsibility, and emotional energy?

6. How much money do you think you are worth annually right now? Take into consideration your special skills and abilities.

7. How much money do you think you will be worth annually in five years? Consider the possibility of skill development, increased responsibilities, and special achievements.

8. What is the minimum salary for which you would be willing to work at the present time?

9. What is more important to you, money earned or feeling happy and successful in your work?

10. How did you feel when you were answering these questions?

Now answer the following questions dealing with the amount of responsibility you would like to have in your job.

1. Where would you place yourself on the scale below in terms of the amount of responsibility you would like to have?

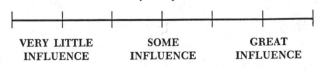

VERY LITTLE RESPONSIBILITY   SOME RESPONSIBILITY   TOTAL RESPONSIBILITY

2. How much influence would you like to have on others in your job?

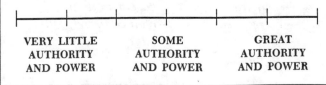

VERY LITTLE INFLUENCE   SOME INFLUENCE   GREAT INFLUENCE

3. How much authority or power would you like to have?

VERY LITTLE AUTHORITY AND POWER   SOME AUTHORITY AND POWER   GREAT AUTHORITY AND POWER

4. Consider the advantages and disadvantages that come with responsibility, influence, authority, and power. Honestly describe their importance to you and the part you want these factors to play in a career.

5. Make a list of any achievements you feel would be important for you in a career. Be as specific as possible.

ARE YOU A MANAGER?

Women are often socialized to be helpers but seldom "bosses" or "managers." A man who aspires to be boss is described as ambitious and on the way up; a woman with the same aspiration is often described as pushy and unfeminine. Therefore, when it comes to career considerations, women often do not consider their managerial aptitude or their desire to use the management skills they may have.

Read each of the questions* below. Which statement following each question do you feel describes you best?

1. Are you a self-starter?

   a. I do things on my own. Nobody has to tell me to get going.
   b. If someone gets me started, I keep going.
   c. I don't put myself out until I have to.

2. How do you feel about other people?

   a. I like people. I can get along with just about everybody.
   b. I can take people or leave them.
   c. Most people bug me.

3. Can you lead others?

   a. I can get most people to go along when I start something.
   b. I can give the orders if someone else tells me what we should do.
   c. I let someone else get things moving. Then I go along if I feel like it.

4. Can you take responsibility?

   a. I like to take charge of things and see them through.

* Questionnaire taken from Wilma C. Rogalin and Arthur R. Pell, *Women's Guide to Management Positions*, copyright © 1975 by Simon & Schuster, Inc. Reprinted by permission of Monarch Press, a Simon & Schuster division of Gulf & Western Corporation.

b. I'll take over if I have to, but I'd rather let someone else be responsible.

c. I prefer to have someone else take the responsibility.

5. How good an organizer are you?

   a. I like to make plans and see them through.

   b. I do all right until things get too confused. Then I give up.

   c. I just take things as they come.

6. How good a worker are you?

   a. I can keep going as long as I have to. I don't mind working hard for something I want.

   b. I'll work hard for a while but when I've had enough, that's it!

   c. I can't see that hard work gets you anywhere.

7. Can you make decisions?

   a. I can make up my mind in a hurry if I have to. It usually turns out okay, too.

   b. I can if I have plenty of time. If I have to make up my mind quickly, I later think I should have decided on the other way.

   c. I don't like to be the one who has to decide things.

8. Can people trust what you say?

   a. You bet they can. I don't say things I don't mean.

   b. I try to be on the level most of the time, but sometimes I say what's easiest.

   c. What does it matter if the other person doesn't know the difference?

9. Can you stick with it?

   a. If I make up my mind to do something, I don't let anything stop me.

   b. I usually finish what I start—if it doesn't get fouled up.

   c. I give up easily when something is difficult or challenging.

10. How good is your health?

    a. I am usually full of energy and vitality.

    b. I have enough energy for most things I want to do.

    c. I run out of energy sooner than do most of my friends.

11. Are you professionally competent?

    a. I know my job and am confident in my work.

    b. I know what I have to know.

    c. I have a basic knowledge of the work.

12. Do you keep up with developments in your field?

    a. I have taken seminars or courses.

    b. I read trade and professional journals.

    c. I just do my job.

13. Are you willing to sacrifice personal activities for your career?

    a. I get my greatest satisfaction from my career.

    b. I balance my career with my other activities.

    c. I love my job, but family and/or social life mean more to me.

14. Are you sensitive about being a woman in a business situation?

    a. In dealing with male business colleagues, I rarely think of my sex.

    b. In dealing with male business colleagues, I try to forget I'm a woman.

    c. In dealing with male business colleagues, I always remember I'm a woman.

15. Can you communicate ideas well?

    a. I communicate easily in writing and speech.

    b. I express myself better in writing than orally (or vice versa).

    c. I have difficulty in communicating my ideas to others.

SCORING: Count 3 points for each *a.* statement you chose, 2 points for each *b.* statement, and 1 point for each *c.* statement. A score of 40 or better indicates excellent managerial potential; 35–40 indicates good managerial potential; below 35, you need to develop your managerial skills before you are ready for a management position.

WHAT KIND OF WORK ENVIRONMENT SUITS YOU?

An important aspect of a career decision is deciding what kind of work environment you would like—the kinds of people you want to work with, the working conditions you would like to have, and where you would like to work geographically.

The first series of questions that follows concerns the work environment made up of people. On the left-hand side of a sheet of paper, write the kinds of people with whom you would *not* like to work. Think of past work experiences or of people you know you would not want as coworkers. Then list the kinds of people you would want to work with on the right-hand side. Compare the two lists. Are the kinds of people you don't want the opposite of those you would want?

Answer the following questions.

1. Would you rather work with groups? Individuals? A combination?
2. With what age group would you like to work?
3. What do you want to do for or with your coworkers?
4. Think about the amount of involvement you want to have with people in a work situation. Choose the appropriate point on the scale below.

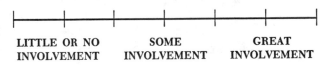

| LITTLE OR NO INVOLVEMENT | SOME INVOLVEMENT | GREAT INVOLVEMENT |

5. List the five most important qualities you would like your coworkers to have.

The next series of questions concerns the working conditions you would like. As before, write out those conditions you would *not* want to have and those you would like to have. Compare the two. Answer the following questions.

1. How much supervision do you want?
2. How much opportunity do you want to work on your own?
3. What kinds of opportunities do you want for advancement?
4. What kind of hours do you want to work? Do you want to punch a time clock? Do you want flexibility? How much vacation do you want?
5. How important is job security?
6. How important are physical surroundings? Do you want to work indoors or outdoors? Do you want your own office? Do you want attractive surroundings?
7. Do you want to travel on your job? How frequently?
8. What kind of benefits do you want?
9. What do you want in terms of professional or occupational development? Do you want on-the-job training? Do you want the company to pay for part of your educational expenses?
10. Summarize the most important things you want in terms of working conditions. List at least five.

The third series of questions concerns where you want to work geographically. How would you answer these questions?

1. Do you know the specific geographic location where you would like to work?
2. Would you be willing to relocate?
3. To what areas would you be willing to relocate? Do you want to work in or near a city? In the suburbs? In the country? Do you want a change of seasons? Do you want to live on the East Coast? The West Coast? In the Midwest? In another country?
4. How far away from your place of work do you want to live?
5. Do you want to be able to use public transportation?
6. Summarize your preferences by listing the geographic location where you want to work. If there are several locations, rank order them from most preferred to least preferred.

Summarize the information you have gathered about yourself so you can use it to make career decisions. To start, list the things you feel you must have and those you could give up in terms of a career. Seldom do people find everything they are looking for in a job. Is there any way you could plan your life so that you could meet some of your needs in your nonworking hours? For example, you may not be able to utilize your interest in music in a career, but you could join a chorus in nonworking hours.

Look at your list again. What careers come to mind that would enable you to have the things that are most important to you?

EXPLORING CAREERS

When it comes to making career decisions, people often fail to do a thorough job of gathering needed information. There may be a career that would be just right for you but if you are unaware that such a career exists, it isn't an option for you. The necessary process, once you have gathered information about yourself, is to generate career alternatives that would meet some of the needs you listed on your summary sheet. Remember, the word *career* is being used in a broad sense—the opportunity to use the skills you want to use and to meet as many of your needs as possible as regards your values, interests, and desired work environments.

The first step is to decide what career possibilities are of interest to you. You are not yet in the final stages of selecting a career, you are simply generating careers about which you would like to learn more. At this stage, do not limit yourself by thinking only of those jobs that have traditionally been associated with women. Certain jobs are typed as female jobs—usually the low-paying, repetitive ones. Other jobs are typed as male jobs—usually those that pay more and allow for some creativity. You may want to explore nontraditional jobs for women such as electrician, plumber, auto mechanic, construction worker, or truck driver.

There are several ways to generate a list of careers that you would like to explore further.

1. Look at your responses to the activities on page 168 that asked you what, if any, careers came to mind.
2. List careers you have thought about when planning for your future.
3. List careers you may have daydreamed about as a child.
4. Think of friends or people you have read about who have careers that interest you.
5. Think of people who have been important to you and their careers.
6. Leaf through books on careers available at your local library. *The Occupational Outlook Handbook* and *The Dictionary of Occupational Titles* would be good books for this purpose.
7. Read the want ads in the Sunday paper.

Now make a list of careers that interest you. List the reason(s) why each career interests you; the reason should be consistent with the things you have learned about yourself through completing earlier activities.

The easiest way to gather information concerning a given career is to ask questions of someone who is in that career. Find someone who has a career that interests you; you might ask friends if they know people, consult the yellow pages, call the chamber of commerce, call professional organizations, look at alumni lists, and so on. Try to find a person in a career that meets the qualifications you desire. For example, if you are interested in learning more about sales careers, which sales careers would be most consistent with the data you listed on your summary sheet? Ask the person the following questions:

1. How did you get into this work?
2. What do you like about it?
3. What do you dislike about it?
4. Where else could I find people who earn a living in this way?

Other questions will probably come to mind when you are talking to the person; you might be interested in the training or education required, books or articles that would tell you more about the career, special skills the job requires, the professional organizations that exist for people in that career field, possible job openings in the next few years, and so on. As you go through this process, you will probably discard some careers as interesting but "not for me." Sometimes you will be able to discard a career area immediately and sometimes it may take talking to several people before you decide it is not for you.

Most people are very willing to talk to others about what they do. If you feel shy or reluctant about asking individuals for a few minutes of their time, you may want to start by conducting a practice interview where you talk to someone who has a hobby or interest you would like to learn more about. When you begin interviewing individuals concerning careers and/or organizations, be sure to keep a file of the interviews. Record with whom you talked, with what organization they were associated, and what you learned. It is also a good idea to write the individual a thank-you note. Even if you don't think the individual would ever be connected to your finding a job, you never know what friends or contacts this person might have. It pays to leave a good impression.

You may also want to read about a given career; contact a professional organization for more information; take a course related to a career; or try a hobby, a part-time job, or a volunteer job that would be similar to the career you are considering.

IS FURTHER EDUCATION FOR YOU?

In gathering information you may have found that you need to expand the skills you already have or gain certain credentials in order to realistically consider using your skills in a certain way.

EXAMPLE
Jane was interested in helping people rehabilitate themselves physically after they had a serious accident or injury. She wanted to have responsibility and to earn at least $35,000 a year. After investigating the physical therapy field and talking to physical therapists, she learned that to become a physical therapist she would need a college degree and a two-year program in physical therapy. The decision Jane was then faced with was whether or not she wanted to get the additional training required to qualify her for this profession.

In investigating career possibilities, many women find themselves faced with the question of further education. Some women decide to go back to school or get additional training. However, this isn't for everyone. Some people know they are not at all interested in investing the time and money required to get further education, even if it would mean a better job eventually. They are willing to put up with career limitations because they hate school. Some women definitely know they want to return to school, regardless of their career goals or the investment involved; they simply want an education.

What do you want in terms of further education? Answering the following questions might help you decide.

1. What was the last year of school or level of education you completed?
2. What does education mean to you?
3. What would education or training do for you in terms of getting a job?
4. Would education or training make you feel better about yourself?
5. What careers or work situations interest you? What level of education or training is necessary for the degree of authority and responsibility you would like to have in these career areas?
6. What careers, jobs, or positions are open to you with the education you presently have?
7. What would further education cost you in terms of time and money? Consider money spent for books and child care as well as the money you could be earning if you weren't going to school.
8. What are the advantages and disadvantages of returning to school or getting additional training?
9. Do you really want to return to school or receive further training? If you do, how are you going to pay for it?

Perhaps the most important decision concerning continuing your education is, *How important is it to you?* If it isn't that important, or if you really don't think it will put you in a better position in terms of a career, you might decide that the sacrifices of time, money, and energy simply are not worth it. On the other hand, there are some women who feel that an education is so important they are willing to borrow money and live on welfare, if necessary, to get one. If you want education or training badly enough, there is usually some way to get it.

Remember, education does not have to mean sitting in a classroom all day. You may want to explore the following educational alternatives:

- Apprenticeship
- On-the-job training
- Military training
- Business trade, or technical schools
- Community, junior, or technical colleges
- Four-year colleges or universities
- Graduate or professional schools
- Adult-education courses
- Correspondence study
- Manpower training programs—federally funded programs to train unemployed and underemployed persons

If you decide that you want more education or training, you have to decide where to get it. Some factors to consider are:

- Quality and reputation of the school or program
- Whether or not the school or program is accredited, enabling you to get a degree or license
- Flexibility of the program in terms of your schedule and needs
- Location of school
- Cost, including availability of financial aid
- Entrance requirements

All of these factors should be weighed when you are considering schools. See the financial aid officer of the school to learn if you are eligible for a scholarship or financial aid. Also, be sure to investigate all possible sources of awards and scholarships—no one gets an award unless he or she applies for it. There are many scholarships available for varying amounts, some with rather unique requirements; go to your local library to consult books listing scholarships. You may just qualify for one and every penny counts! Two books that list scholarship information are *Need a Lift?* and *Financial Aids for Higher Education. Need a Lift?* is available from the American Legion (Dept. S, P.O. Box 1055, Indianapolis, IN 46206) for fifty cents a copy.

If you want to pursue an education, the most important quality you can have is persistence. Even if your grades from the last time you were in school are poor, you can probably present the excellent argument that you are now mature, know what you want, need further training for a career, and have some life experience behind you. Women who return to school have excellent records. Many colleges and universities have special programs designed to meet the needs of women who are entering college after careers as wives and mothers or who are returning to school after their education has been interrupted. These programs are called Continuing Education Programs. Some colleges will grant college credit for life experience if you are able to pass the College Level Examination Program (CLEP) tests. Other colleges have degree programs specifically designed to meet the needs of working adults and award credits for life experience through a special evaluation process. Be sure to investigate this possibility. Regardless of the training or education you seek, be sure to compare schools and programs, since they can vary greatly in cost, requirements, time, reputation, and flexibility.

WHERE DO YOU WANT TO WORK?

Once you have decided what kind of work you want to do and have the credentials, training, and/or education needed, you must decide where you want to work. In your interviews to get information, you probably found that you could employ your skills in a variety of settings. For example, if you wanted to be a journalist, you could write for a large city newspaper, a small-town newspaper, a company newspaper, or a travel magazine, to name a few. The possibilities are limited only by your imagination. In order to decide where you want to work, it is necessary to continue the same interviewing-for-information process that you conducted to learn more about certain careers.

Look at your summary chart for ideas. Can you think of organizations where you can satisfy as many of your desires as possible? Being self-employed or working in your home may be alternatives to consider. Then, contact a person who does what you want to do and ask questions concerning the organizations that you think are appropriate. For example, if you are interested in teaching piano in a junior college, you could contact a person who teaches piano or the head of the music department in a junior college and ask how long the college had offered courses in piano, how many courses were offered, what the goals of the courses were, how many students took the courses, and so on. Then you could ask about junior colleges in the area with similar programs and talk to representatives from their schools. You are still just gathering information at this point—you are not applying for a job. Different sources of information about organizations for which you think you might want to work include:

- Interviewing people who are associated with the organization in different ways: for example, if you want to teach piano in a junior college, you could talk to instructors in other departments, students, people in the community, and so on.
- Company literature: annual reports, brochures, newsletters, magazines
- Newspaper and magazine articles
- Local chambers of commerce directories

- College placement annual or other publications
- Local library

Questions* you may want to ask are:

1. What is the company's major purpose—manufacturing, service, administrative?
2. What products, if any, does it produce? For what markets?
3. Has the company made any significant gains or endured any reversals recently?
4. What is the organizational structure—linear, diversified, or conglomerate?
5. How does it fit into the broad economic structure?
6. Who are some of its major officers, board members, or stockholders?
7. How large is the organization? How many employees, subsidiaries, assets, or profits does it have?
8. What is the organization's major interest in personnel hiring?
9. How old is the organization?
10. What kind of company image does it have?

Among the publications† that provide information concerning organizations and that you may want to consult are:

- *Dun and Bradstreet Million Dollar Directory*
- *Thomas Register of American Manufacturers*
- *MacRae's Blue Book*
- *Moody's Manual of Investments*
- *Standard Corporation Records*
- *The Bankers' Almanac and Year Book*
- *World Space Directory*
- *Literary Market Place*
- *Publishers World*
- *Rand McNally Bankers Directory*
- *The Chemical Buyers' Guide*
- *United States Government Organizational Manual*
- *Encyclopedia of Associations*
- *Industrial Research Laboratories of the United States*
- *Poor's Register of Corporations, Directors, and Executives*

* These questions were adapted from *Career Motivation*, Career Growth Associates, Inc., 1976.
† This list was adapted from *Career Motivation*, Career Growth Associates, Inc., 1976.

- *Guide to Listings of Manufacturers*
- *Standard Advertising Register*
- *McKittrick's Directory of Advertisers*
- *Standard Rate and Data Service*
- *Career*
- *College Placement Annual*
- *National Association of Manufacturers*
- *American Management Association*
- *Society of Automotive Engineers*
- *American Engineering Service*
- *Association of Consulting Management Engineers*
- *America's's Corporate Families*
- *Fortune 500 Directory*

YOUR CAREER GOALS

After you have collected the information you need concerning career possibilities and organizations for which to work and have considered the possibility of further training or retraining for a career that interests you, you should be able to state a career goal. You may already have stated one as you worked through chapter 4, but by now you may be more certain of what you want. Remember, goals don't lock you in, they simply give you a sense of direction. They can change as circumstances change and as you learn more about yourself and career opportunities.

LONG-TERM VERSUS SHORT-TERM CAREER GOALS

Women do not always have the luxury of following a direct career path. They may interrupt their education to get married or have children, quit their jobs when their husbands are transferred, or stop working to raise their children. Often, it is the man whose career comes first, since traditionally he is usually in a position to earn more money. For example, a man rarely takes extended periods of time off to raise the children or to care for a child who is sick. Nor is it as usual for a man to follow his wife when she is transferred or sacrifice his own career goals to support a wife through med school.

Although things are slowly changing in our culture, women often find that they are faced with a kind of "biological destiny" which means that they have the children, accept the responsibility for child care, and somehow fit their career around these life events.

EXAMPLE 1

Beverly majored in biology and had the ultimate dream of getting her M.D. and doing medical research. She married Joel, who was in advertising. First, the children were born (there were three of them), and Beverly postponed her career dreams to raise her children during their early years.

By the time the children were in school—allowing Beverly to start med school—Joel's career pattern had been established. The family made major moves every couple of years when Joel moved to yet another agency, since advertising was a "volatile field" as he put it. He was firmly convinced that the grass was always greener at the next ad firm.

Beverly's life took on a rather predictable pattern: she oversaw the moves from place to place and was the one to choose the home, area to live in, and best school districts for the kids. Joel wasn't much help because all his energy was used in getting acclimated to his new position. The process of being transferred usually took about eighteen months of Beverly's time, and the next year or so was spent trying to establish friends. The children made friends at school and Joel made friends through work. Beverly joined yet another Newcomers' Club and signed up for bridge and tennis. When she got bored with these activities, Beverly would get a job utilizing her biology background as a laboratory technologist, but she did not find this work very satisfying. To her, laboratories were the "sweatshops of the eighties." When she had spent a year or so at the job, it was time to move on, and the cycle started all over again.

Beverly confided to a woman friend at their twenty-fifth reunion that perhaps her friend was lucky to be divorced. That way she could be in charge of her life and move toward the career she wanted.

State your career goals. Where do you want to be in terms of a career, job, or occupation in five years? Now, state your objectives. What steps are you going to take to reach your goals? Be as specific as possible. Decide when (number of months, years, etc.) you expect to reach each objective. You may want to take another look at the examples provided in chapter 4, page 49.

If you need to get a job in the near future, what kind of position do you want to get? What company or companies interest you? It is good to think in terms of long-term career goals (that goal that you would like to reach in five years), and short-term career goals (what you are going to do right now). Short-term goals should in some way relate to long-term goals. Either they should provide experience in a given area leading to a long-term goal or they should provide other conditions in terms of time, money, and flexibility to allow you to move toward your career goal.

EXAMPLE 1

Jessica's long-term career goal was to go into business for herself as a general business consultant. In five years both her children would complete college, enabling her to use her financial resources toward her goal. For the present, she needed the certainty of a predictable salary. She decided to take a job with a major consulting firm which would provide a salary, more experience, and contacts with major corporations that she could use when she had her own business.

EXAMPLE 2

Julia always dreamed of being a lawyer. When she got a divorce, her children were two and four years old and she felt obligated to devote much of her time to them. It would be three years before both her children entered school, thus giving her more time. She received four years of alimony to support her during this period, but it wasn't quite enough to make ends meet.

Julia decided to get a part-time position as a paralegal in a law firm where she could set her own hours, working on individual projects. This would enable her to study for her LSAT (Law School Admission Test). Once she was accepted into law school, she could work her job around a course or two. She decided to follow this route for the next four years, which would move her toward obtaining her law degree. The flexibility of her job and school also enabled her to meet more of her children's needs. Working for a law firm provided experience and contacts in the legal profession.

GATHERING INFORMATION
THROUGH NETWORKING

Networking is talking to people to gather information you need for your individual job search. Networking can be used to gain general information concerning careers or more specific information concerning companies and people within them who are responsible for hiring. It **provides** information concerning strategies (how people get into companies, position themselves in their careers), information about opportunities and organizations, and referrals who can give you additional information.

Make a list of everyone you could talk to to get information concerning your job search. Anyone who can provide insights or who can put you in touch with other contacts can be of help, even if they do not work in a specific area of your interest. Consider people in the following categories for your network list:

1. PEOPLE YOU KNOW WELL—family, friends, neighbors, people you have worked with, people who belong to your church and members of the clergy, people who belong to support groups, community organizations, high-school and college friends.
2. PEOPLE INVOLVED WITH THE PROFESSION THAT INTERESTS YOU—business leaders, professional organization members, trade association executives, union members or leaders, people you met at meetings or conventions.
3. PEOPLE WITH NUMEROUS CONTACTS— government and political leaders, community leaders, well-known community members, your banker, your insurance agent.

Because a person's time is valuable, you should have an idea of the information you hope to obtain from a networking meeting. Do not ask the individual if he or she has or knows of a job for you. This puts people on the spot and will most likely result in rejection. It is not the responsibility of the other person to find you a job. Your job search is your responsibility and the purpose of the meeting is only to provide you with information so you can obtain a position for yourself. If you expect people to do something for you, you are abusing the whole purpose of a job network. Since networking is a give-and-take process, it is a good idea to decide what you can offer the other person.

EXAMPLE

Barbara had five years of work experience as a high-school career counselor. She decided she wanted to earn more money and work with adults, so she was considering using her counseling experience to work in the outplacement consulting field. This field specialized in working with companies to help their employees conduct successful job searches when they lost their positions.

Barbara had a friend who had lost her job and whose company paid for her to participate in an outplacement counseling process. She asked her friend for the name of the company, the counselor she worked with, and if she could use her name. Her friend agreed. This is the telephone script Barbara wrote to ask for a networking interview:

"Hello, I'm Barbara Caldwell. Diane Thomas suggested that you would be a good person for me to talk to in order to learn more about the outplacement industry. I know you may not know of positions available. I am interested in discussing the background required for such a position and the special challenges involved. I have five years of career counseling experience in a high-school environment and would be delighted to share a booklet I prepared in résumé writing for high school seniors. When would it be possible for us to arrange a short fifteen-to twenty-minute meeting? Would sometime next week be convenient?"

In asking for a networking interview be sure to

1. Introduce yourself by stating your name clearly.
2. Mention a contact that the person knows (if you have one). This increases the probability that the person will be willing to take time to talk with you.
3. Assure the person that you are not expecting him or her to get you a job, refer you to a person who can get you a job, and so on. This takes the person off the spot.
4. State the purpose of the networking interview (the information you would like to receive).
5. State what you can offer the other person. Ideally, the networking process is an

exchange between two professionals who both gain something from the meeting.

6. Ask when would be a convenient time to meet with the person. It is good to assume the person will want to meet with you, to indicate how long the meeting will take, and suggest a possible time frame.

While networking may be a new idea for you when applied to job hunting, it is most likely not new to you in day-to-day dealings. People use this process on a regular basis to get accurate information in an efficient way. If, for example, your car broke down and you needed to know the name of the best mechanic in your area to work on your foreign car, you would probably start to ask people: people who own foreign cars, your friends and neighbors, people who run any store selling auto parts and accessories, people in your local gas stations, and so on. You would probably find that one or two names were mentioned more than others. This process is more effective than looking in the yellow pages of your local phone directory because the information is current and you can ask people for the specific information you need. (Is the mechanic reliable? Expensive? Established in the community?)

Networking is a generally accepted process in the business world whereby people exchange information. Approximately 70 percent of people obtain their jobs through informal sources or information obtained through networking. For many people, networking becomes a way of life and keeping contacts current.

NOTE: You may know people who can help you in various ways to get the job you want. You may not like the idea of using your contacts and feel that it is an imposition because you should be able to get a job on your own. If you have information to share or special skills that would benefit an organization, you are doing your contacts a favor by letting them know you are available.

A DIRECT APPROACH TO JOB HUNTING

A direct and very assertive approach to job hunting consists of the following steps:

1. Decide what company or companies interest you.

This requires you to do research through reading and networking to learn as much as you can about companies in the geographical area you have targeted.

2. Talk to the person with the hiring authority.

Finding the appropriate person can be accomplished through networking.

3. Tell the person with the hiring authority what you can do for them, their department, and their organization.

This assumes that you have completed a thorough assessment of your strengths, your skills, interests, values, and personality traits, and can match them with what you know the organization needs from the research and networking you have done. It also assumes that you can make an effective presentation of yourself in an interview or sales situation.

In order to get a position, you have to first know what you want, which requires that you know yourself. This can take some time to decide, particularly if you have never focused on your career. Once you have established a career goal you will have a sense of direction and be able to proceed from there. You cannot expect others to provide you with direction. While they can be helpful by providing you with suggestions and information you need, it is your responsibility to know the career you want.

TRADITIONAL APPROACHES TO JOB HUNTING

There are some common approaches to job hunting that people either try or consider when they are seeking employment. While the great majority of jobs are obtained through networking, the following approaches should not be overlooked.

Listed below are traditional approaches with their advantages and disadvantages. Which approach(es) might you consider? How much time do you think is effective to spend on each approach for your particular job search?

• NEWSPAPER WANT ADS: The want ads can give you a quick sense of available jobs, a rough idea of salary ranges, qualifications required or desired for various positions, position titles, and so on. If you are job hunting, it is good to read the want ads regularly for general information.

Only about 12 percent of all jobs, however, are obtained through the want ads. There are many reasons for this. Although some states may require that ads represent real job openings, in reality, this may not be the case. A company, for example, may have decided who it would like to hire for a given position. Even though it may already have made its decision, it advertises the position in the interest of fairness, in order to meet Equal Employment Opportunity regulations, and so on. Or, an organization may advertise a position and change its mind for a variety of reasons.

Newspaper ads represent only a fraction of the jobs that are out there. When you are looking at the want ads in your career area, so is everyone else who is entering or reentering the job market, as well as those already employed who are considering a change. Therefore, the competition for the jobs that are listed is fierce.

Your chances of obtaining a position through an ad are better if the organization's name is given. That way you can answer the ad, gain information about the company, and try at the same time to network your way into the organization. By all means, answer any ads that are of interest to you. People do get positions this way. But do not spend most of your time on this method of job searching.

- **ADS IN PROFESSIONAL JOURNALS:** The same things that apply to newspaper ads apply to ads in professional journals. By all means, know the professional journals that relate to your career area and answer any ads that interest you.
- **PERSONNEL DEPARTMENTS:** People often think that the best way to get a position in an organization is to go through its personnel department. This is not the case. The personnel department provides a screening function for departmental managers who need to hire someone. If you go to the personnel department first, you may be eliminated and never get to talk to the manager who has the responsibility and authority to hire you and would be your actual boss. While a personnel department provides a valuable function for an organi-

zation, personnel recruiters may not really understand what the job requires or what the manager really wants. It is more effective to talk to the manager directly. Personnel departments rarely have the authority to hire anyone. Therefore, you may decide to submit an application and your résumé to the personnel department as a matter of courtesy and to use your networking contacts or phone the company to learn who the manager is who has the authority to hire you.

- **SCHOOL PLACEMENT CENTERS:** Most universities and professional schools have placement centers to assist their graduates in finding employment. These centers exist to serve the students free of charge, but there may be minimal fees for job bulletin mailings, setting up credential files, and so on. Many companies contact placement centers and make arrangements to interview graduates on campus. While placement centers focus on recent graduates and entry-level positions, they also serve alumni. Be sure to find out what services are available to you if you have attended an educational institution.
- **EMPLOYMENT AGENCIES/EXECUTIVE RECRUITERS:** Employment agencies and recruiters are in the business of finding the best person to fill a position that a company has available. They serve a personnel function for the companies they represent. It is a good idea to obtain the name of several firms that are professional and specialize in placing people in your career area. This information is best attained through networking.

Be aware that employment agencies may charge a fee (usually a percentage of your first year's salary) for performing this service. **Be sure to ask if the employer or employee pays the fee.** Carefully read any documents before you sign them. Most people decide that they are only interested in a position if the employer pays the fee. Under no conditions pay an agency an upfront fee to get you a job. There are always unscrupulous organizations who take advantage of the job hunter. The reality is that employment agencies work for the companies who have the position available. They are only interested in you if they feel you would be an appropriate person for a job order they have to fill.

Some people make the mistake of thinking that an agency or recruiter will get them a job or is working for them. This is a passive and unproductive approach to job hunting. Your job search is your job responsibility. Keep in mind what you want in your desired position. Do not allow yourself to be pressured into accepting a job that isn't right for you.

It is best not to offer the salary you desire to a recruiter. If a recruiter insists that this information is needed, give a salary range. Tell the recruiter that this is confidential information for his or her use only and that you reserve the right to negotiate your own salary.

NOTE: A listing of recruiters and their areas of specialty can be found in *The Directory of Executive Recruiters*. This may be ordered from the publishers at:

Consultants News
Templeton Road
Fitzwilliam, NH 03447
(603) 585–2200, 585–6544

- UNION HALLS: If you belong to a union, be sure to visit your local union hall to see what jobs are available.
- CIVIL SERVICE JOBS: Contact your local civil service office to learn about federal and state civil service positions and to learn the dates of qualifying exams. Do not be intimidated by the exams: you can buy study guides to prepare for them. Be aware that getting a civil service job (even after passing an exam) may involve a long waiting period.
- STATE EMPLOYMENT SERVICE: If you are receiving unemployment compensation, you are required to register with your state employment service. You may want to visit the office nearest you to check the job listings that are available.
- TRAINING SERVICES (Private Industry Council): Federal and state funds are allocated to train unemployed and underemployed people under various legislation such as the Job Training Partnership Act (JPTA). Be sure to learn about training and funding for which you may qualify. Your state employment service should be able to direct you to the appropriate agency.

YOUR RÉSUMÉ

When you begin to hunt for jobs, most people will ask you for a résumé. A résumé is simply a summary of your work history and/or skills. Some employers ask to see a résumé before they see you for an interview. However, if at all possible, try to secure an interview before you submit a résumé. Asking for a résumé can be used as a stalling technique and your résumé could end up in a wastebasket. You might end up without an interview and without the chance to sell yourself in person.

There will, however, be times when you need a résumé. It is a good idea to have ready one that creates a positive first impression. An interviewer may ask to see your résumé before the interview. Interviewers are often tense themselves; they want to select the right person and they may not know how to go about the process or where to begin. It might make them feel more comfortable if they are prepared for the interview by your résumé. After an interview, a résumé can serve as a summary of who you are and the skills you have to offer. A résumé serves as your advertisement; you will want to write a résumé that successfully markets what you have to offer to an employer.

There are two types of résumés: the chronological and the functional résumé. The chronological résumé lists the jobs you have had in chronological order, starting with the most recent, which usually receives the greatest emphasis, and works back to the beginning of your employment history. The functional résumé is organized according to the skills you have. It is also possible to combine the formats by listing your most relevant skill areas and the companies for which you have worked.

To decide which type of résumé would be best for you, decide which of these statements apply to your situation:

CHRONOLOGICAL RÉSUMÉ

—*steady employment record*
—*skill areas are reflected by past jobs*
—*desire to stay in the same field*
—*want to highlight companies and organizations worked for*

FUNCTIONAL RÉSUMÉ

—have never worked
—have employment gaps
—have gone from one job to another
—want to enter new field
—have skill areas not represented by past jobs
—want to play down past jobs unrelated to present career goals
—want to emphasize professional growth

If most of the statements that apply to you can be found in the first list, you may want to prepare a chronological résumé. This format is perhaps the most accepted and familiar one. It is also easiest to prepare since its content is structured by dates, companies, and titles.

If you have never worked, or have gaps in your employment history, you may want to select the functional format. Many women who have never worked or are returning to the working world after a number of years spent as wives and mothers use this format. If you decide to write a functional résumé, you will want to review the skill areas you identified as enjoyable in the activity on pages 162–64. Select your successes that exemplify these skills to build your résumé.

WHATEVER FORMAT YOU SELECT, KEEP IN MIND THE FOLLOWING:

- Your name, current address, and phone number should be at the top of your résumé. If no one is home to answer your phone, be sure to include a number of someone who will be consistently available to take messages, or get an answering machine!
- Your objective should be stated next. It should be appropriate in its scope. If it is too broad or inclusive it will be meaningless. If it is too specific, it may eliminate job opportunities. If you are considering different objectives (e.g., a counseling or a sales position), it is better to write two different résumés. Your objective directs your résumé—everything on your résumé should demonstrate that you can achieve it!
- Include a brief summary of your career and professional strengths. A summary is a "résumé of your résumé" and provides an

overview of who you are. It supports your objective and can serve as a script for the question "Tell me about yourself" which is often asked in the beginning of an interview.
- Use your successes and achievements to build your résumé. In a chronological résumé, list your accomplishments under each position. In a functional résumé, list your accomplishments under each appropriate skill category. For each success or achievement you should do the following:

1. SPECIFY—Tell what you did.
2. QUALIFY—Tell how well you did it.
3. QUANTITY—Show what impact your success had on the organization's bottom line (did it increase profits, save time, save money?) with figures whenever possible.

EXAMPLE

Developed and implemented a marketing plan which increased sales by 50 percent during the first year, resulting in an increase of $300,000 in profits.

SUGGESTIONS

- Start your success statements with past-tense, action-oriented verbs such as:
- directed, increased, managed, sold, initiated, and so on.
- Only state positive points on your résumé.
- Omit personal data such as age, marital status, number of children, health, weight, and height.
- Do not include extra information such as leisure-time activities unless it pertains to your career objective, skills, or is given for a definite reason.
- Keep your résumé short; no longer than two pages.
- Read, reread, and have others read your résumé to make sure it has no spelling or typing errors.
- Look at your résumé and judge its appearance. There should be appropriate white space and it should not look crowded. Pictures, poor quality paper and printing, and colored stock do not create a professional image.

After you have completed your résumé, check it against the preceding suggestions. Also consult the sample chronological and functional résumés on pages 180–83. Check your local library for books that have examples of résumés. Select the format and style that you feel best represents you.

The following questions may be helpful in gathering information you will need to write your résumé:

1. What is your educational background? List schools and dates attended. Did you have any special recognition for educational achievements—honor societies, dean's list, honors degree?

2. Which skills are your strongest? Which do you enjoy using the most? What examples can you give of having used these skills? Can you present these examples in terms of achievements with measurable results?

3. List every job you have held, the skills you have used, and successes for each job which exemplify those skills. Again, try to give examples in terms of measurable results; use figures when possible and be specific.

4. List community, volunteer, and leisure-time activities. List the skills you have used and give examples of times you used these skills.

5. List special abilities such as a reading and speaking knowledge of other languages.

6. List special achievements, awards, and accomplishments.

Two other important pieces of correspondence should be part of your job-hunting portfolio; these are the cover letter and the follow-up letter. The purpose of a cover letter is to introduce an individual seeking a job to a prospective employer. The letter should be no longer than one page in length and should provide just enough information to make the employer want to study the résumé enclosed. Many companies will not respond to résumés sent without a cover letter. Remember to keep copies of all business correspondence.

The cover letter should include

• The name of the recipient, if possible
• How you heard about the job
• Your interest in the specific job—how it relates to your career objectives, skills, and experience

• Your training, education, academic background
• When you are available for an interview
• When you will call the office to arrange an interview date and time
• A statement expressing your appreciation for the recipient's consideration

Use the suggestions above as a checklist when you have completed your cover letter.

If you say that you will call to arrange for a job interview, be sure that you follow up.

The follow-up letter to a first interview should include

• A statement expressing appreciation for the interview
• Job for which you were interviewed as well as the date and place the interview was conducted
• Reaffirmation of your interest in the position and company and what you can offer the company
• Statement indicating willingness to provide any additional information needed
• A suggestion for further action such as when you will be available for additional interviews

After you have written your follow-up letter, check it against the list. Does your letter contain all the relevant parts? If you missed one, revise your letter to include the missing part.

THE JOB INTERVIEW

A "successful" interview is one where enough information has been exchanged between the interviewer and the interviewee to enable both parties to determine whether there would be an appropriate match. Ideally, the company's representative should know what the company and the position needs in an employee. Talking to the person who would be your manager, who has a thorough knowledge of the position that is open, is preferable to interviewing with someone from the personnel department. Ideally, you should be fully aware of your strengths and the kind of position that is right for you.

You may mutually decide that there is the possibility of a working relationship. Or, the company may decide that you are not the best person for the job. You may decide that the job

CHRONOLOGICAL RÉSUMÉ

JOAN ROBERTS
429 Clark Street
Portland, Oregon 97208
(503) 555-8127

OBJECTIVE

Office Manager

SUMMARY

Office manager with over ten years of successful experience coordinating administrative, credit, bookkeeping, and customer relations functions for a $15 million manufacturing company. Prior experience in managing all aspects of a small business. Knowledge of computer applications. Excellent supervision and communication skills.

EMPLOYMENT HISTORY

Specialty Products   1977 to Present
Portland, Oregon

OFFICE MANAGER

Manage sales administration for 8 salespeople. Supervise office staff of 4 to perform all bookkeeping, computer operations, and secretarial work for business forms manufacturing company. Resolve all problems concerning collections, customer relations, and personnel.

Accomplishment Highlights:

- Developed and implemented account analysis system for major customer enabling immediate access to exact figures resulting in prompt and accurate payments.

- Initiated phone-contact calling procedure which reduced overdue receivables by 35 percent within first year of operation.

- Collected over $30,000 in past due monies from major accounts through arranging special payments plans.

- Instituted new computer system which eliminated need for extra office help and streamlined all work procedures.

- Designed and implemented sales tracking system enabling office to obtain immediate and current information concerning all accounts.

Joan Roberts
Avalon Beauty Shop   1972–1977
Portland, Oregon

OWNER

Owned and managed profitable business venture. Hired and supervised 4 employees.

Accomplishment Highlights:

- Established excellent working relationship with suppliers enabling favorable credit and product delivery terms.

- Developed clientele of over 200 customers through successful marketing program.

- Coordinated major renovation of shop enabling business to serve more customers. Renovation completed within three-week vacation period under budget.

- Developed and implemented computerized inventory system enabling greater efficiency and business to maintain optimal inventory for profitability.

Georgia's Restaurant   1971–1972
Portland, Oregon

MANAGER

Managed night crew of 3 cooks and 8 servers for a 24-hour family restaurant. Hired and trained all serving personnel.

Accomplishment Highlights:

- Implemented "Super Server" award which resulted in better customer service and increased employee morale.

- Streamlined food ordering procedures which enabled faster service to customer.

EDUCATION

Portland Community College
A.A. Degree—Business Management, 1972

COMMUNITY ACTIVITIES

League of Women Voters
Treasurer, 1988

Portland Beautification Project
President, 1986–1987

JOAN ROBERTS
429 Clark Street
Portland, Oregon 97208
(503) 555-8127

OBJECTIVE

Office Manager

SUMMARY

Office manager with over ten years of successful experience coordinating administrative, credit, bookkeeping, and customer relations functions for a $15 million manufacturing company. Prior experience in managing all aspects of a small business. Knowledge of computer applications. Excellent supervision and communication skills.

PROFESSIONAL EXPERIENCE

OFFICE MANAGEMENT

- Initiated and implemented sales tracking system enabling sales staff of 8 to obtain immediate and current information concerning all accounts.

- Instituted new computer system which eliminated need for extra office help and streamlined all work procedures.

- Developed and implemented account analysis system for major customer, enabling it to obtain immediate and exact figures resulting in prompt and accurate payments.

PERSONNEL MANAGEMENT

- Managed sales administration for 8 sales professionals and supervised office staff of 4 to perform all functions necessary to ensure success of a $15 million manufacturing company.

- Trained staff to implement phone contact calling procedure which reduced overdue receivables by 35 percent within first year of operation.

- Hired, trained, and managed night restaurant crew of 3 cooks and 8 servers to create a 24-hour family-restaurant operation. Additional operating hours resulted in a $300,000 net profit increase during first year.

BUSINESS MANAGEMENT

- Operated successful small business venture which supported 5 full-time employees and was sold at a profit after five years of operation.

- Implemented new accounting system which saved ten hours each month and enabled more accurate picture of firm's financial status.

- Established excellent working relationship with suppliers enabling favorable credit and product delivery terms.

- Collected over $30,000 in past due monies from major accounts through arranging special payment plans.

EMPLOYMENT HISTORY

Specialty Products   1977 to Present
Portland, Oregon

OFFICE MANAGER

Avalon Beauty Shop   1972–1977
Portland, Oregon

OWNER

Georgia's Restaurant   1971–1972
Portland, Oregon

MANAGER

EDUCATION

Portland Community College
Business Management—A.A. Degree   1972

COMMUNITY ACTIVITIES

League of Women Voters—Treasurer 1988
Portland Beautification Project—President
1986–1987

NOTE: The samples of a chronological and functional résumé are written for the same woman. Since she is looking for a job that is like her present position, a chronological résumé may be more appropriate.

and/or the company does not meet your career needs. Both parties have the power to accept or reject. You are not a powerless victim in the interviewing process.

Women often approach job interviews with apprehension and anxiety. While some nervousness is understandable, job interview anxiety can be diminished by the attitude you take.

How would you complete each of the following statements?

1. Before I go to a job interview I

   a. Picture myself as being nervous, saying all the wrong things, and looking foolish in the interview situation.
   b. Picture myself as being calm, poised, articulate, and making a favorable impression upon the interviewer.
   c. Deliberately focus on something other than the interview such as a magazine.
   d. Am so nervous it's all I can do to remain conscious.

2. When I go on an interview I feel that

   a. If I'm not offered a job, it will mean that I am inferior, unqualified, and a loser.
   b. This is the only job for me and that if I'm not given an offer "I'm finished."
   c. If I'm not offered this job, I'll starve, won't be able to support myself, and will end up a bag lady.
   d. This is one of many jobs and if I'm not offered this one, there will be others.

3. I consider the purpose of an interview to be

   a. For the interviewer to inform me about the company and the job
   b. For me to inform the interviewer about my skills, abilities, and qualifications
   c. An opportunity for an interchange of information between the interviewer, who is an expert on the organization and the job available, and me, who is an expert on my skills, abilities, and qualifications.
   d. An opportunity to get down to the nuts and bolts of a job offer, salary

negotiations, benefits, vacations, and so on.

4. I view the interviewer as

   a. An authority figure who will judge my overall performance in the interview.
   b. A sadist who enjoys my nervousness and discomfort and who will purposely try to put me on the spot.
   c. Someone who is knowledgeable about the organization and the job opening.
   d. A person who is genuinely interested in learning from the interview whether or not an employment agreement would benefit the organization and myself.

5. When I go for an interview I

   a. Expect the interviewer to tell me what my skills are and how I can fit into the organization.
   b. View it as an opportunity to get some free career-counseling from an expert.
   c. Have done some research concerning the job and the organization and know what skills and abilities I can offer the organization.
   d. Don't have any goals for the interview in mind and go in cold.

6. When I go for an interview I feel

   a. Modesty is a virtue and try to minimize my achievements, skills, and abilities.
   b. Uncomfortable talking about my achievements, skills, and abilities.
   c. That if I don't blow my own horn, no one will do it for me so I make an effort to stress how great I am.
   d. Proud about my achievements, skills, and abilities and mention them at appropriate times during the interview.

7. In an interview, I

   a. Dwell upon my positive points.
   b. Dwell on past failures and shortcomings.
   c. Try to hide and cover up shortcomings.
   d. Dwell on my positive points and deal

with past failures and shortcomings if they come up in an honest and straightforward fashion.

8. In an interview, I think I should

    a. "Psych-out" what kind of person the job requires and act as if I were that kind of person even if I'm not.
    b. Try to create a neutral effect so that I can be "all things to all people."
    c. Be myself and emphasize my strong points.
    d. Try to butter up and flatter the interviewer so that the focus will not be on me.

9. I feel that the interview is

    a. Basically the interviewer's responsibility and that I should take a passive stance.
    b. A situation for which I should take some responsibility in terms of what I want from the interview.
    c. An opportunity for me to demonstrate my ability to run the whole show.
    d. An opportunity to discuss the organization with the interviewer and that the responsibility for a productive interview should be shared.

10. In an interview, I

    a. Focus upon myself and what I want to say next.
    b. Focus upon what the interviewer is saying.
    c. Am aware of myself, but also focus upon what the interviewer is saying.
    d. Am oblivious to everything and just praying I'll live through it.

11. I think that an interview is a

    a. Nerve-wracking ordeal.
    b. Necessary evil.
    c. Chance for me to learn more about a job and an organization.
    d. Chance for me to present my abilities, skills, and achievements and to show how I could contribute to an organization.

Women too often view the individual who is interviewing them as an all-powerful person who will reward them with a job if the interview performance is a good one and withhold the job if the interview performance is a poor one. This view, coupled with fears and anxieties you may have if you never worked or have been out of the job market for a time, could cause you to feel passive and timid. Two ways to overcome feelings of passivity and powerlessness in a job interview are to

- Know your skills and what you have to offer
- Know something about the company and what you can contribute

If you have prepared for the interview by knowing your skills and the things you have to offer, you will be in a position to sell yourself.

The following are suggestions for a successful interview:

1. If possible, get a good night's sleep before the interview.
2. Before going on an interview, talk positively to yourself; review your strengths, your successes, and picture yourself as calm, confident, and interested in the interview.
3. Do your homework; know as much about the organization as possible.
4. Know where you are going and plan to be ten to fifteen minutes early for the interview so that you will not feel rushed.
5. Greet the interviewer by name with a firm handshake.
6. Take a pen, paper, and some money with you.
7. Appear interested and alert; look the interviewer in the eye and maintain good posture.
8. Dress in good taste; don't wear heavy makeup or perfume.
9. Be firm about answering only those questions you feel are business-related. If you feel questions are too personal, state your reasons for feeling the way you do.
10. Talk enough so the interviewer gets to know you but don't monopolize the conversation. Stress your positive points.
11. Don't give the impression that you are only interested in the salary. Save questions concerning salary until the inter-

viewer brings up the subject or until a second interview.

12. Be honest; be prepared to deal with questions in a straightforward fashion.

13. Express interest in the position and ask the interviewer when you will hear from him or her again.

14. Be prepared to ask a few questions about things that genuinely interest you about the organization.

15. Be sensitive concerning when the interviewer wishes to end the interview.

QUESTIONS YOU MAY BE ASKED DURING AN EMPLOYMENT INTERVIEW

Interviews and questions asked vary greatly depending upon the person who is conducting the interview and the person who is being interviewed. The person who interviews may not be a trained or experienced interviewer. Since a successful interview is the responsibility of both parties, you should be prepared with points you want to address concerning your strengths and experience. Be sure to have questions prepared about the position and the organization.

Some interviewers feel they can better evaluate you if they ask open-ended questions and encourage you to do most of the talking. Other interviewers will ask you a series of questions and take time to describe the position and tell you about the organization.

You should be aware that because of equal employment legislation, questions concerning your age, race, religion, sex, and ethnic background are not legal. An employer cannot ask questions concerning your plans to have children, the number of children you have, or child-care arrangements you have made. These questions would not be asked of a man. In other words, an employer is not legally permitted to ask questions of a woman that would discriminate against her because she is female.

Regardless of the law, an employer may still ask illegal questions either knowingly or unknowingly. If you are asked what you know is an illegal question, you have several options:

1. Say nothing and answer the question.
2. Refuse to answer the question and point out that it is an illegal question.
3. Politely ask how the question pertains to the job being discussed.

Whether or not you choose to answer an illegal question depends upon how much you need and want the position, your principles, the "spirit" or "intention" with which the question is asked, if you feel the interviewer is aware of the legality of the question, and so on. It is your right not to answer questions that you believe are illegal or personally offensive. From an employer's point of view, it is understandable that the company may want to know if a woman will miss work frequently due to sick children. Or, how many years an employee nearing retirement age has to give a company. Because the questions concerning this information could be illegal, there is no way for an employer to obtain such information unless the candidate offers it. If you feel that an employer has an agenda that cannot be brought out in the open because of equal employment legislation, it may be to your advantage to surface the information. For example, you can say, "I have two children who are both in college. Child care is not a problem." Or, "I have over fifteen years of productivity I can give to a company before I would consider retiring."

The following are questions that are frequently asked during a job interview. Put a check next to questions that you feel would be difficult to answer or you need to consider.

1. Tell me about yourself.

This question is usually asked in the beginning of an interview and used as an opener. Respond by giving a brief summary of your professional history. Your summary from your résumé serves as a good script.

2. What were your responsibilities in your previous positions?

It is a good idea to have a résumé that states where you worked, your titles, your responsibilities, and your successes and achievements for each position. Discussing achievements for each position is more impressive than discussing your job responsibilities. Remember to quantify your achievements. Back them up with figures whenever possible. If your résumé is effectively written it will serve as a script for your interviews.

3. What are your strengths? Why should we hire you for this position?

Be sure you know what strengths you have and mention those you feel will benefit the company the most. Tell your strength and briefly give an achievement that demonstrates that you have the strength. It creates a picture for the interviewer.

For example: "My greatest strength is my sales ability. In my first year with Acme Corporation, I increased sales by forty percent, representing an additional one million, two hundred thousand dollars in sales revenue."

4. What are your weaknesses? What would your manager (or subordinates) state as your weaknesses?

Either reply that you have no weaknesses that would interfere with your performance or select a minor weakness, or one that works to the company's benefit. If you cite a weakness, be sure to add what you are doing to improve in this area.

For example: "Sometimes I expect more of myself than other employees expect of themselves. I become impatient when people around me do not strive to do their best. I have to remember that not all employees have the same work ethic."

5. Why did you leave your last position, company, or change industries?

If you left your last position on unfavorable terms try to be as positive as possible. Do not say negative things about your previous company or supervisor.

6. What kind of position are you looking for?

State your job objective and give one or two strengths or points that support your objective.

7. Did you ever fail at any position? Was your work ever criticized by your manager? What do you most regret about your past?

The purpose of these questions is to surface times that you perceive you were not successful. Do not offer information that will harm your chances for employment. You want to be honest and offer information that works on your behalf. If you share information that could be considered negative, be sure you make it into a positive learning experience.

Example: During a college internship, I was required to gather vast amounts of data. While my work was satisfactory, I had to work long hours alone dealing with data to perform the job. I learned that I much prefer working with people and ideas rather than with facts and figures.

8. How did you get along with your manager? Tell me about a manager you did not work well with and why? What qualities do you look for in someone who manages you?

Answer these questions in a positive way and stress that you can work effectively with a variety of managers. You do not want to share "horror stories" concerning the boss you "hated the most."

9. How much money do you make in your present position? How much money are you looking for?

It is to your advantage not to discuss salary until you are offered the position. If you discuss your present salary, you may be indicating how much money you would be willing to accept. You could be overpaid or underpaid in your present position. Or, the position you are discussing may require more hours, more skills, greater responsibility, and so on. Discussing your present or past salary is not germaine to the position that is open and the salary that is appropriate. You can answer the question by asking the interviewer what the salary range is for the position you are discussing.

10. Where do you hope to be in you career in five years?

This question measures your ambition and expectations. It is good to indicate that you are interested in opportunities for professional growth and development. At the same time, you do not want to appear unrealistic and unwilling to pay your dues.

Example: In five years I want to be an experienced training professional with the ability to effectively design and deliver training programs. I would welcome an opportunity to supervise other training professionals.

SUGGESTION: Be sure to listen to questions carefully and take time to think before you respond. Ask for any clarification you need if you do not understand the questions. Answer as positively and concisely as possible. If the interviewer wants you to go into more detail, he or she will ask you to elaborate.

QUESTIONS YOU MAY WANT TO ASK DURING AN EMPLOYMENT INTERVIEW

It is a good idea to have questions in mind that you would like to ask during the employment interview. An interviewer will usually ask what questions you have. Even if the interviewer was very thorough during an explanation of the job and a description of the company, there should be at least a few questions you would like answered. The following are questions that may be appropriate:

1. Why is the position available?
2. How is the company structured? To whom would I report?
3. What responsibilities are involved with the position?
4. What are the company's goals?
5. What are the plans for the company's immediate future? What are the long-range plans for the company's future?
6. Who are the company's chief competitors? What is their competitive edge?
7. How is performance measured?
8. What are the opportunities for advancement?
9. How is conflict managed in your organization?
10. What do you consider are the most important qualities for the ideal candidate who would fill this position?

HOW TO NEGOTIATE FOR THE HIGHEST SALARY

While people negotiate all the time to reach agreements with other people, they may not consider negotiating to get the best possible salary. Most men negotiate for a salary; most women do not. Women may be reluctant to negotiate because they may feel that they are lucky to be offered the job in the first place, do not want to appear pushy, or believe that the amount that they are offered is set by company policy. The goal of negotiating is to reach a mutual agreement with another party in a way that allows for a positive, ongoing relationship.

There are several reasons why you should consider negotiating for the best salary you can get.

1. Since salary increases are usually calculated by using a percentage of your base pay, it helps to start out earning as much as possible.
2. Even when companies have a stated salary range for a position, there is usually some room for negotiations.
3. Negotiating for the salary you feel you deserve demonstrates that you have a healthy respect for your skills and what you can offer to a company. People usually respect others who demonstrate that they respect themselves and what they have to offer.
4. Most employers, particularly smaller companies, expect to negotiate.

The rules for negotiating the salary that is most favorable for you are similar to rules for other types of negotiation. The individual representing the company will want an outcome that benefits the organization; you want an outcome that will benefit you. Keep the following in mind when you negotiate for salary:

1. Negotiate a win/win contract.

   The ideal is for an employee and a company to negotiate a salary that feels fair to both parties. If you begin working for a company feeling you are underpaid, you may focus on when you can leave the company and can make more money rather than concentrating on doing your best work in the position you have.

2. Do not negotiate for salary until you are offered the position.

   A common question interviewers ask is "How much salary do you expect?" Answering this question before you are offered the position puts you at a disadvantage because it places you in a bidding position for the job that is open. If several people who are more or less equally qualified for a position state the salary they want before receiving an offer, the company will most likely offer the position to the person who gave the lowest salary. Once you are offered the position, you can begin to negotiate salary. If someone asks you what your salary requirement is, ask if you are being offered the position. If the answer is no, state that you prefer to discuss salary when you are offered the position.

3. The person who mentions a salary figure first is at a disadvantage.

Once you are offered a position, if you state the salary you want, it may be higher or lower than the figure the other party has in mind. The individual who mentions a salary figure first shows his or her cards and allows time for the other person to react. When you are offered a position and then asked what your salary expectation is, it is best to answer by asking, "What is the salary range for this position?" When given a range, state that you would be toward the higher end of the range based on your skills, experience, and what you know you can do for the company.

4. Once you are offered a position, negotiate salary first and fringes/benefits second.

Almost everything is negotiable. The number of items that are negotiable depends upon the importance of the position and how much a company wants you. Items such as vacation, when you will have your first performance/salary review, relocation packages, country club memberships, office space, commuting expenses, and parking space may be negotiable. Because some companies are moving toward a "cafeteria approach" where you select the benefits you need, you may be faced with a variety of benefit options. Usually, employees are offered a standard benefit package or a given number of benefit selections, so it is best not to negotiate salary with an idea that you are "getting a benefit" in exchange for money. Be sure to keep in mind, however, how much money benefits represent and are worth to you so you are able to compare total salary and compensation packages when offered more than one position. Because salary and benefits are different topics, arrive at a salary first, and then move on to agree on other negotiable items.

5. Always negotiate in person.

When you are sitting face-to-face with a person, you are able to judge how negotiations are going by reading a person's facial expressions and body language. This is to your advantage. Negotiations should not be conducted over the telephone.

SUGGESTIONS

1. Be sure you know what you want in terms of title, job responsibilities, salary, fringe benefits, advancement potential, and so on.
2. Keep the negotiating on a friendly, collaborative note. You are working toward an agreement that you both will find fair. Remember that you will be working together if you accept the position.
3. If you become "stuck" on a given item during the negotiation process, move on to another area. You can always return to the item later.
4. Do not become negative. Stress that you are interested in the position and that you are certain that you can arrive at an agreement that is mutually beneficial.

WHERE ARE YOU GOING?

In terms of career development, being offered a job is best thought of as a beginning rather than an ending. If you have been offered a job or presently have a job, you may want to consider how this job enables you to meet your goals.

Answer the following questions:

1. Are the expectations and responsibilities of the job realistic for you to fulfill?
2. Are you being given the authority to meet the job responsibilities?
3. Are you being fairly rewarded (financially and in other ways) for the job you will be performing?
4. How does this position meet your immediate needs?
5. How will this position help you achieve your long-range goals?
6. How will this position enable you to develop the skills you enjoy using?
7. What experience will you have as a result of this position that will make you more marketable and valuable in the future?
8. If the position does not relate directly to

your goals, what purpose is it serving?

9. Do you keep a work journal or portfolio of what you have accomplished or contributed that you can use to present your case for a salary increase or a promotion?

10. Do you summarize your work responsibilities and achievements periodically and do you update your résumé?

11. Is there any way you can expand your job in terms of responsibilities and/or training to better meet your career goals?

12. If your ultimate goal is to be self-employed, how is this job helping you to move toward that goal?

SEX DISCRIMINATION

Regardless of how hard you work or how much you contribute to an organization, you will find it difficult to realize your career goals if you are a target of sex discrimination. Women are discriminated against when they are paid less than men who are doing comparable work, when they are promoted less rapidly than men although they are equally qualified, when they have fewer job opportunities and chances for professional growth than men, and when they are considered to be less efficient, able, businesslike, or dependable than men by employers. Employers practice sex discrimination when they have preconceived ideas and prejudicial attitudes concerning women who work. For example, "Women should not be offered promotions involving transfers because they won't move," "Women don't need the money," and "Women are too emotional for responsible positions" all reflect discriminatory attitudes. If you work, it is wise to be aware of sex discrimination and how it operates.

Which statements* do you feel apply to you?

EQUAL PAY FOR EQUAL WORK

1. You are paid less than male employees who do similar work or who are responsible for comparable duties.

2. You were hired to work in a lower-

* This checklist was adapted from *Collegiate Women's Career Magazine* 4 (Spring 1977): 25–28.

paying job than male employees whose qualifications are comparable to or less than your own.

3. You are required to do more work or more complex work than male employees in similar jobs who are earning the same or more than you.

4. The jobs in your grade and salary level predominantly held by women require higher qualifications and skill levels than those in your grade or in higher grades predominantly held by men.

5. You were not hired, appointed, or promoted to a particular job but a man with less tenure and experience was.

6. You have trained men to fill jobs that are higher-paying than your own.

7. You supervise male employees who earn more than you do.

8. You have trained men who supervise you.

9. You were hired or promoted into a job formerly held by a man but are paid less than he was.

10. A male employee is hired or promoted to your present job and is paid more than you were earning.

11. You are an experienced clerical worker and are at the same salary or grade level as inexperienced male clerical workers.

12. You are a secretary and type, take shorthand, and operate office equipment; you are paid at the same or lower rate as male office workers whose jobs require no office skills.

13. You are titled and salaried as a secretary but are actually performing administrative, technical, or other higher-paying duties.

14. You are a college graduate and were hired at the same or lower salary or grade level as male employees who have only a high-school education and with limited work experience.

15. You are titled and paid as an assistant to a department head or administrator, although you perform all the job functions of a department head or administrator (perhaps because such a person does not exist).

16. When you applied for a job, you were only told about or offered clerical or secretarial work.

17. You were denied a job because the appointing authority (department head or personnel office) maintained that a woman could not do the work required by the position.

18. You were not appointed to or offered a position because the appointing authority thought that "you wouldn't be interested in" or that "you would be afraid to do" such a job.

19. When you applied for a job or promotion, your previous or current community, part-time, or volunteer positions were not considered as qualifying work experience.

20. You worked for several years before you took time out to raise your children, but when you returned to work you were hired at a grade or salary level held by inexperienced workers.

21. You were discouraged from taking a promotional exam or from applying for a job because the job description included language and requirements implying that the work was for men.

22. Although you know that you can perform the actual duties of a job that has just become available, the job description includes height, weight, agility, and/or physical strength requirements that you cannot meet.

23. You were advised that you need not apply for or take the test for a job because "they are looking for a man."

24. You were denied a job because "they already have a woman" with that job title.

25. You work in a department or office in which the percentage of female employees is less than 40 percent but no jobs in your department are certified as having bona fide occupational qualifications based on sex.

26. Male employees in your department or office participate in a greater variety of job functions and titles than do women.

27. Jobs in your department or office in which men predominate offer greater promotional opportunities than do jobs predominantly held by women.

28. Your attitude at work is considered to be "too aggressive" while men in your department are praised for being "go-getters," or "dedicated" and "ambitious" workers.

29. Although your work is of good quality, you find that your opinions on policy and administrative matters relating to your work are not taken seriously by your supervisors.

30. Men who are doing the same work or who are performing comparable job functions are given more staff assistance than you are.

31. You are being subjected to greater supervision than men doing comparable work under similar working conditions.

32. Men doing work that is comparable or similar to yours are given more challenging, prestigious, or interesting assignments than you are.

33. You are an administrative assistant, research assistant, or technician and are required to do secretarial work in addition to your other job functions; men in your job title or in similar job titles are not required to perform secretarial tasks.

34. You are not permitted to attend staff conferences; departmental, board, or commission meetings; or community meetings, even though such meetings are related to work for which you are responsible. However, male employees with similar or less involvement in the same work are encouraged to attend such meetings.

35. You are frequently asked to cover the office on skeleton days while male employees in your department rarely work on reduced staff days because, you are told, "it's more professional" to have a woman answering the phone.

36. New jobs or vacancies in your department or office are generally made known through word-of-mouth communication rather than by posting or other formal notification to all employees.

37. You are a secretarial or clerical worker and are allowed to participate only in training programs designed to improve your secretarial skills.

38. You are a secretarial or clerical worker and are not permitted to participate in administrative, management training, or degree programs or in courses although

male employees performing the same job functions do participate in such programs or courses.

39. You are working in a college or neighborhood co-op or work-study program and are assigned to do clerical, secretarial, or receptionist work; male students in your program are given construction, planning, development, or other technical training jobs.

ADVANCEMENT

1. You were the "natural" choice to be promoted to a higher paying job but a man with less experience and tenure was appointed.
2. Very few women hold higher-paying positions in your department or office, although several women are qualified by experience and training to hold such jobs.
3. A majority of the employees in your department or office are women but most of the administrators are men.
4. In your department or office, women participate only at the lower salary levels of high-paying job titles.
5. There are no, or very few, female supervisors in your department.
6. Female supervisors in your department or office generally earn less than do male supervisors.
7. Female supervisors in your department or office do not supervise men.
8. It has taken you and other female employees longer to advance to your present salary level than it took men with similar education and experience.
9. Male employees who started in your department or office as clerical workers at the same time you did are now working in high-paying nonclerical jobs while you are still doing clerical work.
10. Grade by grade, job title by job title, male employees in your department or office advance more rapidly than do female employees.
11. Clerical or secretarial work in your department or office is not counted as work experience that is transferable to nonclerical higher-paying jobs.

EMPLOYEE BENEFITS, LEAVE, AND TERMINATION POLICIES

1. You are not eligible for health and life insurance benefits that wives of male employees enjoy.
2. Your husband and/or family are not eligible for benefits that the families and spouses of male employees receive.
3. Maternity leave is not treated in the same manner as any other normal temporary physical disability. A pregnant woman does *not* have the right to

    a. Continue at work until she determines that her physical condition no longer permits the execution of her work activities.
    b. Use accrued sick time while she remains physically unable to work.
    c. Continue to participate in the department's health and life insurance plans during the period she is unable to work.
    d. Return to the same or a similar job at the same salary and with no loss of seniority or seniority-related benefits.

4. While you are out of work on maternity leave, you are required to pay the total premium for your medical and/or life insurance although male employees who are on leave for extended illness continue to participate in the department's medical and life insurance programs on the same basis as employees not on leave.
5. You have just completed your maternity leave and are told that the department is not required to hold your job, or a similar one, open for you even though male employees who have been on extended leave had their jobs held open until they were able to return to work.
6. Although you are not permitted to work part-time for family or child-care reasons, male employees in your department work on a part-time basis while attending school or convalescing from a prolonged illness.
7. The retirement plan in which your department participates encourages or requires an earlier retirement age for female employees.
8. According to your retirement plan, your

husband is not entitled to the same benefits as the wife of a male employee.

9. During an austerity period, or any other times during which personnel cuts are made, most of the employees terminated in your department are women.

If one or more of the circumstances described on the previous pages apply to you, you are probably being discriminated against on the basis of sex. While it is upsetting to learn you are the object of sex discrimination, awareness of such discrimination will help you make decisions concerning what you plan to do about it. Your alternatives include

- Doing nothing
- Mentioning the matter to your employer and/or personnel manager and asking what can be done
- Getting together with other women in the organization and seeing what can be done
- Taking legal action
- Finding other employment

The decision you make depends upon you and your situation. Only you know the probabilities and risks involved with each alternative.

If you believe you have been discriminated against on the basis of sex, race, color, age, or national origin and decide to take legal action, contact the nearest office of the Equal Employment Opportunity Commission as well as the state or local Human Relations Commission. It is important that your "Charge of Discrimination" be filed as soon as possible after the discrimination takes place, since there are strict time limits for filing complaints.

Laws making sex discrimination illegal include

- **TITLE VII** (1964 Civil Rights Act)—forbids discrimination by all employers, labor unions, employment agencies, or apprenticeship committees. This law is administered by the Equal Employment Opportunity Commission (EEOC).
- **EQUAL PAY ACT**—provides for full-scale investigation on the basis of an anonymous complaint. You can get double back pay instead of simply lost pay as under Title VII. This law is administered by the Wage and Hour Division of the Department of Labor.
- **EXECUTIVE ORDERS**—cover employees of organizations with government contracts that require that victims of discrimination be compensated and that employers develop "affirmative action plans" to correct employment discrimination. These orders are administered by the Office of Health, Education, and Welfare.
- **AGE DISCRIMINATION IN EMPLOYMENT ACT OF 1967**—forbids discrimination against workers aged forty to sixty-five. This law is administered by the Wage and Hour Division of the Department of Labor.

DO YOU WANT TO BE AN ENTREPRENEUR?

Starting your own business may be an excellent alternative to working for someone else. More and more women are starting their own businesses and finding that being an entrepreneur enables them to have the authority, life-style, and rewards that they are seeking. Being in business for yourself should not be a reaction to a job you do not like. It should be a well-thought-out decision that is made considering your strengths, skills, values, interests, and personality.

1. Do you have a realistic evaluation of your strengths? What additional skills will you need to develop (or hire) if you own and manage your own business?
2. Are you willing to invest the energy and hours of work that your own business requires?
3. What kind of business interests you? Would you offer a service? Would you sell a product? Would you buy a franchise?
4. Would you go into business with someone else or a group of people? How would you select business partners? Do their skills, values, and resources complement yours? How would you structure your business?
5. How much capital would you need for start-up operations, that is, buildings, equipment, permits and licenses, and so on? How much capital would you need for your first year of operations? Where would you get it? How much money do you need for personal living expenses?
6. What help would you need to employ? How much would you pay out in annual salaries?

7. What is your competition? What do you offer that is unique?

8. Do you have the support of family and friends for your venture?

9. Do you have the support of other organizations or entrepreneurs who can be helpful?

10. How will you market and sell your business? Do you enjoy selling and have this skill and experience?

11. Do you have a fully developed business plan which presents your business concept, marketing plan, operations plan, financial plan, risk assessment and management, and the supporting documents you need?

12. Have you taken courses or seminars in owning your own business?

There are many resources available for the person who wishes to start a business. The Small Business Association and SCORE (Service Corps of Retired Executives, retired business people available to assist beginning entrepreneurs) are examples. Many universities have centers to aid in small-business development. Be sure if you are considering your own business to take advantage of all the resources available to help you. Most businesses fail because people have not done the proper planning that a business requires. Successful entrepreneurs are calculated risk takers who do their homework and utilize all the resources that are available to them.

TWELVE

DECISIONS CONCERNING YOUR SOCIAL LIFE

Developing a social life when I first got divorced was fun yet overwhelming. The fun part was finding that I was still attractive and sexually desirable to men. The overwhelming part was finding that there are no rules to follow. Dating as a divorced woman today is much different than dating as a teenage girl in the sixties. I realized that as a married woman I had no idea of what social life for a single woman was like.

I found I had become quite selective about who I dated after I was divorced for a while. I learned from dating men who weren't for me, what I really did want. My time is valuable. If I don't enjoy a man's company or if I think a friendship with him is not for me, I won't date him a second time.

One thing I learned after my divorce from the sexual experiences I had was that I was a fully functioning sexual person. For the first time, I began to enjoy my body and the pleasure it could give me. Developing the sexual aspect of my being was an important part in defining myself as a growing person who is able to experience and enjoy life.

Sooner or later, divorced women are interested in establishing a social life for themselves. How soon after divorce they are ready to date and meet new people varies. Some women feel good about themselves and want to date before their divorce is final, others may not be ready for a year or so after their divorce. Your readiness to establish a new social life depends upon factors such as how good you feel about yourself, how you have handled any feelings of hurt and rejection, how long you have been divorced, how you feel about men, and how secure you feel in the other areas of your life. While some women continue to see their married friends socially for a period of time, divorce eventually forces most women to form a new circle of friends. A social life is important for the divorced woman because it encourages her to enter the world as a single person, it gives her an opportunity for some fun and enjoyment, it brings her into contact with people who are likely to be supportive and understanding, and it gives her something to focus on other than herself and her children.

WHAT KIND OF SOCIAL LIFE DO YOU WANT?

Once divorced, some women feel pressured to enter the social scene and experience the new freedom that they have gained through their divorced status. The freedom that you gain with divorce should enable you to say *no* as well as *yes* to new social and sexual experiences. A social life in the broadest sense includes any contact you have with people outside of your family for the purposes of enjoyment; it may include men, women, older people, younger people, people by themselves, and people in groups. Divorced women are often conditioned to think of social life in terms of dating eligible men who might be prospective husbands. This very narrow definition of social life may not always meet your needs. To evaluate how much time you want to devote to a social life and the kind of social life you want, answer the following questions:

1. Approximately how many hours per week do you presently have available to devote to a social life?
2. How much time do you presently devote to your social life?

3. How much time do you *want* to devote to seeing other people?
4. You may wish to spend your social time in some of the following ways. Look at the categories listed and estimate the amount of time you spend on each per week. Then decide how much time you would like to spend on each per week.

   —*seeing female friends*
   —*seeing male friends*
   —*dating potential lovers and/or marriage partners*
   —*going places where you can meet new people*
   —*attending club or special-interest group meetings*
   —*talking on the phone to female friends*
   —*talking on the phone to male friends*

5. How satisfying do you find your present social life? Not very satisfying? Somewhat satisfying? Very satisfying?
6. If "not very satisfying," what is your reason?
7. If you would like your social life to change, in what ways would you like it to change?
8. What goals do you presently have for your social life? What are you doing to meet these goals?
9. Are your goals consistent with the values that you indicated as important to you in the activities in chapter 3? For example, if you listed independence and autonomy as important values, "finding a husband" might be inconsistent as a main social goal.

Many women approach their social life in a hit-or-miss fashion; they never decide what it is they really want or how they are going to get it. Time is a valuable resource for the divorced woman. Therefore, it pays to set goals for your social life and objectives to meet those goals. The questions you just answered should be reviewed periodically since your goals for your social life are likely to change.

Divorced women have made different decisions concerning their social life.

EXAMPLE 1
"I have been divorced for three years, have two daughters, and live with my parents. Right after

the divorce (which I didn't want), I felt hurt, rejected, and confused. I decided to return to college and get my degree, which did wonders for my morale. After college I entered law school and am now in my second year. Frankly, I've been so busy pursuing my own goals that I haven't had much time for a social life. I don't like casual dating yet don't have the time now to invest in a more committed relationship. Right now my classmates at law school fulfill the needs I have for a social life. I expect this to change, however, when I graduate."

EXAMPLE 2

"I have been divorced for two years. Shortly after my divorce, I became involved with a man and we just broke up. Part of the problem was that I just wasn't ready to settle down. Right now I don't feel much like dating and I do things with women friends. When I do begin to date, I want to date a number of men and not become involved with one relationship right away."

EXAMPLE 3

"I have been divorced for four years and have dated lots of men—from truck drivers to Ph.D.'s, from men ten years younger to men twenty years older. Dating different men was important in deciding what I wanted in a relationship because I didn't date much before marriage. I know what I want in a partner now and I'm going out to look for it."

EXAMPLE 4

"I've been divorced for five years and have had several committed relationships with men. I'm tired of the power struggles I seem to encounter and wonder if strict heterosexual relationships are for me. I'm exploring bisexuality and relationships with women."

EXAMPLE 5

"I've always put my male friends first. When I break up with a guy, I have no women friends to talk to because I haven't kept up the friendships. Right now my goal is to develop one or two good friendships with women."

YOUR FIRST DATE—THE SECOND TIME AROUND

The first dates a woman may have after a separation or divorce can be traumatic or they can be

learning experiences. They are less apt to be traumatic if the woman is ready to date, evaluates her expectations, and knows what she wants. To help you decide how you can increase the likelihood that your first dates will be positive rather than negative experiences, answer the following questions:

1. Are you ready to date? Do you want to date?
2. How do you feel when you think of having a date? Nervous? Scared? Hopeful? Excited?
3. What do you think the reasons are for the emotions you may have?
4. What expectations do you have of the person you will be dating?
5. What expectations do you have of yourself for this date?
6. Do you know what you want? Do you know what you don't want? Are you able to comfortably express what you do or do not want?
7. Can you set up the date so that you can leave early if you have nothing in common with the other person?
8. Have you made suitable child-care arrangements? Have you made arrangements for your date to meet (or not meet) your children?
9. Do you have a friend you can call in case of an emergency?
10. Do you have a sense of humor and a friend you can talk to after the date?

The following comments relate to the previous questions; they may help you think about your answers.

Are you ready to date? Do you want to date? If you feel that you are still recovering from your divorce, you may not be ready to date or even to enjoy yourself. If you are not ready to date, or do not want to date, respect these feelings. Why force yourself to date today when you may really want to next month?

How do you feel when you think of having a date? Admitting your feelings to yourself and others is often easier than hiding your feelings. Everyone has a first date and certain apprehensions, fears, and anxieties. Admitting to your date that it is your first date since your divorce and that you are a little nervous may eliminate the feeling that you have to hide what you are experiencing. Your date will probably do his best to make you feel at ease. Remember, he had a first date, too!

What do you think the reasons are for the emotions you may have? Examining the reasons for your feelings may be helpful. For example, you may feel nervous because you want to appear poised or experienced. Or, you may feel that if your date isn't interested in you, all men will find you dull and unattractive. Are the reasons for your feelings rational? Or are you expecting too much of yourself?

What expectations do you have of the person you will be dating? If you expect too much of your date, you may be setting yourself up for a disappointment. Some women are continually disappointed because they expect their dates to be Prince Charming. Be prepared for the possibility that he may not live up to all your expectations.

What expectations do you have of yourself for this date? Expecting to be comfortable, witty, charming, an excellent conversationalist, and so on when you begin to date is unrealistic. Learning to feel comfortable with dating takes time and some people will always feel more comfortable with dating than others. Be kind to yourself; give yourself time to adjust to a new situation.

Do you know what you want? Do you know what you don't want? Are you able to comfortably express what you do or do not want? You will feel more comfortable if you know what you want and if you feel free to express yourself. For example, women often wonder if they will be expected to have sex with their date. They worry about what their date will think about them if they do have sex and what they will think about them if they don't have sex. It is more important to know what *you* want at a given moment. If you decide to let your date decide what you want, you are being unfair to him as well as yourself and you may regret it later.

Can you set up the date so that you can leave early if you have nothing in common with the other person? Since your time is valuable, you might consider meeting someone for coffee, rather than a long dinner for a first date. Then, if you discover you feel uncomfortable with him or have nothing in common, you don't have to devote a whole evening to him. You might also decide to drive yourself and meet your date; that way you will be sure to have transportation home if you decide to leave early.

Have you made suitable child-care arrange-ments? Have you made arrangements for your date to meet (or not meet) your children? If you have young children, you will feel freer to enjoy yourself if you have a reliable sitter. Also, consider the arrangements best suited to you concerning your date meeting your children. Some women prefer to date someone a few times before introducing him to their children. Some children may be openly hostile or ask such questions as "Are you going to be our daddy?" that you may not want to handle on a first date.

Do you have a friend you can call in case of an emergency? If you are feeling timid or if in an adventurous moment decide to spend a weekend at a remote country inn with a man you've dated twice, you may feel more comfortable knowing that you have a friend you can call upon in case of an emergency.

Do you have a sense of humor and a friend you can talk to after the date? If you have a sense of humor, you will probably avoid treating first dates as life-or-death experiences. If you have a particularly enjoyable or disastrous date, it often helps to have a supportive friend with whom to share it.

HOW TO MEET PEOPLE

One of the most frequent complaints of divorced individuals is that there is no way to meet other single people. Yet single people do meet other single people, although the ways of meeting each other, such as singles bars, may be considered by some to be less than satisfactory.

To help decide what ways of meeting people might be best for you, ask yourself these questions:

1. Where (or how) do you presently try to meet people?
2. What kinds of people would you like to meet? With what kinds of people do you enjoy being? Consider personal qualities, level of education, financial status, values, interests, and other things that might be important to you.
3. Are you likely to meet these kinds of people where you are going or through what you are presently doing?
4. What activities are of genuine interest to you?

You might meet people through pursuing the following activities or interests. How do you feel you would best be able to meet people who would interest you?

—*sports*
—*church*
—*professional organizations*
—*special-interest clubs*
—*concerts*
—*Laundromats*
—*newspaper ads*
—*college and adult education courses*
—*therapy groups*
—*libraries*
—*civic organizations*
—*work*
—*singles bars*
—*clubs for single people*
—*lectures*
—*museums*
—*dating services*
—*through friends*
—*trips (including special-interest trips)*
—*encounter groups*
—*book clubs*
—*political activities*

If it were possible to operate a vast clearinghouse for single people wanting to meet other single people with whom they would have something in common, arranging such meetings would not be a hit-or-miss affair. There are ways of increasing the probabilities of your meeting people who would interest you. Unfortunately, women have been socialized to be passive, particularly in meeting members of the opposite sex (remember the song from the Walt Disney version of *Snow White*, "Some Day My Prince Will Come"?). You may have to start a group or become involved in a new activity in order to meet people. For example, if your favorite composer is Richard Wagner and you would love to meet someone who shares your passion, you might start a Wagner Society.

EXAMPLE
When Doris sat down and wrote a description of the people she would like to meet, she came up with the following adjectives: intelligent, creative, articulate, poised, active, and aesthetic. These were the qualities she wanted in the men and women she met. When she thought about how she tried to meet people—through clubs for single parents and by checking out area bars with her women friends—she realized that these were not the best places to meet the people she would be most interested in knowing. She decided to join a local drama club in which she was genuinely interested. This increased her chances for meeting people with whom she would have something in common and at the same time she was doing something that genuinely interested her. As she became involved with acting in plays, she found that she did meet people. Her attention at that point was not focused solely upon meeting people; she was also enjoying herself and going ahead with what she wanted to do. Although she did not immediately meet the "man of her dreams," she felt her chances of meeting men of interest to her through the theater group were better than they would be at a singles' bar.

Loneliness is a problem all divorced people experience at some point in the process. Because women are taught to wait until they are approached, never to call a man, and not to initiate interaction with others, they often take a passive stance in dealing with their loneliness. This often creates a feeling of powerlessness and frustration. Waiting for the phone to ring, for someone to have **a** party, or for a stranger to begin a conversation results in giving the responsibility for one's social life to other people.

ARE YOU APPROACHABLE?

Some women seem to have a knack for meeting people; others never seem to meet anyone. Make an attempt to examine how approachable you are and experiment with ways to approach other people. You might go to a party, a social gathering, or any place you normally go to meet people. Take a friend and ask that friend to observe you briefly at different times during the evening. Ask your friend to answer these questions:

1. What kind of feelings did I transmit? How did I transmit them—through facial expression, eye contact, body posture, or body language?
2. Did I attract people by the way I was dressed? What kinds of people?

3. What was I doing that attracted people? Repelled people?
4. Did I seem interested in the people to whom I talked? Did I talk to them in an animated way?
5. When I was by myself, what impression did I convey? Discomfort? Loneliness? Enjoyment?
6. When I was with a group, did I give the impression that other people were free to join us?
7. Did I seem passive—waiting for something to happen—or active—contributing to my own enjoyment?

Or you might want to assess your approachability by going to a public place such as a restaurant, zoo, park, or museum. Deliberately look in a friendly way at one or two people; don't stare. You could try smiling and looking cheerful or you could look at them as if something about them interested you.

1. How did you feel when you looked at the person?
2. What did you notice about the person at whom you looked? Expression? Physical characteristics? Clothing?
3. What reaction did the person have once he or she noticed you were looking at him or her?
4. What was your reaction when the person looked at you?
5. Did you find that you looked down or away from people? Did you avoid eye contact with others?

Women may focus on their own feelings of shyness and awkwardness without realizing that men may be just as shy. One way to be approachable is to take the initiative and approach others. Begin a conversation with a person in a public place—while waiting for a bus, on a train, in a supermarket, at a museum. To open the conversation you could

- Ask a question requiring more than a yes or no answer, preferably a question that you would really like answered and that would stimulate further conversation. For example, "I noticed you got on the train at Oak Park. What do you think about that community?"
- Refer to a common experience. For example, "The conductor on this train is a char-

acter; he really seems to enjoy his job."
- Express a positive feeling about the people or setting. For example, "This transportation system is certainly efficient—it really makes it easy to live in the suburbs and work in the city."

Then ask yourself these questions:

1. How did you feel before you initiated the conversation?
2. How did you feel after you initiated the conversation?
3. How did the other person react?
4. What did you learn about yourself?

Once you are able to initiate conversations under conditions that are less threatening to you, try to initiate them in settings or with people you find more stressful. For example, if you went to a party and saw a man you found attractive, how would you initiate a conversation? Think of three examples of things you could say.*

Some women collect openers to use; others wait until they are in a particular situation before they decide what they will say. The important thing is to discover your particular style of initiating conversations and to feel natural about it. One woman may be able to carry off, "Aren't you the one who won the Don Johnson look-alike contest?" Another would feel ridiculous. The most important thing is to be yourself and say what is comfortable for you.

CAN YOU TAKE THE INITIATIVE?

To learn how comfortable you feel in taking the initiative in social situations, rank order the following suggestions according to the difficulty you would experience in carrying them out.* The suggestions you would find easiest should be numbered "1." You may assign the same ranking more than once. Disregard suggestions that don't apply to you.

- Introduce yourself to a new person in your office building, the grocery store, or in a class.

* Adapted from *Asserting Yourself*, by Sharon Anthony Bower and Gordon H. Bower, copyright © 1976, by permission of Addison-Wesley Publishing Co., Reading, Mass.
* From a doctoral dissertation, "A Comparative Study of Friendship Behaviors," by Peggy H. Smith (Stanford University, 1974).

- Invite someone who is going your way to walk with you.
- Ask to join the next game or bull session you see in progress. If you work in an office, join a coffee-break talk group.
- Conduct a personal opinion survey. Ask ten people their opinions on a certain topic; ask each person the same question.
- Ask someone you don't know if you can borrow twenty-five cents for a phone call. **Arrange to pay him or her back.**
- Find out the name of a man in your office, class, or social club. Call him on the telephone and ask about the latest work issue, class assignment, or upcoming event.
- Go to a coffeehouse. Smile and nod at the first three people who look at you. Strike up a conversation with at least one person of the same sex.
- Stand in a line at a grocery store, bank, or movie theater. Strike up a conversation about the line with the person nearest you.
- Converse with the gas station attendant as he or she is filling your tank and checking the oil.
- Sit down beside a man who looks interesting—in a bus, lounge, or class. Make some sort of opening comment.
- Ask three people for directions. Shift at least one of them into general conversation for a minute or two.
- Go to a jogging track, beach, or swimming pool and converse with two or three strangers.
- Notice someone who needs help in your neighborhood, class, or office. Offer to help.
- Carry a copy of a controversial book with you for one day. Count the number of people who start a conversation about it.
- Organize and throw a small party, say three to five people. Invite at least one person you don't know well.
- The next time you have a problem, find someone who is not close to you and ask his or her advice.
- Invite someone to go eat with you, someone with whom you have not eaten before.
- Decide to say "Hi" to five people you would not normally greet. Smile and try to get them to respond.

YOUR SEXUAL CONDITIONING

Unfortunately, most women were socialized not to take responsiblity for their sexual enjoyment and development. In order to become sexually responsive, women often have to overcome negative messages and experiences concerning sex. It didn't take long for most women to learn, for example, that there were different sexual rules for girls and boys. Many women who divorce report that their sex lives while married were unsatisfactory, thus further conditioning them to believe that "sex isn't much fun" or that they are in some way "sexually deficient." One way to begin to examine who you are as a sexual person is to ask yourself what negative sex attitudes you have developed. Try to find out where they came from. One positive aspect of divorce is that you have the freedom to examine and make decisions about your sexuality without the consequences such behavior might have if you were married.

If possible, sit down with a close female friend and describe to one another your sexual attitudes and the experiences you had while you were growing up and while you were married that influenced your present sexual identity. The following questions* could serve as a guide for your discussion. Spend five to ten minutes on each question. If it is not possible to discuss the subject with a friend or if you feel uncomfortable doing so, answer the questions for yourself.

1. What were your parents' attitudes toward sex? What was your mother's attitude? What was your father's attitude? How were these attitudes communicated to you?
2. What attitude did your friends have toward sex as you were growing up?
3. When and how did you learn about menstruation? What was the attitude of the person who told you? Were you frequently uncomfortable? Did you have cramps? Were you ever embarrassed by an incident involving menstruation?
4. When and how did you learn about masturbation? Do you remember when you

* Excerpts from *For Yourself: The Fulfillment of Female Sexuality,* by Lonnie Garfield Barbach. Copyright © 1975 by Lonnie Garfield Barbach. Reprinted by permission of Doubleday & Company, Inc.

first masturbated? Did anyone tell you that masturbation was wrong or harmful?

5. When and how did you learn what sex really was? Were you shocked?

6. What were the circumstances of your first real sexual experience? What was it like for you? How did you feel about it?

7. Did you have any sexual traumas such as child-adult sexual contact or rape?

8. Did you enjoy sex during marriage? What was your husband's attitude toward sex? What was your attitude? Did either of you experience sexual problems? How did you deal with those problems?

9. Did you feel free to discuss sex with your husband?

10. What sexual experiences have you had as a divorced person that have contributed to your present attitude toward sex and your sexual identity?

Consider your answers. What attitudes have you developed that might interfere with your enjoyment of your own sexuality? What did you learn about women's attitudes toward sex and toward the way they *should* behave, act, or feel sexually? Do these interfere with your enjoyment of your own sexuality or do they no longer apply to your present life-style as a divorced person? Do you have any sexual attitudes you would like to change? If there are sexual attitudes you would like to change, make a contract with yourself telling how you plan to change them.

EXAMPLE
I want to change my attitude that women should play a passive role and never initiate sexual activity. The next time I am with John and feel sexual, I'm going to let him know by verbal or physical actions that feel natural to me at the time.

*Signed*_____

Being sexually liberated means using the freedom you have to choose the sexual values and activities that are right and pleasurable for you. Sexual and personal liberation often go together. Taking control of one's life, at the intimate, personal, and fundamental level of one's sexuality seems to lead to taking control of the other areas of one's life as well.

SEXUAL STAGES

In their book, *The Divorce Experience* (New York: McGraw-Hill, 1977), Morton and Bernice Hunt state that they found divorced people to be fairly open about their sexual behavior, that nearly all took advantage of their new sexual freedom, that most had more partners than they ever expected to have, and that divorced women responding to their 1974 study had intercourse four times as often as those answering their 1940 survey. The Hunts stated that most divorced people found their postmarital sexual experiences to be more pleasurable and satisfying than their marital ones had been. Nearly three fourths of the men and two thirds of the women in the sample reported that they had had at least some casual sex after divorce.

Being sexually liberated means having the freedom as a divorced woman *not* to have sexual relationships if you do not feel they will meet your needs and values. The purpose of this activity is to encourage you to examine your sexual behavior as part of the total adjustment process that divorce requires. In *The Divorce Experience*, the Hunts stated that postmarital sexual behavior is basically a reconstructive process— "what appears to be mere self-indulgence is actually a means to the essential ends of ego-repair, the discovery (or rediscovery) of one's mature sexual self, and its integration with the formerly married's emergent, changing personality."

Three major stages describing how sexual behavior can function as a reconstructive process are listed here. Some people may skip over one stage, or even two. Many divorced people go through the three stages in sequence. Which stage, if any, best describes you at this time?

STAGE 1: EGO REPAIR
In this stage, the divorced woman is interested in learning if she is desirable to others, can function sexually, and can successfully give and receive pleasure. Most women find that their first sexual experiences are reassuring and affirming. Women who felt "cold," "frigid," and "unwomanly" often begin to feel alive, confident, and able to like themselves. The divorced woman is primarily interested in sexual affirmation and

feeling good about herself. There are seldom any deep emotional ties to sex partners during stage 1; the enthusiasm for sex on a primarily physical level is typical of this stage. Stage 1 rewards divorced women by letting them know that they are fully functioning physically and that they can still desire and be desired.

STAGE 2: EXPLORATION

In this stage, the divorced woman explores her own sexuality as well as that of others. For women who married long ago and/or had little premarital experience, it provides a needed sexual education; for women who have had some experience in the era of sexual liberation, it provides a refresher course. Women use this stage to educate themselves to be more adequate sexual partners in the future. Women learn that there is great variety in styles of sexual response, that their partners' bodies can vary greatly, that different partners have different idiosyncrasies, and that their partners' moods can vary greatly. When women experience variety during this phase, they are able to decide which style of sexuality suits their needs. This stage also teaches women that there are different techniques of lovemaking and that no two people use identical techniques. Women who have had a few partners may be exposed to techniques they have not previously tried. The divorced woman gains from this stage an increased sexual knowledge, an enhanced sexual identity, and an expanded realization of her ability to respond and evoke response in a partner.

STAGE 3: RECONSTRUCTION

Sooner or later, most women discover that sex and affection go together and reinforce each other. They begin to want something more than recreational sex; they want to care for their partner. They want to have sex only with someone who cares in return. The length of time women take to feel this way varies. For most women, such a feeling is a result of a gradual process in which casual sex slowly becomes less exciting and satisfying. The need for emotional as well as physical intimacy begins to appear. Sex is united with deep caring and love, the total personality of the woman, and with commitment to the partner. Sometimes this stage may be reached with a single partner; usually, it is a gradual process

that requires a number of trials of various sorts. Such trial relationships are an essential part of self-discovery and development. Most women have several imperfect or abortive love relationships before entering one that seems right and deep enough to be a realistic basis for remarriage. An acknowledged, truly loving, and exclusive relationship is possible when stage 3 has been completed.

The Hunts cite a woman's experience illustrating the sexual reconstuction process.

I needed some experimentation with sex after a long and sexually disappointing marriage. I had several experiences with men I was attracted to, but I wasn't seriously interested in them, nor were they with me. But it gave me a chance to discover that yes, I could function, my body worked okay, that I was attractive. I needed that time to get ready for a more important relationship.

Now I find casual sex less satisfactory than sex in the context of a relationship. I've had several, but only one has been serious. He and I have gone together for a year, off and on. We have love for each other but he is fearful of a committed relationship and tends to feel trapped; when things get very intensive between us he disappears for a few weeks. Then we get back together.

I wonder at my own desire to continue with him; he's a poor marriage prospect. Perhaps he protects me from facing remarriage. But even if it were to end this time, I would feel that I've benefited—I've learned a lot about relating sexually and emotionally, I've gained increased self-esteem as a female. *

Hospital administrator, 36, in a southwestern city

Do you think you have experienced any of the stages that were described? Do you feel any of the stages describe you presently? If you feel a stage describes you presently, how do you feel about being in that stage? What can you do to accept yourself and to accept the stage you are in?

* Morton and Bernice Hunt, *The Divorce Experience* (New York: McGraw-Hill, 1977).

"SAFE SEX" IN THE AIDS ERA

While some divorced women may experience the three sexual stages previously described, others will find that they do not want to engage in sexual relationships unless they know their partner very well and there is the possibility for an ongoing relationship. Women are becoming much more cautious about sexual activity because of the threat of contracting AIDS and other sexually transmitted diseases.

There are conflicting and changing reports as to what is considered "safe sex" and how great your chances are of contracting AIDS as a heterosexual woman. There are two "truths" concerning AIDS:

1. The only way to be 100 percent sure that you will not contract AIDS sexually is if you remain sexually abstinent.
2. AIDS is deadly and there is presently no known cure.

These two facts are sobering thoughts for the woman who is getting a divorce and may want to experience her sexuality through new associations. The reality is that few women will decide to abstain from sex to ensure that they will remain healthy. Being sexual today, however, brings higher risks and different decisions.

If you are considering having sex with a partner, think about the following questions:

1. How well do I know this man? Do I feel I know and like him enough that there may be the possibilitiy of an ongoing relationship?

It is important to consider if you like a man enough to risk being sexual with him. While knowing a man well will not ensure your protection from AIDS, it can help you decide if an affair is worth the risk. While some people are in a high-risk group (homosexuals, bisexuals, intravenous drug users, and clientele of prostitutes), it is impossible to be sure if a man has AIDS just by knowing him.

2. Do I know for sure that I am not an AIDS carrier?

If you are sexual, it is your responsibility not to pass AIDS to your partner. Be sure you insist that your partner use a condom regularly. Use a spermicide for added protection. (It is believed that spermicide contains an antiviral/bacterial agent which may protect you from AIDS and other venereal diseases.)

1. Do I feel comfortable enough to discuss precautions to ensure "safe sex"?

If you do not know a person well enough or do not feel comfortable discussing the requirements for "safe" sexual activity, the best thing is to wait until you know the person better.

4. Am I assertive enough to insist a man use a condom when he may not want to or offers objections?

Your health is your responsibility. This is one situation where not being assertive could be life threatening. Insist that your partner wear a condom. If he refuses, he is not good relationship material. He is either not concerned with your welfare or avoiding present sexual reality. Men may insist that they do not have AIDS, that they are sure you are "safe," that condoms interfere with their pleasure, and so on. If you and your partner are both concerned, you will cooperate in safe sex practices.

It is difficult to surrender yourself to the pleasure of a sexual relationship if you are worrying that you might be putting your health in jeopardy. Take care of yourself. That way you are more likely to enjoy a sexual relationship and can avoid nagging doubts afterward.

Some women believe that the AIDS crisis has supported them in their desire to be selective concerning their sexual partners. During the sixties and seventies, there was a trend toward sexual experimentation and the attitude, "If it feels good, do it." This trend tended to support the sexual stages of "ego repair" and "exploration" that many divorced women experience.

Other women found that they became involved sexually before they really wanted to. Once they were sexual, they were somehow "hooked" into a relationship that was not necessarily good for them. Because people are concerned for their health, there is more societal support today for knowing a person well before one enters into a sexual relationship.

ARE YOU IN AN ADDICTIVE RELATIONSHIP?

If a woman has divorced a man because she felt the relationship was not good for her, she may be surprised when she finds herself in a relationship that is similar to the relationship she had with her ex-husband. It is not accidental that women find that they have a pattern of becoming involved with alcoholics, men who are passive, men who are emotionally unavailable, men who are not capable of intimacy, and so on. While we may say we want a different kind of man when we divorce, we may find ourselves with a man who has similar problems because we have experienced this kind of relationship before, have learned the "rules" of such a relationship and feel somehow comfortable with the same patterns.

If you are involved in a relationship that does not genuinely enhance your life in many areas, you need to ask yourself what the payoff is for you. A payoff may be an advantage that may not always be obvious when one considers the obvious disadvantages of the relationship.

Just as people can be physically and emotionally addicted to alcohol and drugs, people can become addicted to relationships. A person is addicted when his or her attachment to a substance, a sensation, or a person interferes with the ability to deal effectively with oneself and one's environment. When we become addicted, we become increasingly dependent upon that experience as our only source of gratification.

An addiction serves many purposes and provides payoffs. If you think you may be addicted to a relationship, consider the following statements and check those that apply to you:

1. The relationship provides me with immediate relief from anxiety. When I am alone or by myself, I feel on edge and unable to participate in meaningful activity for extended periods of time.
2. The relationship structures my time. I do not have to make decisions concerning my future.
3. When I focus on the relationship, I can avoid and escape problems that exist in other parts of my life.
4. The relationship and its dynamics give me the security of predictable patterns and outcomes.
5. Predictable crises of the relationship creates a kind of high where my resources are mobilized. Once the crisis is over I am faced with my real problems which seem even more overwhelming.
6. I use sex in the relationship to escape from the problems we have and avoid other problems in my life. I seem to need sex as an escape more than as an expression of caring, pleasure, and celebration.
7. The relationship gives me a sense of identity. I would be lost without it.
8. When I think of the loss of the relationship, I become panicky, suffer physical distress, and feel that I would be unable to survive. (A feeling that goes far beyond the normal grief experienced at the loss of a loved one.)
9. Even though I know in rational moments that my relationship is not good for me and my friends agree, I am unable to end the relationship. When I try to end it I keep going back to him.
10. I create reasons for staying in the relationship even though I know the reasons for ending it are much stronger.

In a healthy relationship, people choose to be together because they enhance each other's lives. The relationship provides caring, mutual support, tenderness, affection, and an opportunity to develop into the best person you can be. It is sad when a woman has the courage to end one relationship in divorce, only to find herself in another destructive relationship. Because women are socialized to feel responsible for their relationships, not make waves, and be dependent, there is often societal and cultural support to stay in harmful relationships. If you feel you are addicted to a harmful relationship, get the help you need to move on through counseling or a support group. Robin Norwood's book, *Women Who Love Too Much* (Los Angeles: Tarcher, 1985), is an excellent resource.

WHAT MEN ARE RIGHT FOR YOU?

After they have been divorced for a while and have had some dating experiences, divorced women find that they become more selective concerning who they date. The great majority of divorced people do remarry. Many of those who state they would like to remarry have not done so because they are either still working on their personal adjustment to divorce and their personal growth or because they feel that they have grown and adjusted to their divorce and only need to find the right person. Some people who feel they are ready for a committed relationship choose people who are not right for them because this makes them *safe;* these people are not really ready for a serious relationship. Whether or not you are ready for a committed relationship, it helps to keep in mind the qualities you are looking for in men as you become more selective in the dating process. How would you answer these questions?

1. What did you like about your ex-husband? What did you dislike?
2. Think about the men you have dated. What qualities or personal characteristics stand out that you would like to have in a partner?
3. Which qualities or personal characteristics did you dislike in men you have dated?
4. Which of the men you dated seemed to bring out the best in you? Which brought out the worst in you? What qualities do you need in a partner in order to feel the way you want to feel—good about yourself, alive, full of energy, comfortable, spontaneous?
5. Think about your answers to the first four questions. Some of the qualities you listed as being important to you may have been listed more than once. List these and rank order them. If you listed a number of qualities, can you combine some of the qualities into categories?
6. Do you feel that you have adjusted to your divorce and your life as a single person? Which stage of the adjustment process applies to you?
7. Do you feel you have the time and energy to devote to a committed relationship? Have you experienced personal growth, resolved problem areas, and completed goals?
8. Do you have a firm sense of who you are?
9. Do you feel confident and secure in your ability to support yourself and be an independent adult?
10. Have you had the dating and other experiences you want as a single person? Do you feel you will not be missing anything if you devote your time to a committed relationship?

If your answers to questions 6 through 10 are yes, you are probably ready for a committed relationship(s). How ready are you for a committed relationship? If you have dated people who are not right for you, do you feel you have selected these people because you are not really ready for a committed relationship? Are the qualities you listed as being important in a man consistent with the values you listed as most important to you in chapter 3? Are the qualities consistent with those you decided were important in friends in chapter 1?

THINKING OF REMARRIAGE?

To appraise your readiness for remarriage and the likelihood of the marriage's being a success, answer yes or no to the following statements:

- You are happy as a single person.
- You are financially able to support yourself.
- You have a job you enjoy.
- You feel you are both ready for remarriage.
- The person shares your values.
- The person has the qualities that are important to you.
- You have dated other people.
- You have dated for at least a year and have seen the person in a variety of situations.
- Your friends like the person.
- Your friends can "see you two together."
- Your parents like the person.
- You like the person's family (parents, children).
- You have common interests.
- You have common goals.
- Your children like the person.
- The person likes your children.
- You have spent long periods of time with the person in the family situation you will have.

- You have the same level of education.
- You have similar religious beliefs.
- You have discussed how you will handle problems concerning children and agree.
- You have discussed financial arrangements.
- You have discussed whether or not you want to have children and the means of birth control you will use.
- You have a satisfying sexual relationship.
- You have discussed the degree of freedom each of you will have in the marriage.
- You have shared expectations you may have of each other when you marry.
- You have discussed honestly and openly special health or emotional problems either of you may have.
- Each of you is aware of problems you had in your former marriage(s); you both feel you will be able to avoid or work out similar problems that might arise in a future marriage.
- You have had several fights and are familiar with how the person fights and makes up.
- You both feel you have fully adjusted to your divorce(s).
- You have accepted your partner as he is, not as you would like him to be.
- You believe the marriage has a good chance for success.
- You feel you are ready for marriage.
- You feel your partner is ready for marriage.

The more questions you could answer yes, the greater the probability that both you and your partner are ready for marriage and that the marriage will be successful. Answer the following questions by determining the appropriate points on the scales provided. *Do not share your responses with your partner.*

1. How ready do you feel you are to marry again?

NOT READY   SOMEWHAT READY   VERY READY

2. How ready do you feel your partner is to marry again?

NOT READY   SOMEWHAT READY   VERY READY

3. How successful do you think your marriage will be?

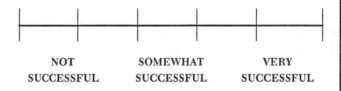

NOT SUCCESSFUL   SOMEWHAT SUCCESSFUL   VERY SUCCESSFUL

Now, ask your partner to evaluate how he feels about these questions by providing him with an unmarked copy of the scales. Have him indicate his responses on the scales. Compare your responses with those of your partner.

Now ask yourself these questions:

1. Do your responses generally agree?
2. What are the reasons for your respective responses?
3. If your responses differ radically, what can be done to bring them closer together?
4. What do you think a comparison of your responses suggests?

USING ASSERTIVENESS TO IMPLEMENT DECISIONS

I used to try to please everyone. I would never say no to a request and was afraid that people wouldn't like me if I were honest and direct. I don't know how I appeared to others, but for a time I had the feeling that I didn't really exist. Divorce forced me not only to make decisions but to stand up for my right to make decisions and carry them out. Basically, I do what I want to now. I have a better sense of who I am and am happier. Somehow, I have the feeling that others respect me more, too. If they don't, I've learned that I can survive their disapproval. I'm doing what's right for me!

The preceding chapters have encouraged you to consider and make some of the decisions necessitated by divorce. The gap between making a decision and implementing it can be a large one. Not only do you need to consider the skills needed to make decisions, you must also consider the skills needed to carry out those decisions. Some women become discouraged when, after making decisions for themselves, they are faced with obstacles in implementing their decisions.

Since many women have been socialized to be passive and dependent upon others, it is understandable that when it comes to carrying out the decisions they have made, they are often faced with obstacles. Women may face internal obstacles when they are unable to say no, stand up to authority figures, express anger, or tell someone that his or her behavior is bothering them. Women may face external obstacles when other people stand in the way of what they want. The principles of assertiveness training can help women act on their decisions and deal with obstacles effectively.

Assertiveness training tries to help women discard self-defeating, nonassertive or aggressive behavior and to adopt healthier, more direct behavior. In the process, a woman is able to develop self-esteem. She may not always be able to achieve her goals but she at least has the satisfaction of knowing that she has tried to get what she wants in a straightforward fashion. She increases her self-esteem when she learns she is able to act to change situations; she need not only react to the situations. Being able to initiate action increases one's sense of personal power, autonomy, and independence. While everyone could benefit from the principles of assertiveness training, it is particularly relevant for women.

Women are often rewarded by society for nonassertive behavior; they are called "sweet," "demure," "feminine," and so on. Similar nonassertive behavior used by men would be labeled as "wishy-washy," "passive," and "unmanly." Because women have been socialized to be nonassertive, even mental-health professionals have differing standards of what is "mentally healthy" for men and "mentally healthy" for women. Men are encouraged to become assertive; they are told they are "stronger," more "ambitious," and should "stand up for their rights." When women become more assertive they are accused of being "too independent," "selfish," and "castrating." This double standard approves of nonassertive behavior for women but not for men. Other unwritten rules also keep women from being assertive; it is all right to be intelligent, but not more intelligent than men. Women can work and earn money, but they should not hold better positions nor earn more money than men. Many women who are intelligent and successful find it necessary to hide these facts. The sad fact is that, although women are often rewarded for their nonassertive behavior, they are rewarded at a tremendous cost to themselves. At the same time they are being praised for being feminine, they feel powerless, dependent, incapable, ignorant, depressed, and unable to maintain control of their own lives. For these reasons assertiveness training is of utmost importance to women; it offers a healthy alternative to nonassertive and aggressive behaviors.

In this chapter, you will be asked to examine special difficulties you may have in getting what you want and will learn to use the principles of assertiveness to overcome these difficulties. The chapter is only a brief introduction to assertiveness training. You may want to refer to other books or, better yet, take a course that allows you to practice being assertive!

NOT ACTING UPON DECISIONS

Everyone has had the experience of making a decision and then not being able to act upon it. Perhaps it was a major decision, such as getting a divorce, and you found guilt feelings kept getting in your way. Or perhaps it was a split-second decision, such as not wanting to watch your best friend's children for three hours on the one afternoon you had for yourself, but you found yourself unable to say no. Being assertive about your decisions means being able to go after what you want and simultaneously respecting the rights of others. Everyone has certain problem spots when it comes to standing up for what they want.

To evaluate the kinds of decisions you have failed to act upon, answer the following questions:

1. Think of decisions you have made and failed to act upon and/or situations where you have wanted something but failed to act accordingly. Make a list of these.
2. What did you do or fail to do that resulted in your not getting what you wanted?
3. What feelings kept you from doing what was necessary to get what you wanted?
4. What were you afraid would happen if you acted to get what you wanted?
5. When you did not act on your behalf, how did you feel about yourself? If other people were involved, how did you feel about them?

ASSERTIVE, NONASSERTIVE, AND AGGRESSIVE BEHAVIOR

Basically, people use three types of behavior to get what they want: assertive behavior, nonassertive behavior, and aggressive behavior. Read the following descriptions and decide which one applies to your usual behavior.

ASSERTIVE BEHAVIOR

Characteristics of assertive behavior include expressing your feelings, needs, ideas, and rights in ways that don't violate the rights of others. Assertive behavior is usually honest, direct, expressive, spontaneous, and self-enhancing. The assertive woman makes her own choices, is confident, and feels good about herself while she is being assertive and afterward. She usually achieves her goals; when she doesn't, she still feels good about herself because she knows she has been straightforward. Acting assertively reinforces her good feelings about herself, improves her self-confidence, and creates free, honest, and open relationships with others.

NONASSERTIVE BEHAVIOR

Characteristics of nonassertive behavior include not expressing your feelings, needs, and ideas; ignoring your rights; and allowing others to infringe upon them. Nonassertive behavior is usually emotionally dishonest, indirect, inhibited, and self-denying. The nonassertive woman often lets other people choose for her and ends up feeling disappointed in herself and angry with them; at best, she can be described as passive, at worst as a doormat. She chooses nonassertive behavior to avoid unpleasant situations, tension, conflict, and confrontation.

AGGRESSIVE BEHAVIOR

Characteristics of aggressive behavior include expressing your feelings, needs, and ideas at the expense of others. The aggressive woman stands up for her rights but ignores the rights of others; she may dominate or humiliate other people. While this behavior is expressive, it is also defensive, hostile, and self-defeating.

The aggressive woman tries to make choices for herself and for others. She usually ends up feeling angry, self-righteous, and guilty. She uses aggressive behavior to vent her anger and to achieve her goals, at least for the present. Her behavior often turns people away and she ends up frustrated, bitter, and alone. Because an aggressive woman is viewed as unfeminine in our society and because the passive woman also suffers, a woman may become indirectly aggressive; she may develop ways to get what she wants by indirect means. She may use trickery, seduction, or manipulation. When she is angry, she may use sneaky ways to get revenge rather than express her anger directly.

The alternative answers to the following example indicate possible assertive, nonassertive, or aggressive responses to a situation. Which behavior do you feel best describes your usual behavior? Can you think of examples of situations in which you used aggressive, assertive, and nonassertive behavior? How did you feel about yourself when you used each type of behavior? Which type of behavior worked best for you?

EXAMPLE

Your children are with their father for the weekend and you are looking forward to spending a weekend alone. You have not had a day to yourself for a long time and you feel you really need one. Your best friend, who is also divorced, calls. Her baby-sitting arrangement has fallen through at the last minute and she wonders if you would be willing to take her four-year-old for the weekend so she can go on the ski trip she had planned. You really don't want to because you want to be alone.

RESPONSES

1. "Well . . . uh . . . I guess I could . . . (pause) . . . uh . . . O.K."
   (Nonassertive: nonverbal pauses with apparent hesitancy)
2. "I'd love to take care of her, but this is the weekend I promised I'd spend with Aunt Martha helping her clean her attic. I'd take your daughter with me but Aunt Martha gets nervous around children."
   (Nonassertive: excuses)
3. "You have a nerve asking someone else to devote a weekend to taking care of your child."
   (Aggressive: attacking with an attempt to make the requester feel guilty)
4. "I understand that the ski weekend is very important to you, but I really need this weekend to myself."
   (Assertive: direct refusal)
5. "What's the matter—am I the only person you can find who can put up with your child for a weekend?"
   (Aggressive: sarcastic)
6. "I really had planned and needed to have this weekend for myself. I understand how long you have planned and counted on your ski weekend. I will take your daughter this weekend if you will take my children next weekend so I can have some time for myself."
   (Assertive: compromise)

YOUR BASIC RIGHTS

Many books on assertiveness training list a "bill of rights" in which women must believe if they are to learn to assert themselves and feel good about it. Women sometimes overlook these basic rights when they are passive and fail to stand up for what they want. If others fail to respect these rights, assertive responses may be necessary.

Read the following list of rights. Which apply to you? Can you think of any others?

- The right to be treated with respect
- The right to have and express your own feelings and opinions
- The right to be listened to and taken seriously

- The right to set your own priorities
- The right to say no without feeling guilty
- The right to ask for what you want
- The right to get what you pay for
- The right to ask for information from professionals
- The right to make mistakes and be responsible for them
- The right to say "I don't know the answer"
- The right to say that you need some time to think it over
- The right to self-fulfillment
- The right to accept challenge
- The right to determine your own life-style
- The right to change—your mind, yourself, your behavior, your values, your life situations
- The right to privacy
- The right to be intelligent
- The right to offer no reasons or justifications for your behavior
- The right to judge whether or not you are responsible for finding solutions to other people's problems
- The right to choose not to assert yourself

Which of these rights have you failed to defend assertively? Think of specific examples. What assertive responses could you have made in each situation?

If you find you are resentful of your children, can you think of any rights you may not be defending? Sometimes the divorced mother forgets that she has the right to privacy, the right to time for herself, the right to adult companionship, the right to a social life, and so on.*

HOW ASSERTIVE ARE YOU?

AN ASSERTIVE CHECKLIST†
Read the list of items below. How would you rate yourself? Indicate whether you would never, rarely, sometimes, usually, or always respond in a given fashion. Write down your responses.

* This exercise was adapted from Lynn Z. Bloom, Karen Levin Coburn, and Joan Crystal Pearlman, *The New Assertive Woman*, pp. 32–33. Copyright © 1975 by Lynn Z. Bloom, Karen Levin Coburn, and Joan Crystal Pearlman. Reprinted by permission of Delacorte Press.
† Taken from Susan M. Osborn and Gloria G. Harris, *Assertive Training for Women* (1975), courtesy of Charles C. Thomas, Publisher, Springfield, Illinois.

1. I do my own thinking.
2. I can be myself around wealthy, educated, or famous people.
3. I am poised and confident among strangers.
4. I freely express my emotions.
5. I am friendly and considerate of others.
6. I accept compliments and gifts without embarrassment or a sense of obligation.
7. I freely express my admiration of others' ideas and achievements.
8. I readily admit my mistakes.
9. I accept responsibility for my life.
10. I make my own decisions and accept the consequences.
11. I take the initiative in personal contacts.
12. When I have done something well I tell others.
13. I am confident when going for job interviews.
14. When I need help, I ask others to help me.
15. When at fault, I apologize.
16. When I like someone very much, I tell him or her so.
17. When confused, I ask for clarification.
18. When someone is annoying me, I ask that person to stop.
19. When someone cuts in front of me in line, I protest.
20. When treated unfairly, I object.
21. If I were underpaid, I would ask for a salary increase.
22. When I am lonely or depressed, I take action to improve my situation.
23. When working at a job or task I dislike intensely, I look for ways to improve my situation.
24. I complain to the management when I have been overcharged or have received poor service.
25. When something in my house or apartment malfunctions, I see that it is repaired.
26. When I am disturbed by someone's smoking, I say so.
27. When a friend betrays my confidence, I tell that person how I feel.
28. I ask my doctor all of the questions I want answered.
29. I ask for directions when I need help finding my way.
30. When there are problems, I maintain a

relationship rather than cutting it off.

31. I communicate my belief that everyone in the home should help with the up-keep rather than doing it all myself.

32. I make sexual advances toward my sex partner.

33. If served food at a restaurant that is not prepared the way I ordered it, I express my dissatisfaction to the food server.

34. Even though a clerk goes to a great deal of trouble to show merchandise to me, I am able to say no.

35. When I discover that I have purchased defective merchandise, I return it to the store.

36. When people talk in a theater, lecture, or concert, I am able to ask them to be quiet.

37. I maintain good eye contact in conversations.

38. I would sit in the front of a large group if the only remaining seats were located there.

39. I would speak to my neighbors if their dog was keeping me awake by barking at night.

40. When interrupted, I comment on the interruption and then finish what I am saying.

41. When a friend makes plans for me without my knowledge or consent, I object.

42. When I miss someone, I express the fact that I want to spend more time with that person.

43. When a person asks me to lend something and I really do not want to do so, I refuse.

44. When a friend invites me to join him or her and I really don't want to do so, I turn down the invitation.

45. When friends phone and talk too long, I can terminate the conversation effectively.

46. When someone criticizes me, I listen to the criticism without being defensive.

47. When people are discussing a subject and I disagree with their points of view, I express my difference of opinion.

48. When someone makes demands on me that I do not wish to fulfill, I resist the demands.

49. I speak up readily in group situations.

50. I tell my children the things I like about them.

51. When my children make endless demands on my time and energy, I establish some firm notions about the amount of time I am willing to give.

52. When one friend is not meeting all of my needs, I establish meaningful ties with other people.

53. When my own parents, in-laws, or friends freely give advice, I express appreciation for their interest and concern without feeling obligated to follow their suggestions.

54. When someone completes a task or job for me with which I am dissatisfied, I ask that it be done correctly.

55. When I object to political practices, I take action rather than blaming politicians.

56. When I am jealous, I explore the reasons for my feelings, and look for ways of increasing my self-confidence and self-esteem.

57. When a woman tells me she envies me, I accept her comments without feeling guilty or apologetic.

58. When I am feeling insecure, I assess my personal strengths and then take action designed to make me feel more secure.

59. I accept my lover's interest in other people without feeling I must compete with them.

60. I insist in following safe sex practices even though my partner may be reluctant to do so.

Give yourself one point for every "never," two points for "rarely," three for "sometimes," four for "usually," and five for "always." Now total your score. The higher it is, the greater your degree of assertive behavior.

Did the quiz bring to mind any situations in which you found it difficult to be assertive? What were they?

"WHO DONE IT?"*

Think of a particular situation in which you acted nonassertively. Which of the items below caused you to behave nonassertively? Make a list of these items to use in guiding your progress toward assertive behaviors.

* From Stanlee Phelps and Nancy Austin, *The Assertive Woman.* Copyright © 1975. Impact Publishers, Inc., San Luis Obispo, California. Reprinted by permission of the publisher.

1. Who made you feel passive or nonassertive?

—*a spouse*
—*a relative*
—*an employer*
—*a teacher*
—*a police officer*
—*an acquaintance*
—*children*
—*friends*
—*an employee*
—*a doctor*
—*a sales clerk*
—*waiters or waitresses*

2. Have you felt nonassertive when you *ask* for

—*cooperation from children, employer, employees?*
—*a loan of money or of an item?*
—*a favor?*
—*a job?*
—*a raise?*
—*love and attention?*
—*directions?*

3. What subject(s) has caused you to behave nonassertively?

—*sex*
—*women's rights*
—*others' accomplishments*
—*expressing positive feelings*
—*politics*
—*your accomplishments*
—*your mistakes*
—*others' mistakes*
—*expressing negative feelings*

4. Group size might be a factor in causing you to behave nonassertively; did the situation involve you and

—*one other familiar person?*
—*one other unfamiliar person?*
—*two or more familiar persons?*
—*two or more unfamiliar persons?*
—*a group of familiar persons?*
—*a group of unfamiliar persons?*

WHICH TRAPS SNARE YOU?

Women often fall into certain traps that make it difficult for them to stand up for what they want.

The following are traps that snare many women who would like to be assertive. Which apply to you? Think of situations in which you may not have acted assertively because of one of these traps. Add examples in each category that may apply.

FEMININE STEREOTYPE TRAP: You learned that

· Girls are helpless
· Girls need to be protected and taken care of
· Girls are fearful
· Girls are dependent
· Girls find greatest fulfillment as wives and mothers
· Girls need a man in order to be happy
· Girls are passive
· Girls are weak and easily hurt
· Girls are obedient
· Girls are illogical
· Girls are poor in math
· Girls aren't mechanical

FAMILY TRAINING TRAP: You were taught

· That you were Daddy's little girl
· That girls don't "rock the boat"
· To act sweet, cute, and "like a lady"
· That nice girls don't argue or talk back
· That girls don't fight
· That if you can't say anything nice, don't say anything at all
· Not to bother Daddy
· Not to "touch yourself down there"
· That girls should play quietly

BODY TRAP: You learned that

· Girls should sit still
· Girls should have their hands in their laps
· Girls should not look at a man first
· Girls should not stare
· Girls should smile sweetly
· Girls should talk softly
· Girls don't masturbate
· Girls should stand with their legs together

THE APPROVAL TRAP: You need to be seen as

· The good or perfect wife
· The good or perfect mother
· The good or perfect housekeeper
· The good or perfect lover

- The good or perfect daughter
- The good or perfect daughter-in-lawThe good or perfect corporate wife
- The good or perfect friend
- The good or perfect student

THE COMPASSION TRAP: You feel you

- Exist to serve others
- Must provide tenderness, compassion, and sympathy at all times
- Must serve humanity
- Must keep the family together
- Must work in the helping professions
- Must support and stand behind a man
- Must be nurturing for others
- Must put others first
- Must care for sick, aged relatives
- Must satisfy your lover's sexual needs
- Must help in an emergency

THE RESPONSIBILITY TRAP: You feel you are

- Responsible for your children's happiness
- Responsible for your husband's happiness
- Responsible for your parents' happiness
- Responsible for your friends' happiness
- Responsible for your lover's sexual fulfillment and potency
- Responsible for your children's behavior
- Responsible for other people's feelings
- Responsible for your children's intelligence

THE AUTHORITY TRAP: Because you see others as authorities, you

- Feel you are inferior and know less
- Won't say no to your parents
- Won't question your doctor
- Won't question the mechanic's judgment and bill
- Won't complain to the headwaiter
- Won't set limits for your ex-husband
- Won't ask your boss for a raise or a promotion
- Find it nerve-wracking to go on job interviews
- Won't speak up in class

YOU'LL BE DEVASTATED TRAP: You'll be devastated if

- People say no to a request
- Your parents get angry
- Your boss criticizes you
- Your children don't love you
- You don't get a promotion
- People laugh at you
- People think you're stupid

Which traps apply to you? In what situations? To what extent do they prevent you from acting assertively? Do you act at all? Do you act but feel nervous?

Think of a situation in which you wanted or needed to be assertive but were afraid to be. Ask yourself these questions. Did you

1. Stop yourself from acting assertively because of beliefs concerning how you should or shouldn't act?
2. Have evidence from past experience to support any of the beliefs that kept you from being assertive?
3. Feel assertive actions have only unpleasant, devastating, and wrong outcomes?
4. Feel assertive actions could have positive, constructive, and favorable outcomes?
5. Have evidence from personal experience concerning the outcomes of assertive behavior?
6. Feel that you couldn't handle the results of your assertive behavior if they were unpleasant or problematic?

YOUR VULNERABLE AREAS

Many of the traps women fall into when they want to be assertive come from feelings within themselves that get in their way. You may find that you have internalized the expectations that others have of you or of women in general. The first step in handling these traps is to examine your beliefs. People who have a stake in your continued nonassertive behavior may act to play upon your feelings and to manipulate you.

EXAMPLES

The doctor, who can make more money if less time is spent answering questions, may cultivate a rushed and superior manner.

The headwaiter who doesn't want you to question the service or the bill may act superior and aloof.

Your mother, who wants you to eat every Sunday meal with her, may appear pitiful.

Your friend, who wants you to baby-sit for her children at a moment's notice, may sound hurt if you refuse.

The president of the PTA, who wants you to serve as cake chairperson for the annual dinner, may sound desperate.

Think of other examples, ones that get to you.

If you continue to live according to the beliefs that lead you into certain traps, others will be able to manipulate you. One way to avoid traps is to be aware of your vulnerable areas. Which areas or spots are particularly vulnerable for you?

- Being told you hurt someone's feelings
- Being told you are stupid or ignorant
- Being told you are overweight, underweight, and so on
- Being teased about your appearance
- Being told you disappoint someone
- Being told you are selfish
- Being told you are a bad mother

Manipulation requires two people, one person to aim at a vulnerable spot and another to react and be manipulated. Ways to respond when people aim at one of your vulnerable spots include:

- Not reacting
- Describing what the person is doing, expressing how you feel, asking the person to stop, and informing the person what you will do if he or she does not stop
- Agreeing with the person
- Responding to what the person is feeling, thus getting the manipulator to be honest about what he or she really wants
- Responding to what is said rather than to the attempt to manipulate you

EXAMPLE

Your mother says, "I think you are very selfish and inconsiderate not to be willing to eat dinner with your father and me on Sunday. You know how much we look forward to it." You might react in one of these ways.

1. Ignore the fact that your mother is trying to make you feel guilty. (If you are not willing to react, she will be unable to manipulate.)
2. "I really feel you are ignoring my right to spend a Sunday by myself and are trying to make me feel guilty. I don't like that. Please stop it. If you continue to use this

approach, I won't feel like spending any Sunday with you." (You are describing what your mother is doing, why you don't like it, and what you will do if she doesn't stop.)
3. "You're right. I may be selfish and inconsiderate." (You are refusing to fall into the need for approval trap.)
4. "You sound disappointed and hurt because I won't be having Sunday dinner with you." (You remain firm about what you want but your response could lead to a more honest exchange concerning your mother's feelings.)

   For example, she might respond with, "That's all right, dear (sigh). I know you need to have a Sunday now and then to yourself. Your father and I will be able to get along by ourselves."
5. "Gee, that's great you understand my need to have some time for myself. I know you and Dad can make it without me for one Sunday." (By responding to what is said rather than the "poor me" sighs and hurt voice, you are avoiding the compasssion trap.)

Give an example of a statement someone has made, or could make, that hit one of your vulnerable areas. List several assertive replies you could have made.

ASSERTIVENESS TECHNIQUES

There are several techniques you can use to assertively state what you want so as to avoid manipulation by others. Some techniques were discussed in the last activity, others are discussed here. Read the descriptions of these techniques. After reading them, think about the situations in which you could use one or a combination of the techniques to assert yourself.

1. Broken record technique: be persistent and keep saying over and over again what you want without getting angry, irritated, or loud. For example,

   You: I'd like Tommy to be home by eight o'clock.
   Ex-husband: He's never had to be back at a definite time before.

You: I know that. I want him home by eight o'clock tonight, tomorrow is a schoolday.

Ex-husband: That will cut into what I had planned.

You: That may be. I want him home by eight o'clock.

Ex-husband: You're being unreasonable.

You: That may be. I want him home by eight.

2. Don't answer questions and don't respond to statements—just repeat what you want without responding to questions designed to manipulate you. For example,

You: I don't want to make love tonight.

Date: You didn't feel that way last night.

You: That's right. I don't want to make love tonight.

Date: What's the matter, you have your period?

You: I don't want to make love.

Date: You frigid or something?

You: I don't want to make love.

3. Share your feelings.

Friend: Could you loan me your car tomorrow?

You: I really worry when I loan something that is important to me and which I can't replace. I have to say no.

Friend: But you know I'd be careful. I'd fix it if anything happened.

You: I know that, but I'd still worry. I really would feel better not loaning you my car.

4. Agree with the truth, principle, or the odds to cope with manipulative logic, argument, guilt-and-anxiety-inducing statements without being sarcastic.

Mother: The children mention that Jerry is sometimes there in the morning.

You: That's right, Mom, he is.

Mother: If you have him stay overnight, the neighbors will lose respect for you. It might not be good for the children.

You: You may be right, Mom. The neighbors might not respect me and it might not be good for the children.

5. Parroting: repeat what is said to you. Don't respond to statements intended to manipulate you as in the previous example.

6. Compromise: offer a workable compromise to the other person if you feel that your self-respect is not in question.

Date: Where do you want to eat?

You: I'd really like to eat Italian food. How about you?

Date: I'd prefer steak.

You: I'll go to the steakhouse tonight as long as we go to the Italian restaurant next time.

7. Let the other person know you hear and understand him or her. Tell the person how you feel, tell the person what you want.

Ex-husband: I'm in a financial pinch right now and I know you've just been paid. Can I give you the support money two weeks from now?

You: I realize that things may be difficult for you financially right now but I really want to be able to count on the child support the first of the month. I'd like it now.

By using this format, you respect the other person but also state what you want. Sometimes the first two steps are not necessary; however, following them in involved interactions encourages you to consider the other person as well as yourself.

Think of a situation in which you wanted to be assertive but found yourself unable to be. How could you have used one or more of the techniques described to assert yourself? How could you use one or more of these techniques in a present situation in which you want to assert yourself?

CAN YOU SAY NO?

A woman who is assertive can say no to requests when she is already busy, or she can say "Let me think about that—I'll get back to you" when she wants to decide whether or not she wants to do someone a favor. She examines her resources, decides which she wants to protect, and decides how she can be assertive about protecting them. Which of the following* apply to you?

1. On which of these activities do you spend a large part of your time?

   —*cooking, laundry*
   —*studying, reading*
   —*working away from home*
   —*driving*
   —*attending school*
   —*caring for children, family members*
   —*pursuing hobby*
   —*watching TV, movies*
   —*entertaining*

2. What specific requests are regularly made of you?

   —*driving*
   —*running errands*
   —*working overtime*
   —*attending meetings, accepting leadership positions*
   —*talking with friends, counseling friends*
   —*donating time or volunteering for worthy causes*
   —*traveling*

3. With which activities do your family and friends frequently expect you to help?

   —*housecleaning*
   —*cooking*
   —*chauffeuring*
   —*watching the children*
   —*loaning money*
   —*visiting and caring for relatives*

Are you satisfied with the amount of time you spend on each activity? What changes, if any would you like to make?

In what ways would you like to protect more of the resources you have—time, energy, money? Which specific requests would you like to refuse? Write out assertive responses to these requests. Remember that you have the right to say no and that the other person has the right to make a request.

Too often, women do not value their time enough. The divorced woman comes to realize that she has more to do and less time to do it in. Every minute wasted is an opportunity lost to work toward a goal, acquire a skill, earn money, think, plan, or enjoy some well-deserved leisure. Be aware of people who try to conserve their time by imposing on yours. If you find you are running lots of errands for others, ask yourself whose time is more important.

Men take it for granted that they will have uninterrupted blocks of time. Women have settled for bits and pieces of time, fitted in and around other people's priorities. Women are expected to adjust their schedules to the convenience of banks, utility companies, repairmen, doctors, dentists, schools, and so on. The first thing you can do is learn to respect and value your own time. The second thing is to educate others to respect and value your time. When you make an appointment, you can ask the doctor's receptionist how long you will have to wait to see the doctor and inform her that you have another appointment or must return to work. You can complain to the doctor if you are kept waiting longer than promised. You can take a firm stand with people who automatically assume that you have all day to wait for something to be delivered, repaired, or installed. You can ask "Why?" when people say, "You have to come in to the office." There is no reason why a great deal of business can't be handled by telephone. Remember, your time is an important and valuable resource!

BODY SIGNALS

Sometimes your body may signal the need for assertive behavior on your part. The following symptoms could be related to the anxiety or impatience felt by a person needing to assert himself or herself. Which apply to you?

—*pacing*
—*foot swinging or jiggling*

—*covering mouth with hand while speaking*
—*teeth grinding*
—*nail biting*
—*finger or foot tapping*
—*frozen smile*
—*artificial or nervous laughter*
—*insomnia*
—*stomach churning*
—*increased breathing*
—*jaw tightening*
—*headache*
—*tight neck muscles*
—*tightness in throat*
—*difficulty in speaking*
—*blushing*
—*weakness*
—*dry mouth*
—*perspiration*
—*fatigue, weariness*
—*poor eye contact*
—*playing with jewelry or clothing*

ASSERTIVE ANGER

At some point in the divorce process, most women feel anger or outright rage; usually the anger is directed toward their ex-husbands. They may feel anger as a result of feeling rejected, abandoned, discarded, and unappreciated. If you have been trained to hold back angry feelings and feel that it is unfeminine to be angry, you may be frightenend by the intensity of your feelings. Expression of anger is an important part of the adjustment process. Women who are able to express their anger at some point find it easier to separate from their partners. Anger can be used to mobilize your strengths and to serve as an impetus to strike out in your own direction. It can be expressed in aggressive, indirect, passive, and assertive ways. Aggressive anger is expressed to hurt or destroy another person. Anger expressed aggressively can be seen in the forms of insulting, physically abusive, and even violent behavior. Anger can be expressed through indirect means. Since women have been trained to hold back their anger, they may express it through silence, sarcasm, sexual disinterest, slamming doors, patronizing and condescending attitudes, and attempts to get others to feel guilty. Women who assume a passive stance toward anger are frequently depressed; depression is anger that one is unable to express and is turned inward on oneself. A woman who is depressed often feels resigned, hopeless, and powerless about her situation.

Assertive anger is directly stated but in a way that is neither physically nor verbally abusive. The woman is as specific as possible about what is bothering her, why it is bothering her, and how she feels. This kind of anger is often expressed in terms of "I" rather than in terms of "you," which sounds blaming and accusatory. For example, "I really get angry when you keep me waiting for an hour. My time is valuable to me!" rather than, "You are inconsiderate and selfish to keep me waiting for an hour."

When you divorce, you may have reasons for being angry and may realize that you have never allowed yourself to deal with your anger assertively. Or, through the women's movement, you may come to realize that you have accumulated years of stored anger and suddenly find yourself going through an "angry phase" in which you are angry a great deal of the time. This is very normal. Eventually, you will probably find your anger diminishing and will find it easier to use your energy to express your anger in assertive rather than aggressive ways. Some women find they are not able to use their anger assertively until they have expressed anger aggressively. Although you may be frightened when you find yourself expressing your anger aggressively, this could be a positive sign; you may be moving from a passive stage in which you felt stepped on and depressed to an active stage, one in which you are able to express your anger.

Four steps are involved with expressing anger assertively.

- Recognizing and accepting your anger; realizing you have a right to be angry.
- Identifying the origin of your anger—sometimes it is easier to blame someone else for our anger. It may also be displaced anger; it is easier to express anger toward your child than your ex-husband who isn't around.
- Identifying the real reason for your anger. Sometimes it is easier to be angry over something incidental than to face the real cause, which may hurt more.
- Deciding if you want to assert yourself. There are times when you may choose not to assert yourself: when others are very

sensitive, when they would interpret your assertiveness as aggression, or when they are in a more powerful position.

Think of your most recent experience with anger. How would you answer the following questions?

1. Did you recognize your anger and allow yourself to feel angry?
2. Did you identify the origin of your anger?
3. Were you able to identify the reason you were angry?
4. What did you decide to do about your anger? Was your behavior typical of the way you handle anger?
5. Did you feel good about the way you handled your anger? If not, how could you have handled it differently?

Now answer these questions with a "yes" or "no".

1. Do you usually keep quiet when you are angry?
2. Do you walk away from a person when you are angry?
3. Are you afraid to express your anger because people won't like you?
4. When you are angry, do you feel anxious and confused about what you want to say?
5. Do you "simmer" for days and then vent your anger in a big blowup?
6. When you are angry, do you drop hints about your feelings, hoping that the other person will get the message?
7. Do you express your anger by making sarcastic or caustic comments?
8. Do you appear to feel hurt when you are actually angry?
9. Do you take out your anger on someone other than the person with whom you are angry?
10. Do you express your anger directly and firmly without labeling the other person?
11. When you are angry, do you cry?
12. Do you feel hurt and withdraw when someone is angry with you?
13. When someone is angry with you, can you respond directly and effectively, with composure and without tears?
14. Can you listen and try to understand another person's grievance?
15. Do you apologize when someone is angry even though you do not feel you are wrong? Are you able to apologize if you feel you are wrong?
16. When someone is angry with you, do you feel that person does not like you?
17. When someone is angry with you, do you feel angry or guilty?
18. When someone is angry with you, do you try to make a joke out of it or try to smooth it over?
19. Do you feel you have a right to understand why a person is angry with you and respond accordingly?

Think of a present situation that makes you angry. If you are unable to think of one, try to imagine a situation that would make you angry. How could you deal with your anger assertively?

WHAT DO YOU DO WITH YOUR POWER?

Women have been conditioned to see themselves as powerless rather than powerful. Being assertive involves having a sense of your own power and using this power to stand up for yourself and what you want while respecting the rights of others. There are many things you can do to avoid using your power; many people use the methods described here. Which do you use?

- Keep peace—don't get angry, don't challenge others, don't differ from others
- Don't pay attention to yourself—spend all your time trying to understand what other people are feeling
- Bow to authority—assume that everyone knows more than you about everything
- Be passive rather than active—always allow others to initiate actions
- Don't make decisions, express choices, or state priorities—just let things happen
- Don't focus on the present—glorify or regret the past, think or worry about the future
- Act confused—never state issues or problems clearly
- Act according to stereotypes that state how you "should act"
- Wait for others to express your ideas, feelings, and intentions
- Always follow the rules and norms other people establish

- Do not allow your facial expressions and body actions to be consistent with what you are saying—keep people guessing
- Say nothing when you need information or are unsure of something
- Always speak in a timid voice—sound like a little girl
- Always apologize for everything—when you are stating what you want, when you are asking a question, when you are angry
- Procrastinate—wait long enough to avoid having to act; wait long enough so that others will act for you

There are payoffs or initial advantages to taking a passive stance and refusing your own power; there are also costs of such behavior. The following statements indicate some of the payoffs and costs of nonassertive behavior:

- "When I act helpless, I get protection and people are willing to help me. But I also lose my feeling of competence and independence."
- "I avoid risks and feel safe when I do not express my ideas and opinions, but I also feel like I don't exist and have no control over my life."
- "When I don't express myself because I fear the criticism of others, I feel safe but I also feel dishonest."
- "When I don't stand up for myself, I avoid conflict but I also lose respect for myself."
- "When I don't take the initiative, I avoid possible mistakes, but I also don't get to use my abilities and implement my good ideas."
- "I am passive to avoid conflict, but inside me a war is going on."
- When I don't express my anger I may avoid initial unpleasantness, but I finally explode or get so angry that I want to end a friendship anyway."
- "I may avoid a confrontation by holding my anger in, but I become depressed."

Examine the payoffs and costs you may be experiencing due to acting nonassertively.

The following columns* list payoffs and costs of nonassertive behavior. Which have you expe-

rienced? Can you add others that apply to you? Try to think of specific situations in which you have experienced these payoffs and costs of nonassertive behavior.

PAYOFFS

—*protection from others*
—*sympathy from others*
—*praise for conforming*
—*security from familiar patterns*
—*avoid responsibility*
—*avoid conflict*
—*avoid others' anger*
—*avoid rejection*
—*avoid risks*
—*praise for putting others first*
—*avoid unpleasant activities*
—*avoid possibility of failure*
—*blame others for your unhappiness*
—*avoid decisions*
—*less effort initially*

COSTS

—*lose independence*
—*feel victimized*
—*lose sense of identity*
—*neither grow nor have new experiences*
—*lose control over life*
—*don't resolve problems with others*
—*lose respect for your rights and preferences*
—*lose inner tranquillity*
—*lose ability to influence others*
—*unable to initiate and carry out plans*
—*lose opportunity to utilize talents and abilities*
—*lose control of emotions*

Do the payoffs of nonassertive behavior outweigh the costs? If so, in which situations? Remember, there are times when it may be wise to be nonassertive—when a thief has a gun and asks for your wallet.

Who do you know who will support, encourage, and understand your assertive behavior? How can assertive behavior help you to achieve your goals and implement your decisions?

* This exercise was adapted from Lynn Z. Bloom, Karen Levin Coburn, and Joan Crystal Pearlman, *The New Assertive Woman*, pp. 80–81. Copyright © 1975 by Lynn Z. Bloom, Karen Levin Coburn, and Joan Crystal Pearlman. Reprinted by permission of Delacorte Press.

ASSERTIVENESS CHECKLIST

Use the following checklist* to determine under which conditions you are prepared to assert yourself. Which of these points apply to you?

- Have a clear grasp of the situation and/or the issue
- Know your goal, what you want to accomplish
- Know how assertive behavior will help you to accomplish your goal
- Know what you would usually do to avoid asserting yourself
- Know what traps may be stopping you from asserting yourself and identify what your rights are in the situation
- Know your anxiety level and how you can reduce it to a manageable level
- Have the information you need to assert yourself
- Assert yourself so that you:

—*let the other person know that you hear and understand him or her*
—*let the other person know how you feel*
—*let the other person know what you want*

Important points to remember in asserting yourself are similar to the steps involved in the decision-making process. You may want to review these by referring to chapter 6.

Think of a situation in which you want to assert yourself and go through the checklist to prepare yourself to be assertive.

Good luck!

* This exercise was adapted from *The New Assertive Woman.* Copyright © 1975 by Lynn Z. Bloom, Karen Levin Coburn, and Joan Crystal Pearlman. Reprinted by permission of Delacorte Press.

BIBLIOGRAPHY

A vital step in the decision-making process is collecting information. Much of the information you need when you are making decisions can be found in your local library. Many women do not consider turning to the library and the books available to help them. While this may not be your response in a crisis situation, it is a good idea to develop the library habit. There are hundreds of books on coping with life that can be valuable for the divorced woman. There are also many books on the subject of divorce itself. To locate books that can be helpful to you, consult your library's computer, catalog, or the bibliographies provided in some of the books listed here.

The following is a brief list of books that divorced women have found helpful. Those with an asterisk (*) are particularly helpful. Most of the books have been published in paperback editions.

GENERAL

Belli, Melvin, and Krantzler, Mel. *Divorce*. New York: St. Martin's Press, 1988.

Fisher, Bruce. *Rebuilding: When Your Relationship Ends*. San Luis Obispo, Calif.: Impact Publishers, 1981.

Gould, Roger L., M.D. *Transformations: Growth and Change in Adult Life*. New York: Simon and Schuster, 1978.

Krantzler, Mel. *Creative Divorce: A New Opportunity for Personal Growth*. New York: New American Library, 1975.

————. *Learning to Love Again*. New York: Crowell, 1977. A helpful book for the woman who has adjusted to divorce and is ready to develop meaningful and caring relationships with others.

Napolitan, Catherine, and Pellegrino, Victoria. *Living and Loving After Divorce*. New York: Rawson Associates, 1977.

Sheehy, Gail, *Passages: Predictable Crises of Adult Life*. New York: Dutton, 1974.

Trafford, Abigail. *Crazy Time: Surviving Divorce*. New York: Bantam Books, 1982.

Vaughan, Diane. *Uncoupling: How Relationships Come Apart*. New York: Vintage Books, 1987. Provides interesting insight into the patterns that exist when couples separate.

* Viorst, Judith. *Necessary Losses: The Loves, Illusions, Dependencies and Impossible Expectations That All of Us Have to Give Up in Order to Grow*. New York: Bantam Books, 1986. An excellently written and researched book which puts into perspective the losses with which we all deal during our lifetimes.

Weiss, Robert S. *Marital Separation*. New York: Basic Books, 1975.

Yates, Martha. *Coping: A Survival Manual for Women Alone*. Englewood Cliffs, N.J.: Prentice-Hall, 1976.

REFERENCES

Paulsen, Kathryn, and Kuhn, Ryan A. *Woman's Almanac: 12 How-to Handbooks in One*. New York: Lippincott, 1976. An excellent reference book containing articles on health, sex education, working, child rearing, money, and other areas of importance to women. A woman's directory, which lists more than 1,500 local and national women's services, resources, and special-interest organizations is included.

Ullman, Jeffrey. *The Singles Almanac: A Guide to Getting the Most Out of Being Single*. New York: World Almanac Publications, 1986. A practical and upbeat approach to being single.

Women in Transition, Inc. *Women in Transition: A Feminist Handbook on Separation and Divorce*. New York: Scribner's, 1975. A must for every divorced woman. Has an excellent chapter on emotional supports and deals with virtually every facet of being on your own. Also includes helpful advice for women on welfare.

MAGAZINES

DIVORCE
A bimonthly magazine that deals with topics of interest to those separated and divorced.

LEAR'S: FOR THE WOMAN WHO WASN'T BORN YESTERDAY.
A bimonthly magazine that has interesting articles for the mature woman.

MONEY
An excellent resource on how to use your money wisely. The June 1988 issue has an excellent article on divorce and finances which has a state-by-state guide telling how property distribution is handled. It also discusses how to determine the true worth of your divorce settlement as affected by the new tax laws.

MS.
Deals with issues, subjects, and legislation of interest to women.

NEW WOMAN
Devoted to personal growth and development of women.

SAVVY
A magazine for the executive woman. Will send you a complete, nationwide listing of networks of interest to women. Send a $2 check or money order and a stamped self-addressed envelope to: Professional Connections, Savvy Magazine, 111 Eighth Avenue, New York, NY 10011.

SINGLE PARENT
Monthly magazine of Parents Without Partners.

WORKING MOTHER
Devoted to issues of working mothers.

WORKING WOMAN
Helpful articles on coping with a career and family.

PERSONAL GROWTH

* Bailey, Linda J. *How to Get Going When You Can Barely Get Out of Bed*. Englewood Cliffs, N.J.: Prentice-Hall, 1984. An excellent book that helps women deal with depression and develop personal power.

Brown, Sharon C., Paulson, Pat A., and Wolf, JoAnn. *Living on Purpose*. Glen Ellyn, Illinois: Phoenix Rising Press, 1988.

Cowan, Dr. Connell, and Kinder, Dr. Melvyn. *Women Men Love, Women Men Leave: What Makes Men Want to Commit*. New York: Signet, 1987.

Dowling, Colette. *Cinderella Complex: Women's Hidden Fear of Independence*. New York: Summit Books, 1981. This book examines the issues of dependence and independence with which many women struggle.

Dyer, Wayne M. *Your Erroneous Zones*. New York: Avon, 1977. An easy-to-read book that encourages you to take responsibility for yourself. Some of the author's suggestions about dealing with anger can be questioned.

———. *Pulling Your Own Strings*. New York: Avon, 1978. Helpful for women who want to stop being victims and take charge of their own lives.

Ellis, Albert, and Powers, Milvin. *A New Guide to Rational Living*. Hollywood, Calif.: Wilshire Book Company, 1977.

Greenwald, Jerry. *Be the Person You Were Meant to Be*. New York: Dell, 1974. Very helpful. Deals with the roadblocks we create for ourselves and how they can be removed.

Hill, Napolean. *Think and Grow Rich*. New York: Fawcett Crest, 1960. A "classic" dealing with personal achievement, financial independence, and general well-being.

Jongeward, Dorothy, and Scott, Dru. *Women as Winners*. Reading, Mass.: Addison-Wesley, 1976. Utilizes a transactional approach to women's growth and development.

Newman, Mildred, and Berkowitz, Bernard. *How to Be Your Own Best Friend*. New York: Ballantine, 1974.

Rusk, Tom, M.D., and Read, Randy, M.D. *I Want to Change But I Don't Know How!* Los Angeles: Price, Stern, Sloan, 1988.

Russianoff, Penelope. *Why Do I Think I Am Nothing Without a Man?* New York: Bantam Books, 1983. Deals with the feelings of desolation and fragmentation many women experience unless they are connected to a man.

LEGAL MATTERS

Sack, Steven M. *What's Love Got to Do with It? A Legal Guide to Marriage, Divorce, Custody & Living Together*. New York: McGraw-Hill, 1987.

Samuelson, Elliot D. *The Divorce Law Handbook: A Comprehensive Guide to Matrimonial Law*. New York: Human Science Press, 1988.

NEGOTIATIONS

Fisher, Roger, and Ury, William. *Getting to Yes: Negotiating Agreement Without Giving In*. New York: Penguin Books, 1983.

CHILDREN

Berger, Stuart, M.D. *Divorce Without Victims: Helping Children Through Divorce with a Minimum of Pain and Trauma*. New York: New American Library, 1986. A helpful book for parents who are going through divorce. Chapters are included on remarriage, children, and stepfamilies.

Bonkowski, Sara. *Kids are Non-Divorceable*. Chicago: Buckley Publications, 1987.

The Boston Women's Health Collective. *Ourselves and Our Children: A Book by and for Parents*. New York: Random House, 1978. A good, general reference for parents.

Dreikurs, Rudolf, and Soltz, Vicki. *Children: The Challenge*. New York: Wyden, 1970. A good basic book on child rearing, designed to encourage children to take responsibility for themselves and their actions.

Gardner, Richard A. *The Boys and Girls Book About Divorce*. New York: Bantam Books, 1971.

———. *The Boys and Girls Book About One-Parent Families*. New York: Putnam, 1978.

———. *The Parents Book About Divorce*. Garden City, N.Y.: Doubleday, 1977.

Gordon, Thomas. *Parent Effectiveness Training*. New York: Hawthorne, 1964.

Hope, Karol, and Young, Nancy. *Momma: The Sourcebook for Single Mothers*. New York: New American Library, 1976. A book every divorced mother should have on her shelf.

* Hunter, Evan. *Me and Mr. Stenner*. New York: Lippincott, 1976. A sensitive and beautifully written story

about the problems of an eleven-year-old girl when her parents divorce and her mother remarries. A delightful experience for both mothers and daughters.

Jong, Erica. *Megan's Book of Divorce: A Kid's Book for Adults.* New York: New American Library, 1984.

Krementz, Jill. *How It Feels When Parents Divorce.* New York: Knopf, 1988.

LeShan, Eda. *What's Going to Happen to Me? When Parents Separate or Divorce.* New York: Macmillan, 1986. A book for children covering concerns they have when parents divorce.

Mayle, Peter. *Why Are We Getting a Divorce?* New York: Crown, 1988. A book for young children on divorce.

Prokop, Michael S., and Fogartz, Michelle D. *Divorce Happens to the Nicest Kids: A Self-Help Book for Kids and Adults.* Warren, Ohio: Alegra House Publishers, 1986.

Richards, Arlene, and Willis, Irene. *How to Get It Together When Your Parents Are Coming Apart.* New York: David McKay, 1976. This book is particularly good for adolescents trying to cope with their parents' marital problems and/or divorce.

Rogers, Fred. *Mister Rogers Talks with Families About Divorce.* New York: Berkley, 1987.

Salk, Lee. *What Every Child Would Like Parents to Know About Divorce.* New York: Harper & Row, 1978.

Satir, Virginia M. *Peoplemaking.* Palo Alto, Calif.: Science and Behavior Books, 1972. An excellent book that deals with family process. There is a chapter on "one-parent" and "blended" families.

Sinberg, Janet. *Divorce Is a Grown Up Problem.* New York: Avon, 1978. An excellent book for elementary children.

Sullivan, Maria. *The Parent-Child Manual on Divorce.* New York: St. Martin's Press, 1988.

FINANCES

* Ashton, Betsy. *Betsy Ashton's Guide to Living on Your Own.* Boston: Little, Brown, 1988. A valuable and complete guide for the consumer covering taxes, loans, leases, warranties, phone service, credit records, and much more.

Auerbach, Sylvia. *A Woman's Book of Money: A Guide to Financial Independence.* Garden City. N.Y.: Doubleday, 1976. The author is particularly sensitive to the insecurities some women have about managing money.

Briles, Judith. *The Dollars and Sense of Divorce: A Financial Guide for Women.* New York: Master Media Ltd., 1988. A financial guide for individuals in the process of divorce.

Laut, Phil. *Money Is My Friend.* San Francisco, Calif.: Trinity Publications, 1979.

Lewin, Elizabeth S., C.F.P. *Financial Fitness Through Divorce: A Guide to the Financial Realities of Divorce.* New York: Facts on File Publications, 1987. A workbook approach which helps you deal with the realities of divorce and your financial situation.

Nelson, Paula. *The Joy of Money: The Guide to Women's Financial Freedom.* New York: Stein and Day, 1975. An excellent book for women who want financial independence, to operate in the black, to understand financial principles, and to think in terms of financial goal setting.

* Van Caspel, Venita. *Money Dynamics for the 1990s.* New York: Simon and Schuster, 1988. A comprehensive directory to personal investing and financial planning for the 1990s.

CAREERS

Anderson, Nancy. *Work with Passion: How to Do What You Love for a Living.* New York: Carroll & Graf, 1984. An excellent and thorough book on career planning.

* Bolles, Richard Nelson. *What Color Is Your Parachute? A Practical Manual for Job-Hunters and Career-Changers.* Berkeley, Calif.: Ten Speed Press, 1988. An absolute must for any woman who is trying to get a job or make career decisions.

Sher, Barbara, and Gottlieb, Annie. *Wishcraft: How to Get What You Really Want.* New York: Ballantine Books, 1979. This is an excellent book to help you focus on what you really want, how to set goals, and how to follow through on achieving the goals you have set. The book has an excellent resource section.

* Wendleton, Kate. *The Five O'Clock Club Guide to Changing Jobs.* 1987. May be ordered from:
The Five O'Clock Club
210 Fifth Avenue
New York, NY 10010

This is must reading for anyone who is conducting a job search. The author includes many thought-provoking quotations that apply to career decisions.

HEALTH

* The Boston Women's Health Book Collective. *The New Our Bodies, Ourselves.* New York: Simon and Schuster, 1984. A valuable book for the divorced woman who realizes how important it is to take care of herself. Discusses related health topics such as sexuality.

Kaplan, Helen Singer, M.D., Ph.D. *The Real Truth About Women and AIDS: How to Eliminate the Risks Without Giving Up Love and Sex.* New York: Simon and Schuster, 1987. A helpful book. Some of the information presented may not be accurate or up-to-date in light of present research.

Siegal, Bernie S., M.D. *Love, Medicine and Miracles: Lessons Learned About Self-Healing from a Surgeon's Experience with Exceptional Patients.* New York: Harper & Row, 1986.

U.S. Department of Health & Human Services. *Understanding AIDS.* Rockville, Md.: Public Health Service Centers for Disease Control, 1988. This is a helpful pamphlet prepared by the surgeon general (HHS Publication No. (CDC) HHS-88-8404).

SEXUALITY

* Barbach, Lonnie Garfield. *For Yourself: The Fulfillment of Female Sexuality.* Garden City, N.Y.: Doubleday, 1975.

Heiman, Julia; LoPiccolo, Leslie; and LoPiccolo, Joseph. *Becoming Orgasmic: A Sexual Growth Program for Women.* Englewood Cliffs, N.J.: Prentice-Hall, 1976.

Hill, Justine. *Women Talking: Explorations in Being Female.* Secaucus, N.J.: Lyle Stuart, 1976.

Kline-Graber, Georgia, and Graber, Benjamin. *Woman's Orgasm.* Indianapolis: Bobbs-Merrill, 1975.

These books stress the need for a woman's taking responsibility for her sexual pleasure and knowing and enjoying her body.

ASSERTION

Baer, Jean L. *How to Be an Assertive (Not Aggressive) Woman in Life, in Love, and on the Job.* New York: Rawson Associates, 1976.

Bloom, Lynn Z.; Coburn, Karen Levin; and Pearlman, Joan Crystal. *The New Assertive Woman.* New York: Dell, 1981.

Bolton, Robert. *People Skills: How to Assert Yourself, Listen to Others, and Resolve Conflicts.* New York: Simon and Schuster, 1979. An excellent all-around book which provides information concerning communication, building relationships, and asserting yourself.

* Bower, Sharon Anthony, and Bower, Gordon H. *Asserting Yourself: A Practical Guide for Positive Change.* Reading, Mass.: Addison-Wesley, 1976. An excellent book in workbook format.

Fensterheim, Herbert, and Baer, Jean. *Don't Say Yes When You Want to Say No.* New York: Dell, 1975.

Phelps, Stanlee, and Austin Nancy. *The Assertive Woman.* San Luis Obispo, Calif.: Impact, 1975.

Smith, Manuel J. *When I Say No, I Feel Guilty.* New York: Bantam Books, 1975.

ENDING RELATIONSHIPS

Carter, Stephen, and Sokol, Julia. *Men Who Can't Love: When a Man's Fear Makes Him Run from Commitment.* New York: Berkley, 1987.

Forward, Dr. Susan. *Men Who Hate Women and the Women Who Love Them: When Loving Hurts and You Don't Know Why.* New York: Bantam Books, 1986.

Halpern, Howard. *How to Break Your Addiction to a Person.* New York: Bantam Books, 1983.

Hootman, Marcia, and Perkins, Patt. *How to Forgive Your Ex-Husband (and Get on with Your Life).* New York: Warner Books, 1985.

Nicarthy, Ginny. *Getting Free: A Handbook for Women in Abusive Relationships.* Seattle: Seal Press, 1982. A detailed and compassionate guide for the battered woman who is building a new life for herself. Also highly recommended to victims of emotional abuse. It contains self-assessment activities that help women clarify their experience and goals.

* Norwood, Robin. *Women Who Love Too Much.* Los Angeles: Tarcher, 1985. Necessary reading for any woman who is in a harmful or addictive relationship.

Peele, Stanton, and Budsky, Archie. *Love and Addiction.* New York: Signet, 1976.

Phillips, Debora, and Judd, Robert. *How to Fall Out of Love.* Boston: Houghton Mifflin, 1978.

Wanderer, Zev, and Cabot, Tracy. *Letting Go.* New York: Warner Books, 1978.

RESOURCES

There are many resources available for women dealing with a variety of problems. The best way you can learn about resources that will be of help to you in your community is to network—call groups in your area that are concerned with women's issues, tell them what you need, and ask for referrals. Places you can call are:

NOW Chapters
YWCAs
Community Colleges
Health or Family Services Agencies
Human Services Directories (often in the yellow pages of your telephone book if you live in a metropolitan area)

WOMEN'S YELLOW PAGES
A number of states have yellow pages that advertise businesses owned by women and groups offering special services of interest to women.

The following are examples of centers that offer special services for women who are going through separation or divorce. Since centers are funded by grant monies, some may have closed if their funding has not been renewed. Other centers may have opened.

CALIFORNIA

FEMINIST LEGAL SERVICES
YWCA Building
1122 17th Street
Sacramento, CA 95814

Provides humanist legal referral services, workshops on doing your own divorce, and low-interest loans for individuals needing legal assistance.

COLORADO

BEYOND DIVORCE INC.
620 Federal Boulevard
Denver, CO 80204
(303) 623–3288

Provides support groups for individuals.

DENVER METROPOLITAN YWCA
535 16th Street
Denver, CO 80202
(303) 825–7141

Has a legal clinic and workshops on pro se divorce.

DIVORCE SUPPORT GROUP
19650 East Main Street
Parker United Methodist Church
Parker, CO 80134
(303) 841–3979

Provides support groups for separated and divorced individuals.

WOMEN'S CRISIS CENTER
OF DOUGLAS COUNTY
P.O. Box 369
Castle Run, CO 80104
(303) 688–8484

Provides counseling and help for women in crisis.

WASHINGTON, D.C.

AMERICAN ASSOCIATION OF UNIVERSITY
WOMEN (AAUW)
2401 Virginia Avenue N.W.
Washington, D.C. 20037
(202) 785–7700

For women with college degrees. The organization has chapters throughout the United States which have study groups, consider public policy concerning women, and meet to explore common interests.

D.C. CITYWIDE WELFARE RIGHTS
ORGANIZATION, INC.
220 Highview Place S.E.
Washington, D.C. 20032
(202) 574–8400

This organization provides assistance and workshops for welfare recipients to help them understand their rights and cope with the system.

NATIONAL ORGANIZATION OF WOMEN
1401 New York Avenue N.W.
Suite 800
Washington, D.C. 20005

NATIONAL WOMEN'S LAW CENTER
1616 P Street N.W.
Washington, D.C. 20036
(202) 328–5160

Provides counseling concerning sex discrimination, child support, social security, welfare rights, and employment issues.

NEIGHBORHOOD LEGAL SERVICES
PROGRAMS
701 4th Street N.W.
Washington, D.C. 20001

This organization has a domestic relations unit and provides free legal representation for individuals who meet the guidelines and are below the poverty level. They also have a referral service.

PROJECT ON THE STATE AND EDUCATION OF WOMEN
Association of American Colleges
1818 R Street, N.W.
Washington, D.C. 20009
(202) 387–3760

Publishes a financial aid "self-help" book for women. The guide can be purchased for $3.50 a copy.

WOMEN'S LEGAL DEFENSE FUND
2000 P Street N.W.
Suite 400
Washington, D.C. 20036

This organization provides legal counseling free of charge and will make referrals for similar services in other states.

ILLINOIS

THE DIVORCE HOTLINE
West Surburian YWCA
Lombard, IL 60148
(312) 969–4806 (hotline)
(312) 629–0170

Provides a 24-hour hot line, information on emergency shelter, and other services for women.

LEGAL ASSISTANCE FOUNDATION
Women's Law Project
343 S. Dearborn St.
Chicago, IL 60604
(312) 341–1070

Provides legal services for indigent people and pro se *divorce information.*

MIDWEST WOMEN'S CENTER
53 W. Jackson
Suite 1015
Chicago, IL 60604
(312) 922–8530

Provides job training, placement and referral services for women. Has a library concerning women's issues and concerns.

MASSACHUSETTS

CHILD CARE RESOURCES AND REFERRAL CONSORTIUM

Provides information on child care and parent support groups. There are four area offices:
Prospect Hill Parents and Children Center.
Waltham, MA
(617) 890–8781

Warm Lines
West Newton, MA
(617) 964–2256

Family Connection
Roslindale, MA
(617) 325–3919

Magic Unicorn
Burlington, MA
(617) 229–6420

DIVORCE AND MEDIATION CENTER
334 Broadway
Suite #2
Cambridge, MA 02139
(617) 492–3533

Provides mediation, counseling, support groups, and psychological testing.

EVERYWOMAN'S CENTER
506 Goodell Hall
University of Massachusetts
Amherst, MA 01002

This center provides support groups, legal listings and referrals, and a resource library.

SINGLE MOTHERS
Tanager Street
Arlington, MA 02174

WOMEN'S EDUCATIONAL CENTER, INC.
46 Pleasant Street
Cambridge, MA 02139
(617) 354–8807

This center offers a variety of resources such as counseling, self-defense courses, and referrals.

MICHIGAN

THE GRYPHON PLACE
1104 S. Westnedge
Kalamazoo, MI 49008
(616) 345–3036 (crisis line)

WOMEN'S COUNSELING CENTER, INC.
13000 W. Seven Mile Road
Detroit, MI
(313) 861–3939

MINNESOTA

WOMEN'S RESOURCE CENTER
Normandale Community College
9700 France Avenue South
Bloomington, MN 55431
(612) 831–1144

Provides free legal clinic and referrals.

NEW MEXICO

WOMEN'S CENTER
1160 Mesa Vista Hall
University of New Mexico
Albuquerque, NM 87131
(505) 277–3716

NEW YORK

NATIONAL ORGANIZATION OF WOMEN (NASSAU CHAPTER)
Divorce Information Center
148 Greenwich Street
Hempstead, NY
(516) 485–8902

Offers free legal counsel and psychological services (by appointment).

NOW LEGAL DEFENSE AND EDUCATION FUND
99 Hudson Street
New York, NY 10013
(212) 925–6635

ROCKLAND COUNTY WOMEN'S NETWORK
145 College Road
Suffern, NY
(914) 947–3130

THE SISTERHOOD OF BLACK SINGLE MOTHERS
1360 Fulton Street
Suite 423
Brooklyn, NY 11216
(718) 638–0413

Offers group and individual sessions, parenting courses, and a fatherhood collective.

UNION CENTER FOR WOMEN
8101 Ridge Boulevard
Brooklyn, NY 11209
(718) 748–7708

Offers support groups of interest to women.

OHIO

DIVORCE EQUITY
3130 Mayfield Road
Cleveland Heights, OH 44118
(216) 321–8587

A nonprofit organization that offers research, advocacy, and education in the divorce process.

PENNSYLVANIA

WOMEN'S ALLIANCE FOR JOB EQUITY (WAJE)
1422 Chestnut Street
Suite 1100
Philadelphia, PA 19102
(215) 561–1873

Provides programs on sexual harassment prevention, pay equity, career development, and career issues.

WOMEN'S LAW PROJECT
125 S. 9th Street
Philadelphia, PA 19107
(215) 928–9801

Provides free legal counseling over the phone.

WOMEN IN TRANSITION
125 S. 9th Street
Philadelphia, PA
(215) 922–7500 (hot line)

Provides counseling, advocacy and referrals for women on domestic violence, separation, divorce, careers, and substance abuse.

WASHINGTON

UNIVERSITY YWCA
4224 University Way, N.E.
Seattle, WA 98105
(206) 632–4747

Offers resources and referrals of interest to women.

ABOUT THE AUTHOR

Christina Robertson is a counselor, consultant, and training specialist with over fifteen years of experience helping individuals and organizations effectively manage change. She has counseled men and women experiencing divorce to use the experience for personal development and to create opportunities for their futures as single individuals. The author has graduate degrees in Counseling Psychology and Organizational Development and has had extensive experience in seminar design and delivery, adult education, and career counseling. Presently, she is a consultant with a national consulting firm and works with corporations and employees who are in career transition. She has been divorced for fifteen years and has two children, Amanda, age twenty, and Nathaniel, age sixteen.